Lois —
Hope this
becomes one of
your favorites!
Lori Lacey

IN GOOD TASTE
RENO / TAHOE

A Restaurant Guide & Restaurant Recipe Cookbook
Written and compiled by Lori Lacey & Sonnie Imes

IN GOOD TASTE
RENO / TAHOE
1ST Printing, 2000
ISBN 0-9676606-0-2
$14.95

Cover design by Tina Tyrrell
Printing by Publishers Press

Printed in the United States of America

DEDICATION

Out of self-preservation, Sonnie dedicates this book to her Mother, Ann Weiser, who used her oven to store paper bags.

Lori dedicates this book to her Mother, Bonnie Shacter, who taught her the love of cooking through the use of cookbooks.

Love you Mom

INTRODUCTION

One of the greatest pleasures is to share good food with good friends, and that's what "In Good Taste" is all about. We invite you to come with us as we dine in elegant surroundings and kick-back casual settings, to share the delights of a catered party or a spur-of-the-moment picnic. The Lake Tahoe-Reno area is our home, and we want to show you around, from the hot spots to the hidden treasures.

Good times are worth remembering, too. So, we've filled "In Good Taste" with recipes to savor, to bring back memories of places you've been, and whet your appetite for places yet to be explored. Chefs from the restaurants included in "In Good Taste" have generously shared their culinary secrets, with delicious, easy-to-prepare recipes that are destined to become family favorites.

The Reno-Tahoe area offers snow-covered mountains that attract skiers from all over and the beautiful mountain lake that attracts visitors all year 'round. The high desert of the Great Basin still holds the charm of the old west and the Comstock era, when silver drew the world to Nevada. Silver is still a lure in the glittering casinos in Reno, and on Tahoe's North and South Shores. In the flower-strewn grassy valleys east of the Sierra Nevada, you can still see buckaroos moving their herds to pasture. On the wooded slopes, you might find the tree-markings left by Basque sheepherders.

Downtown Reno is bisected by a railroad tract that runs through high mountain tunnels toward the Pacific Ocean – tunnels blasted into rock by Chinese workers more than a century ago. In Reno's parks, you'll find bocce ball courts, established by homesick Italian immigrants. Hispanics even gave their name for cowboy, "vaquero," to the Nevada "buckaroo".

Immigrants, explorers, adventurers, dreamers, and entrepreneurs have made this area truly cosmopolitan. Nowhere is that more apparent than in the variety of restaurants that reflect this happy amalgam of cultures. But the real hallmark of Northern Nevada-California is the warm western hospitality and small-town friendliness. "In Good Taste" can guide you to a restaurant, but it is the good food and genuine welcome that will bring you back again and again.

(Continued on next page)

If you are visiting, or new to this area, you'll find "In Good Taste" an invaluable guidebook. Long-time residents will discover new and exciting things too, like the Truckee eatery that names its 57 kinds of omelets after local folk, the inn that delivers breakfast to your door, the restaurant with a 40,000 bottle wine cellar you can dine in, the places that offer valet parking – for your boat!

Find out where to go to pick up a really great deli meal – or have it catered. Discover where you can get Chinese and Italian cuisine on the same menu. If you're looking for a romantic rendezvous, a place to dine with a really fine view, or a no-frills joint with award-winning barbecue, you'll find them all in "In Good Taste".

We're always looking for what's new and different, and we always enjoy returning to old favorites. We hope you'll feel the same, that you'll make some new friends among these pages, and find some old ones well worth the keeping.

"In Good Taste" makes a great gift for any occasion, because it will bring pleasure for years to come, and even if you can't visit our beautiful home, the recipes will bring a taste of it to you.

Enjoy!

Sonnie Imes & Lori Lacey

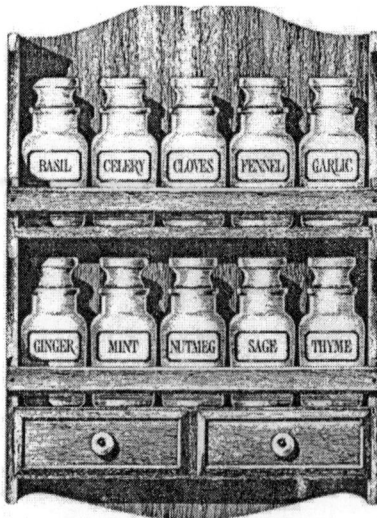

ACKNOWLEDGMENTS

Our sincere thanks to the restaurant owners, managers and chefs, who so willingly cooperated by taking time out of their busy schedules to share their fabulous recipes. They are the real movers and shakers of the book.

A very special thank you to:

Viola Cody, for her creative computer artistry, and her valued friendship. JoAnn Myers, who changed the restaurant lingo and made it compatible for the home cook. Barbara Wies, who transcribed our ramblings, organized our thoughts, and made sense of it all. Mike Barron, for his countless hours and patience in teaching us typesetting skills. Chuck Morales, for his expertise with transporting the logos.

And finally to our families, for their encouragement, inspiration and enthusiasm while tasting our "proofing" of the chef's recipes.

TABLE OF CONTENTS

Reno

BRICKS RESTAURANT & WINE BAR 13

    BRICKS BBQ PEPPER PRAWNS 14
    PROVOLONE SAUTÉ 15
    BUTTERNUT SQUASH & LEEK SOUP 16
    CHICKEN PESTO 17
    PEAR, GINGER, HAZELNUT TART 18

RAPSCALLION SEAFOOD HOUSE & BAR 21

    SPANISH CEVICHE 22
    COCO PRAWNS 23
    CLAM CHOWDER 24

VIAGGIO 25

    MEDITERRANEAN RED CLAM CHOWDER 26
    OSSOBUCO 27
    WHITE CLAM SAUCE 28
    LORETO'S MARINARA SAUCE 29
    ITALIAN RUM CAKE 30

ANDIAMO 31

    GRILLED ASPARAGUS AND CHILI OIL 32
    PICKLED RED ONION 33
    ROAST PEPPERS 33
    CHILI OIL 34
    CANDIED ORANGE 34
    RICOTTA GELATO WITH GRILLED STONE FRUIT 34
    CANDIED BASIL 35
    SPINACH SALAD 36
    MUSHROOM VINAIGRETTE 36
    ANDIAMO'S BRULEÉ 37
    KEY LIME PIE 37
    FLOURLESS CHOCOLATE CAKE 38

PLANET HOLLYWOOD (ADDITIONAL LOCATION IN SOUTH LAKE TAHOE) 41

    CHOPPED COBB SALAD 42
    YAKI SOBA 42
    GRILLED TUSCAN CHICKEN 43
    PORTOBELLO MUSHROOM BURGER 43
    FIRE-GRILLED PIZZA 44
    WHITE CHOCOLATE BREAD PUDDING WITH WHISKEY SAUCE 45
    WHISKEY SAUCE 46

LA VECCHIA **47**

    LENTIL SOUP 48
    FETTUCCINE WITH QUAIL AND SHIITAKE 48
    VENISON RAVIOLI 50
    RISOTTO RADICCHIO & SCALLOPS 51
    OSSOBUCO 52

PANE VINO **53**

    PANEVINO CIOPPINO 54
    WHITE BEAN MINESTRONE 55
    COCO CHICKEN 56
    CREMOSA POLENTA ROSSO 57
    CIOCCOLATI MOUSSE 57
    CAPPUCCINO CHEESECAKE 58

ATLANTIS SEAFOOD STEAKHOUSE **59**

    PRAWN TROPICALE 60
    VEAL AND LOBSTER ROULADE 61
    PORT WINE AND MOREL MUSHROOM SAUCE 61
    CORAL REEF CHICKEN 62
    TARRAGON CREAM SAUCE 63

NAPA SONOMA GROCERY COMPANY **65**

    BUTTERNUT SQUASH SOUP 66
    TORTELLINI SALAD WITH DIJON MUSTARD VINAIGRETTE 67
    DIJON MUSTARD VINAIGRETTE 67
    GRILLED MEDALLIONS OF PORK WITH BOURBON APPLE BUTTER 68
    BOURBON APPLE BUTTER 68
    LEMON HERBED BREAST OF CHICKEN 69

CAFE SOLEIL **71**

    CAFE SOLEIL LAMB SHANKS BRAISED IN RED WINE 72
    CAFE SOLEIL BASIC POLENTA 73
    GRILLED SALMON, POT AU-FEU (POT ON THE FIRE) 74
    CAFE SOLEIL ROASTED BELL PEPPER SAUCE 75
    CAPPUCCINO PANNA COTTA 76
    RASPBERRY SAUCE 77
    BASIC BREAD PUDDING WITH PRALINE TOPPING 77

HILLTOP BAR & EATERY **79**

    HILLTOP VEGETABLE SOUP 80
    HILLTOP HOUSE VINAIGRETTE 80
    CHICKEN CALIFORNIA SANDWICH 81

FRESCO'S PIZZA **83**

    CALZONE 84
    STROMBOLI 85

ELEGANT PARTY CATERING 87

GRANDMA DOT'S EASY STIR FRY VEGETABLES 88
CHICKEN EGGPLANT PARMESAN CASSEROLE 88
BAMBI'S MACARONI AND CHEESE 90
SEAFOOD STUFFED CROISSANTS 90
SUMMER TORTELLINI SALAD 91
YOGURT BERRY PIE 92

BAVARIAN WORLD 93

POTATO CABBAGE SOUP 94
ROULADEN 95
PORK ROAST IN BEER SAUCE 96

MONTEVIGNA 97

SALMONE AI CARCIOFFI 98
CHARDONNAY BUTTER SAUCE 98
LINGUINI PESCATORA 99
ANATRA AL BALSAMICO 100
BALSAMIC PEPPERCORN SAUCE 101

THE GRILL AT WOLF RUN 103

CAESAR SALAD 104
SHRIMP SCAMPI 105

RICKSHAW PADDY 107

ASIAN BISTRO BOUILLABAISSE 108
SZECHWAN DUCK BREAST SALAD 109
TIGER PRAWNS AND SWORDFISH 110
SPICY BASIL CHICKEN 111

NIK-N-WILLIES PIZZA AND DELI (COMSTOCK PIZZA CO. IN DAYTON) 113

GARLIC BREAD 114
GARLIC CHICKEN DIJON PIZZA 114
GOLD PAN PIZZA 115

TEXAS LONGHORN 117

TEXAS-STYLE RIBS 118
RASTA RIBS 120
TEXAS-STYLE PULLED PORK 121
TEXAS-STYLE BARBECUED BRISKET 122
JAMAICAN JERK MARINADE 123
QUICK GARAM MARSALA 124

NOTHING TO IT CULINARY CENTER 125

BABY GREENS WITH STRAWBERRIES AND SUGARED ALMONDS 127
CLASSIC CAESAR SALAD* 128
HOMEMADE GARLIC CROUTONS 129
ROASTED RED POTATO SALAD 129
CHICKEN AND GRAPE PASTA SALAD 130

LONGNECK'S BAR & GRILL..133

    LONGNECK'S ITALIAN DIP SANDWICH 134
    MARINATED MUSHROOM SALAD 134
    LONGNECK'S TURKEY AND SWISS CHEESE SANDWICH......135
    CRANBERRY HORSERADISH MAYO 135
    LONGNECK'S BLACKENED CHICKEN CLUB SANDWICH......136
    CITRUS CILANTRO MAYO..137

TOUCAN CHARLIE'S BUFFET AND GRILLE...............139

    SPICY CRAB SALAD...140
    ANTIPASTO SALAD 140
    GARLIC CHICKEN 141
    SALSA 142

Sparks

B. J.'S BAR-B-QUE 145

    GRILLED PORK TENDERLOIN....................................146
    B. J.'S BBQ'D BEANS 146
    SWEET POTATO TARTS 147

GREAT BASIN BREWING COMPANY 149

    WISCONSIN STYLE BEER CHEESE SOUP 150
    WILD HORSE ALE CINNAMON BREAD.........................151
    NEVADA GOLD CUCUMBER SALAD............................153
    JAMAICAN JERK-STYLE PORK MEDALLIONS 154
    SALMON TACOS WITH FRESH MANGO SALSA 156
    MANGO SALSA 156

Carson City

GLEN EAGLES 161

    VICKY SHRIMP 162
    NEPTUNE SAUCE 162
    CREME BRULÉE...163

ADELE'S RESTAURANT & LOUNGE...........................165

    LOUISIANA OYSTER FRITTER SALAD 166
    CAESAR DRESSING...167
    PICKLED ONIONS...167
    SEARED SALMON SALAD..168
    SALMON FUSILLI 169
    MOROCCAN LAMB 170
    MOROCCAN SPICE MIXTURE...................................172
    VEAL JOSHUA...173

MOLLY'S CATERING..175
    SEAFOOD STUFFED MUSHROOMS...176
    CHICKEN & SHRIMP WON TONS WITH CHILI SWEET & SOUR SAUCE 176
    CHILI SWEET & SOUR SAUCE 177
    CRAB & SHRIMP COCKTAIL LAHVOSH 178
    BRIE WRAPPED IN PUFF PASTRY STUFFED WITH WILD MUSHROOM & MAUI
    SWEET ONION FILLING 178
    GARLIC CHILI BEEF WITH PARMESAN BAGUETTE CROUTE......................180
    PARMESAN BAGUETTE CROUTES 180
    SPICY THAI CHICKEN BITES 181
    SHORTBREAD 182

B'SGHETTI'S 183
    PASTA E. FAGIOLI 184
    FRESH BASIL BRUSCHETTA..185
    RAVIOLI FRITTA..186
    LEMON BASIL CHICKEN 187
    TIRAMISU..188

Carson Valley

RIVER BEND GRILLE AT GENOA LAKES GOLF CLUB 191
    ITALIAN SAUSAGE STUFFED MUSHROOMS.............................192
    PASTA AL BORO 192
    SHRIMP BLT WITH A LEMON CAPER DILL MAYO.......................193
    TEQUILA LIME MARINADE..194
    PAPAYA CILANTRO SALSA 194
    CHOCOLATE MOUSSE 195

D. W.'S RESTAURANT 197
    GENERAL GRANT'S PEPPER STEAK....................................198
    ROASTED RED BELL PEPPER CHICKEN.............................199

THE WILD ROSE INN BED & BREAKFAST 201
    CURRANT SCONES 202
    LEMON CURD..203
    WILD ROSE MORNING CASSEROLE 203
    TOAD IN THE HOLE 204
    SEAFOOD LASAGNE 204

CARSON VALLEY COUNTRY CLUB 207
    OXTAIL STEW IN BROWN GRAVY 208
    GRILLED LAMB CHOPS..209
    CHICKEN AND RICE..209
    BASQUE BEANS...210

Incline Village

LONE EAGLE GRILLE 213

    CAESAR SALAD 214
    CAESAR SALAD DRESSING 214
    BRAISED LAMB SHANKS 215
    YELLOW TOMATO TOMATILLO SALSA 216
    ROOT BEER FLOAT PIE WITH PASTRY CREAM.................216

CIAO MEIN TRATTORIA..219

    ROASTED PORTOBELLO MUSHROOMS WITH BALSAMIC REDUCTION 220
    TEMPURA PRAWNS..221
    LEMON GRASS-JALAPENO PONZU SAUCE.........................222
    MONGOLIAN BEEF..222
    POLLO RIPIENO 223
    CRAB TOPPED SWORDFISH WITH SESAME CILANTRO.......225
    SESAME-CILANTRO AIOLI 226

SIERRA CAFE 227

    FAJITA WRAP 228
    COCONUT SHRIMP 229
    SWEET & SOUR DIPPING SAUCE.......................................230

AUSTIN'S (ADDITIONAL LOCATION IN RENO) 231

    CHICKEN FRIED STEAK 232
    SIERRA CHICKEN STEW...233
    TEXAS TACO SALAD 234
    MOUNTAIN PINTO BEANS...234
    ANDY'S INCREDIBLE APPLE PIE 235

CHINA WOK 237

    HOT & SOUR SOUP...238
    BEEF PEPPER STEAK...239
    EGGPLANT AND HOT GARLIC SAUCE 240

Tahoe Vista

SUNSETS ON THE LAKE..243

    SPINACH & MUSHROOM LASAGNE WITH TOMATO/MUSHROOM AND BÉCHAMEL SAUCE 244
    TOMATO/MUSHROOM SAUCE..244
    BÉCHAMEL SAUCE 245
    WOODFIRED PORK TENDERLOIN WITH MINTED COUSCOUS , CINNAMON BURGUNDY SAUCE & VANILLA GLAZED VEGETABLES 246
    MINTED COUSCOUS..247
    CINNAMON BURGUNDY SAUCE 247
    VANILLA GLAZED VEGETABLES 248
    SPIT ROASTED GARLIC CHICKEN WITH GRILLED POLENTA AND VEGETABLES 248

POLENTA...249
CRISPY SAFFRON RISOTTO CAKES 250
MUSHROOM SAUCE..251
GORGONZOLA AND PEAR SALAD 252
BASIC VINAIGRETTE 252
CHOCOLATE, BOURBON, PECAN TART WITH HOMEMADE CINNAMON ICE
CREAM 253
CINNAMON ICE CREAM 254

BOULEVARD CAFÉ **255**

GRILLED SWEETBREAD SALAD WITH WILD MUSHROOMS 256
POTATO RAVIOLIS WITH PORCINI, REGGIANO AND WHITE TRUFFLE OIL 257
FRITELLE WITH CRAB AND SHRIMP...................................258
ALMOND PANNA COTTA 259
NUT MERINGUE COOKIES 259

CAPTAIN JON'S SEAFOOD..**261**

OYSTERS ROCKEFELLER 262
SALMON EN CROUTE 263
FISH MOUSSE..263
LOBSTER WHISKEY 264
BERRIES ROMANOFF 264

BLUE ONION CATERING & EVENT PLANNING...................**265**

CARAMELIZED GINGER SCONES..266
ORANGE PISTACHIO BISCOTTI 267
ROSEMARY BRIOCHE DINNER ROLLS 268
THAI COLE SLAW..269

Tahoe City

JAKE'S ON THE LAKE..**273**

SEAFOOD GUMBO 274
RACK OF LAMB 275
DIJON HERB PASTE 276
CHUTNEY BUTTER 276
MEDITERRANEAN CHICKEN SANDWICH.............................277
OLIVE TAPANADE 277
HERB MAYONNAISE...278
TORTILLA GRILLED FRESH FISH 278
TORTILLA BREADING CRUST 279
AVOCADO AIOLI 279
AHI POKE 280

SUNNYSIDE RESORT CHRIS CRAFT DINING ROOM **281**

SUNNYSIDE AHI FISH TACO 282
CORN HUSK SALMON..282
CHICKEN CHILI RELLENO WITH ROASTED TOMATO SALSA 283
SALSA 284
BLACK BEAN CHILI...285

7

SUNNYSIDE'S SEARED AHI...286
GARLIC ROASTED SMASHED POTATOES..286
ROASTED RED BELL PEPPER CREAM..287

Truckee - Squaw Valley - Northstar

SQUEEZE IN...**291**

GRILLED LOLA..292
CASA DIA...292
ERIC SANDWICH..293
BLACK BEAN SOUP 294

GRAHAM'S...**295**

GRILLED SALMON WITH ORANGE SAFFRON GLAZE 296
SUMMER VEGETABLE MEDLEY 296
BLUEBERRY CRISP 297

MARTIS VALLEY GRILLE **299**

GRILLED JUMBO SHRIMP DRIZZLED WITH LEMON CHIPOTLE BUTTER.........300
BROILED MAHI MAHI WITH GRILLED PINEAPPLE SALSA AND LEMON 301

TIMBERCREEK @ NORTHSTAR...**303**

BLACK AND BLUE CAESAR SALAD...304
MEDITERRANEAN SEAFOOD PAELLA WITH HERB AIOLI.............................305
BROTH BASE 306
SAFFRON COUSCOUS 306
HERBED AIOLI..307
PEPPERED AHI SASHIMI WITH BLACKBERRY HOISIN SAUCE 307
DOUBLE PORK CHOP WITH SUN-DRIED APRICOT AND CHILE CHUTNEY 309
PAN ROASTED MUSCOVY DUCK ATOP THAI RED CURRY SAUCE 310
THAI RED CURRY SAUCE 311

South Lake Tahoe

PRIMAVERA **315**

FENNEL SAUSAGE AND WILD MUSHROOM LASAGNA 316
SAUTÉED PRAWNS WITH GARLIC, SAGE AND LEMON 317
ARTICHOKE BRUSCHETTA..318
ROASTED STRIPED BASS WITH FENNEL AND ARTICHOKES.............................319
TWO COLORED LINGUINI WITH FOUR CHEESES 319
STRAWBERRIES IN AMARETTO SABAYON...320

THE CORK & MORE...**321**

HOUSE TORTE STUFFED MUSHROOMS 322
BASIL GORGONZOLA TORTE 323
GERMAN POTATO SALAD..324

THE CHRISTIANIA INN **325**

TOMATO BRUSCHETTA..326
CHRISTIANIA CAESAR SALAD 327

8

GRILLED SALMON ON A BED OF BLACK BEANS WITH GREEN CHILE APRICOT
CHUTNEY 328
ROSEMARY CABERNET NEW YORK STEAKS 329
ROASTED GARLIC GREEN PEPPERCORN BUTTER 329
SALMON GRAVLAX 330
DILL SAUCE 330
SPICED TOMATO SOUP 331
CRANBERRY ORANGE MUFFINS 332
PUMPKIN BRULÉ 333

Sonnie and Lori's Favorite Recipes

SONNIE'S FAVORITES..337

SALMON SPREAD 337
TOMATO BISQUE.. 338
CHINESE COLE SLAW 339
CALICO SALAD 340
PEA SALAD 340
HARVARD BEETS 341
CHEESY POTATOES 342
SWEET & SOUR SAUCE 342
SONNIE'S ALMOND ROCO 343
BARB'S LEMON CAKE... 343
GROUND ALMOND TORTE.. 344

LORI'S FAVORITES...345

CRAB QUICHE 345
SPINACH BALLS 345
CURRIED STUFFED EGGS.. 346
LAYERED MEXICAN DELIGHT 347
DELUXE POTATO SALAD.. 348
SMOKED TURKEY TETRAZZINI.. 349
CHICKEN MOZZARELLA 350
CHICKEN CORDON BLEU... 351
CRANBERRY-STUFFED CORNISH HENS 352
CHICKEN BREAST FLORENTINE... 353
CARROT BREAD 354
HAWAIIAN BANANA NUT BREAD.. 354
CHOCOLATE CHEESECAKE... 355
MOCHA CHIP CHEESECAKE... 356

INDEX..358

ORDER FORM 372

ABOUT THE AUTHORS 374

RENO

Bricks Restaurant & Wine Bar

1695 South Virginia Street
Reno, Nevada 89502
(775) 786-2277
Reservations: Suggested

Bricks is a unique blend of elegant charm and friendly hospitality. The exterior bricks for which the restaurant is named were rescued from a Comstock-era building in Carson City. The stones of the back bar came from a Reno ranch and the welcoming brick fireplace makes you feel at home in Bricks. The beautifully appointed dining room with its cozy floral tapestry covered booths sparkles with leaded glass and brass accents. A friendly, knowledgeable staff tells you about the nightly features.

Bricks' menu provides a fine selection of fresh fish dishes, meat, pork tenderloins, lamb and steaks. There are always a few vegetarian selections on the menu. Roasted rack of lamb is a specialty. So is fresh ahi tuna crusted with freshly cracked pepper and sauced with a wasabi beurre blanc. Dinner entrees are served with a choice of soup of the day, mixed green salad or Caesar salad, and it's a hard choice to make, when all are so consistently good.

The bar has an excellent wine cellar, as well as an outstanding selection of premium beverages. At lunch, you'll find a tempting choice of appetizers, soups, salads, sandwiches, and entrees.

Specialties:
American, Rack of Lamb, Seafood, and Steaks

Hours:
11:30 AM - 2:00 PM, Mon. – Fri.
5:00 PM - 10:00 PM, Mon. – Sat
Closed Sunday

Credit Cards Accepted:
All major

Bricks BBQ Pepper Prawns

1 Tbsp. olive oil
4 large shrimp
All purpose flour for dusting shrimp
¼ c. mushrooms, sliced
1 green onion, sliced
2 Tbsp. cold butter
½ tsp. fresh garlic, chopped
½ c. dry white wine
1 tsp. Worcestershire sauce
Juice from ¼ lemon
½ tsp. Creole Seasoning (recipe follows)
½ tsp. cracked black pepper

Heat the olive oil in a sauté pan. Dust the shrimp in flour and sauté on both sides over moderate heat until lightly brown. Add the mushrooms and green onions, cook for 1 minute. Add the remaining ingredients and reduce until slightly thickened. Garnish with French bread for dipping.

Creole Seasoning
1 c. salt
¼ c. granulated garlic
¼ c. ground black pepper
1 tsp. cayenne pepper
1 tsp. thyme
1 tsp. oregano
¼ c. paprika
1 Tbsp. granulated onion

Blend all ingredients in a mixing bowl. Store in a sealed container.

Serves 1

Provolone Sauté

1 Tbsp. olive oil
3 oz. Provolone cheese (¼" thick slice)
1 egg, beaten
Flour seasoned with salt & pepper to dust the cheese
3 Tbsp. cold butter, cubed
2 Tbsp. sun-dried tomatoes, sliced
3 leaves fresh sweet basil, julienned
¼ c. dry white wine
½ tsp. fresh lemon juice
French bread

Heat the olive oil in a non-stick sauté pan. Dip the Provolone in the egg and dredge in flour. Shake off excess flour and sauté on both sides until cheese just begins to melt. Remove from the skillet and transfer to a small warm serving plate. Add the butter, tomatoes, basil, white wine and lemon juice. Reduce over medium heat for a few minutes and pour over the cheese. Serve with a crusty French bread for dipping.

Serves 2

Butternut Squash & Leek Soup

4½ lb. butternut squash, halved lengthwise
5 Tbsp. unsalted butter
4 large leeks, white & tender green parts, coarsely chopped (thoroughly soaked and cleaned)
7 sprigs fresh thyme or 1 tsp. dried
5 c. chicken stock
1¼ tsp. salt
½ tsp. freshly ground pepper

Garnish:
½ c. sour cream
3 Tbsp. chopped chives
8 slices bacon, fried crisp & crumbled

Preheat oven to 350°. Place the squash, cut side down, on a baking sheet and bake until tender, about 40 minutes. Let cool slightly. Using a spoon, scoop out and discard the seeds. Scrape the squash from the skin. Meanwhile, in a large heavy saucepan, melt the butter over low heat. Add the leeks and thyme and cook, stirring occasionally, until soft and browned, about 40 minutes. Discard the thyme sprigs. Stir the stock in with the squash. Simmer over moderate heat for 20 minutes. In a blender or food processor, puree the soup in batches until smooth. Pour the soup back into the pan and season with the salt & pepper. (The recipe can be prepared up to 2 days ahead. Reheat the soup before proceeding). To serve, ladle the soup into bowls and garnish each serving with 1 tablespoon sour cream, 1 teaspoon chives and a sprinkling of the bacon.

Serves 8

Chicken Pesto

2 Tbsp. olive oil
All purpose flour for dusting chicken
2 (8 oz.) boned and skinned chicken breasts
6 Tbsp. cold butter
10 leaves fresh basil, julienned
6 Tbsp. sun-dried tomatoes, julienned
2 tsp. fresh garlic, chopped
2 Tbsp. toasted pine nuts
½ c. dry white wine
1 tsp. lemon juice
½ c. heavy cream
½ c. grated Parmesan cheese
1 lb. linguini, cooked al dente
Freshly cracked pepper & salt to taste

Heat the olive oil in a sauté pan. Dust the chicken in flour and sauté on both sides over moderate heat until golden brown. To the chicken add the butter, basil, tomatoes, garlic, pine nuts, white wine and lemon juice. Reduce until the chicken is cooked through. If the dish becomes too dry, add more white wine. Add the heavy cream, 6 Tbsp. the Parmesan cheese and the linguini. Reduce until slightly thickened. Salt and pepper to taste. Serve in a pasta bowl and sprinkle with the remaining Parmesan cheese.

Serves 2

Pear, Ginger, Hazelnut Tart

2 pears (Comice, D'Anjou) cut in half, peeled, cored and sliced thin crosswise

Pastry:
1 c. flour
1 Tbsp. sugar
¼ tsp. salt
¼ c. toasted hazelnuts, chopped
½ c. butter, chilled and cut into small pieces
¼ tsp. lemon juice
⅔ tsp. vanilla
2 Tbsp. water

In a food processor, combine flour, sugar, salt and hazelnuts. Add butter and mix until dough resembles coarse meal. Mix together the lemon juice, vanilla and water and add to the dough and mix until it forms a ball. Gather ball together and flatten into a circle, wrap in plastic and allow to rest for 30 minutes. Roll out dough to fit a 9" removable tart pan. Place tart shell in freezer for 1 hour or longer.

Custard for Tart:
½ c. sugar
⅓ c. whipping cream
3 egg yolks
⅛ tsp. lemon juice
¼ tsp. Vanilla

Mix all ingredients together and pour into unbaked tart shell. Add the pears.

Pear, Ginger, Hazelnut Tart (Cont.)

Candied Ginger:

½ c. finely chopped ginger, sprinkled evenly over custard.

Apricot Jam for Glaze:
1 Tbsp. mixed with a little water and warmed until easy to spread.
Brush baked tart with warmed apricot jam.

Serves 6-8

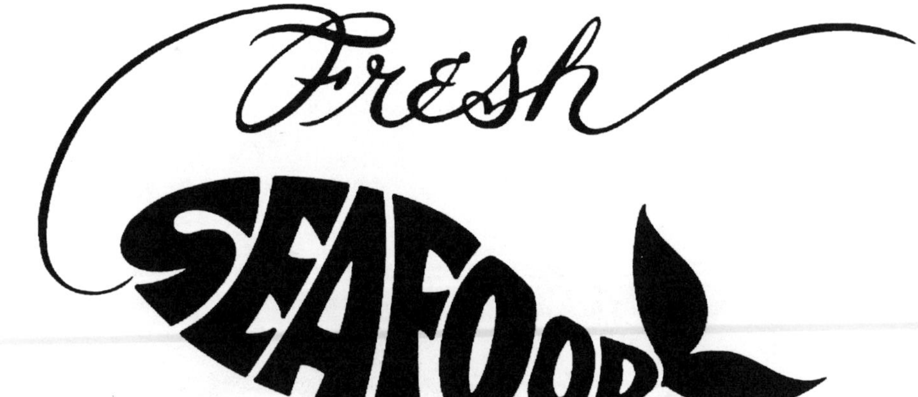
Fresh
SEAFOOD

Rapscallion Seafood House & Bar

1555 South Wells Avenue
Reno, Nevada 89502
(775) 323-1211
Website: www.rapscallion.com
Reservations: Suggested

Rapscallion has the look and feel of a Comstock-era San Francisco restaurant. The entire dining area feels like a private oasis. Along one wall, partitions surround "private cabins". The lighting is subdued. San Francisco architect Pat Kuleto designed the attractive wood and brass combined with a stained and etched glass interior. The lively lounge boasts a big stone fireplace. Adding to the "old San Francisco" feeling is the menu which changes daily, depending on what kinds of fresh fish are available. One can always find old favorite dishes like steaks, rack of lamb, pork chops, chicken, and burgers, but the star of the show is seafood - really fresh seafood. Lunch specials are included on the daily menu, too.

Daily specials show a global awareness with touches of Thai, Cajun, and the Caribbean - among others. On Sunday nights there is a Rapscallion clambake which includes steamed Maine lobster, sweet Italian sausage, Manila clams, corn on the cob, and new potatoes. Rapscallion's wine list is comprehensive and interesting, with a respectable by-the-glass selection. In fine weather, you can dine outside on the patio.

Specialties:
Fresh Seafood

Hours:
11:30 AM - 4:00 PM, Mon.-Fri.
10:00 A M - 2:00 PM, Sunday Brunch
5:00 PM – 10:00 PM (to 10:30, Fri. & Sat.)

Credit Cards Accepted:
American Express, Visa, MasterCard

Spanish Ceviche

1 c. lemon or lime juice
1 c. white wine
½ c. salad oil
¼ c. chopped parsley
¼ c. diced red bell peppers
¼ c. diced green bell peppers
2 Tbsp. diced yellow onion
½ tsp. fresh garlic
½ tsp. fresh shallots
Add to taste: black pepper, granulated garlic, seasoning salt, 1 bay leaf, crumbled, thyme & basil
1 1b. assorted white fish

Mix all ingredients (except fish) together. Cut fish into bite-size pieces. Add fish to remaining ingredients and gently toss. Cover and refrigerate stirring occasionally for 1 day. Serve as a first course, hors d'oeuvre, or salad.

Serves 4

Coco Prawns

Prawn Batter:
½ c. flour
¾ tsp. cayenne pepper
¾ tsp. paprika
¾ tsp. white pepper
½ tsp. sugar
½ tsp. salt
½ c. beer
¾ lb. very large prawns
¼ c. shredded coconut

Mix first 6 ingredients together. Add beer and mix thoroughly until smooth. Add more flour if not thick enough. Coat prawns in batter then roll in coconut. Deep fry in hot oil until done.

Coco Prawn Sauce

1 ½ c. orange marmalade
¼ c. Major Gray's chutney
1 c. soy sauce
1 Tbsp. granulated garlic
1 Tbsp. white pepper
1 Tbsp. ground ginger
dash Tabasco
¼ c. horseradish
dash cayenne pepper

In a food processor, mix the orange marmalade and chutney together. Add soy sauce and mix well. Add the rest of the ingredients and mix thoroughly. Place on side as dipping sauce. Serve as appetizer.

Serves 2

Clam Chowder

2 stalks celery
1 large peeled yellow onion
1 large carrot
¼ lb. bacon
4 cans (6½ oz. size) chopped clams
2 c. hot water
½ tsp. whole fennel seed
½ tsp. ground sage
½ tsp. granulated garlic
¼ c. white wine
1 large potato, peeled, large diced, boiled until fork tender
2 Tbsp. cornstarch mixed with 5 Tbsp. water
white pepper to taste
1½ c. half and half

In a food processor, chop celery, onion, carrot and bacon together. Sauté in large kettle until bacon is almost crisp and onion is tender. Add chopped clams with clam liquid and water. Add all spices and white wine and bring to a boil. Add cooked potatoes. Thicken with cornstarch mixture. Add pepper to taste. Add half and half and cook for 3 minutes

Serves 6-8

Viaggio

2309 Kietzke Lane (inside Franktown Corners)
Reno, Nevada 89502
(775) 828-2708
Reservations: Suggested - especially on weekends

The owner, Brett Roselli says that Viaggio is more than just an Italian restaurant. It is also a retail wine shop with a large selection of wines by the glass and offers a wine of the month club plus wine tastings. The cuisine is from Abruzzo on Italy's northern Adriatic coast and the menu includes heritage recipes that have survived from generation to generation. The preparation is based on sound principles of using fresh ingredients of the highest quality, thus preserving their inherent goodness and flavor. Fresh pasta is a specialty here and appears in many delicious variations including ravioli, gnocchi, and cannelloni. Veal is well represented, as are seafood dishes. There are nightly specials, too.

A large, attractive wine display is a feature of the warm-hued dining room. Your server is knowledgeable about the wines and can help you choose the perfect accompaniment from the more than 900 selections on hand.

Your experience at Viaggio will take you through a "journey" of great food, service, and wine and is meant to be fun, filling, and delicious, so sit back and enjoy the flavors! Buon Appetito!

Specialties:
Northern Italian

Hours:
11:00 AM to 4:00 PM, Monday through Friday
From 5:00 PM, Nightly

Credit Cards Accepted:
American Express, MasterCard, Visa, Discover

Mediterranean Red Clam Chowder

4 bacon slices, diced
1 c. onions, diced
1 c. carrots, diced
1 c. celery, diced
2 Tbsp. parsley, chopped
1 (1 lb. 12 oz. can) tomatoes
2 (11½ oz. jars) minced clams
4 c. water
2 tsp. salt
4 whole black peppercorns
1 bay leaf
½ Tbsp. dried thyme leaves
3 medium potatoes, pared and diced

In a large pot, sauté bacon until almost crisp. Add onions. Cook until tender, about 5 minutes. Add carrots, celery and parsley. Cook over low heat 5 to 10 minutes, stirring occasionally. Drain tomatoes, reserve liquid. Add tomatoes to vegetables in kettle. Drain clams, set aside. Add salt, peppercorns, bay leaf, thyme, water and reserved liquids. Bring to boil, reduce heat, cover and simmer 1 hour. Add potatoes, cover and cook approximately 20 minutes. Add clams to chowder. Simmer, uncovered, 15 minutes.

Serves 10

Osso Bucco
"Braised Veal Shanks"

1 c. finely chopped yellow onions
⅔ c. carrots, finely chopped
⅔ c. celery, finely chopped
¼ c. butter
1 tsp. garlic, finely chopped
2 strips lemon peel
½ c. oil
8 pieces veal shanks
¾ c. all purpose flour, spread out in shallow pan
1 c. dry white wine
1½ c. homemade meat broth or canned beef broth
1½ c. Italian tomatoes, coarsely chopped with their juices
1 tsp. dried thyme
4 leaves fresh basil (optional)
2 bay leaves
3 sprigs fresh parsley (Italian if possible)
6 twists of pepper mill (approximate)

Preheat oven to 350°. Using a three quart Dutch oven, sauté onions, carrots and celery in butter over medium heat for 8 to 10 minutes, adding the garlic and lemon during the last two minutes. Set aside. In another skillet, heat oil to a medium to high heat. Dredge veal in flour shaking off any excess and brown on all sides in the hot oil. When browned, remove the veal and place in a standing position on top of the cooked vegetables. Remove excess fat from the skillet. Add wine, boiling briskly for 3 minutes, pour over veal pieces. In the skillet, bring broth to simmer and pour over casserole. Add last 6 ingredients (enough broth to come to the top of the veal shanks). Bring contents to a simmer on top of stove, cover tightly and place in the oven for about 2 hours, basting veal every one half hour.

Serves 4

White Clam Sauce

2 (6 ½ oz. cans) chopped clams
¼ c. olive oil
1 Tbsp. garlic, minced
3 Tbsp. parsley, chopped
salt and black pepper to taste
juice from ½ fresh lemon
¼ c. butter
½ c. good dry white wine
Cooked pasta

Drain clams, reserve juice. In a large skillet, heat olive oil, add garlic. Sauté garlic to a light golden brown. Quickly stir in parsley. Add the drained clams and stir well. Cook lightly over medium heat. Add salt and black pepper and stir well. Add lemon juice, stir again. Add butter, stir in gently until all butter is melted. Add white wine, stir in gently, add reserved clam juice. Let come to a slow boil, then turn heat down to a simmer. Let simmer for 10 to 15 minutes. Turn off heat. Pour over cooked pasta.

Serves 6

Loreto's Marinara Sauce

½ c. olive oil
1½ c. onions, coarsely chopped
1 c. carrots, peeled and cut into rounds
3 large garlic cloves, chopped
6¾ c. tomatoes, with their liquids
salt and pepper to taste
pinch fresh parsley, minced fine
1½ tsp. dried oregano
2 tsp. dried basil
Cooked pasta

Pour oil in a sauce pot. Heat oil to medium high. Add the onions, carrots and garlic. Cook, stirring, until vegetables turn a golden brown. Add the tomatoes to the vegetables in the pot. Season with salt and pepper to taste. Bring the sauce to a boil then turn the heat down to a simmer. Partially cover the sauce pot and simmer for 1 to 1½ hours. When cooled, puree in a food processor and pour back into pot. Add remaining ingredients. Serve over cooked pasta.

Serves 8-10

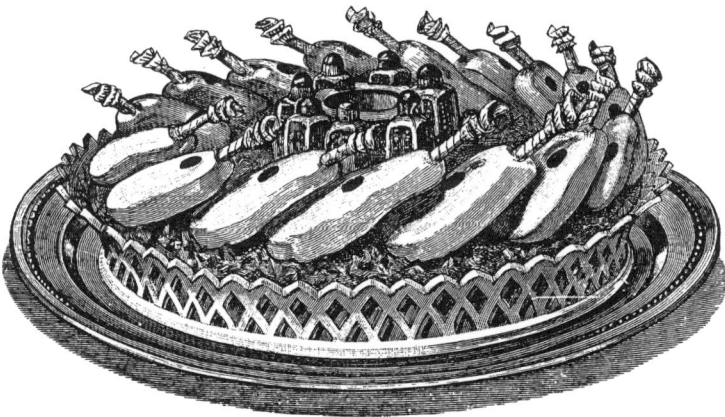

Italian Rum Cake

Cake:
1 c. pecans or walnuts, chopped fine
1 (18½ oz. pkg.) yellow cake mix
1 (3¾ oz. pkg.) Jell-O instant vanilla pudding mix
4 eggs
½ c. cold water
½ c. Wesson oil
½ c. 80 proof dark rum

Glaze:
½ c. butter
¼ c. water
1 c. granulated sugar
½ c. 80 proof dark rum

Preheat oven to 325°. Grease and flour a 10" tube or 12 cup bundt pan. Sprinkle nuts over bottom of pan. Mix all cake ingredients together. Pour batter over nuts. Bake 1 hour. Cool. Invert on serving plate. Prick top with a fork.

Make glaze: Melt butter in saucepan. Stir in water and sugar. Boil 5 minutes, stirring constantly. Remove from heat, stir in rum. Drizzle and smooth glaze evenly over top and side. Allow cake to absorb glaze. Repeat until glaze is used up.

Serves 8-10

Andiamo

Reno Hilton
2500 East Second Street
Reno, Nevada, 89502
(775) 789-2267
Reservations: Suggested

Whether you dine in Andiamo's sleekly modern outer dining room and bar, or the brick-vaulted main dining room, you'll find Italian food as exuberant as an Italian opera. The artfully conceived menu includes appetizers, soups, salads, pizza, pastas, and entrées with seasonal changes. There is always a fish of the day, and the Tenderloin of Beef in Gorgonzola red wine sauce with Cabernet shallot whipped potatoes is a show-stopper. You might find Asparagus Vegetarian Risotto with sun-dried tomatoes, Mushroom Lasagna with truffle oil, or Semolina Gnocchi with Cambozola cream sauce and fried parsley. Don't miss the Baby Spinach Salad tossed with mushroom vinaigrette, truffle oil, pancetta and toasted walnuts.

Andiamo's wine list is brief but thoughtfully chosen. Most are in the moderate price range, with a few very fine vintages. Desserts deserve their own separate menu, and they are memorable.

Specialties:
Fine Italian food with a California influence

Hours:
5:00 PM - 10:00 PM, Sun. - Fri.
5:00 PM - 11:00 PM, Sat.

Credit Cards Accepted:
American Express, MasterCard, Visa, Discover

Grilled Asparagus and Chili Oil

5 spears asparagus, grilled
1 tsp. balsamic vinaigrette
3 rings Pickled Onion (recipe follows)
½ red bell pepper, roasted (recipe follows)
1 tsp. extra virgin olive oil
pinch salt & pepper
3 slices shaved asiago (for garnish)
1 tsp. Chili Oil (recipe follows)
1 slice Candied Orange, chopped (recipe follows)

To grill asparagus, toss asparagus in dressing. Let sit for 5 minutes. Season with salt & pepper and grill over hot coals for 5 minutes, rolling them every 2 minutes. Toss asparagus, onion and roasted pepper in olive oil with salt & pepper. Arrange on plate and garnish with asiago. Drizzle Chili Oil on plate and serve after sprinkling with orange. Note: Serve vegetables at room temperature.

Pickled Red Onion

4 c. red wine vinegar
1 c. sugar
2 c. cold water
10 black peppercorns
2 red onions, ½" slices
3 sprigs thyme
3 bay leaves

Dissolve vinegar and sugar. Add all other ingredients and slowly heat, making sure onions are covered with liquid. When mixture starts to boil, remove from heat and let onions cool in liquid.

Roast Peppers

5 red bell peppers
2 tsp. oil

Lightly coat each pepper with oil. Place peppers on a sheet pan and bake at 500°. Shake pan every 15 minutes to rotate peppers. Pull out when skin is charred, usually 1 hour. Put in plastic bag and refrigerate. When cool, remove from bag and peel. Clean seeds out with your hands. Cut the pepper in strips. Do not rinse peppers.

Chili Oil

1 c. Pomace oil
2 tsp. red chili flakes
1 tsp. paprika

Heat oil slowly to 140°. Add chili flakes and remove from flame. When oil is lukewarm, add paprika, mix in and strain through fine strainer. Note: Do not add paprika when oil is hot because it will burn.

Candied Orange

5 orange slices, ¼" thick
1 qt. simple syrup (12 c. sugar & 8 c. water), mixed well

Cover oranges with simple syrup. Heat and slowly reduce to three-fourths. Drain. Fill pot (use only enough water to cover oranges) and reduce again. Pull oranges out and dry on a sheet pan overnight. Note: Do not refrigerate oranges as they will weep.

Ricotta Gelato with Grilled Stone Fruit

5 egg yolks
½ c. superfine sugar
5 tsp. cognac
1 lb. fresh ricotta
1 apricot, halved
2 tsp. sugar
1 peach, halved
2 c. balsamic vinegar
Candied Basil (recipe follows)

Ricotta Gelato with Grilled Stone Fruit (Cont.)

Put egg yolks and sugar into blender and blend until fluffy and pale. Add cognac and ricotta and blend to a light cream. Line mold with plastic wrap. Pour mixture into mold and cover with another piece of plastic wrap. Freeze for at least 4 hours. Meanwhile, using very ripe fruit, cut in half and remove pit. Sprinkle with sugar and let sit for 15 minutes. Put flesh side down on hot grill and grill for 5 minutes. Remove and cool. Do not refrigerate. In a sauce pan over low flame, reduce balsamic vinegar to ⅓ cup. Arrange gelato and fruit on plates, top with balsamic glaze and garnish with candied basil.

Candied Basil

2 egg whites
4 basil leaves
1 tsp. sugar

Beat egg whites until loose. Lightly brush the basil leaves with the egg white on both sides and sprinkle with sugar. Put on plate and dry.

Serves 2

Spinach Salad

¼ c. pomace oil
5 cremini mushrooms, sliced
1 tsp. salt
½ tsp. pepper
33 leaves baby spinach
3 Tbsp. Mushroom Vinaigrette (recipe follows)

In a sauté pan heat oil and add sliced mushrooms. Season with salt and pepper and cook for 10 minutes, stirring well. Toss remaining ingredients into bowl with Mushroom Vinaigrette and coat the leaves well . Arrange on a plate.

Mushroom Vinaigrette

⅓ c. strong mushroom stock
1 tsp. shallots
10 leaves parsley, chopped
1 tsp. salt
½ tsp. ground black pepper
½ c. champagne vinegar
2 c. olive oil
2 tsp. truffle oil

Combine ingredients in a bowl and mix well.

Serves 1

Andiamo's Bruleé

1 c. milk
1 vanilla bean, split
2 eggs
2 egg yolks
¼ c. sugar
1 c. heavy cream
1 ripe banana
2 oz. Baker's chocolate, chopped
1 Tbsp. sugar

Scald milk with split and seeded vanilla bean. Blend eggs, egg yolks and ¼ c. sugar together. Add heavy cream and milk. Mash banana and stir in. Use ¾ c. Serving dishes. Distribute chopped chocolate evenly. Distribute bruleé mix evenly. Bake in a water bath at 320° for 35 minutes or until set. Finish by placing 1 Tbsp. of granulated sugar on top of the bruleé. Heat with torch or place in a preheated 400° oven until sugar becomes caramelized.

Serves 2

Key Lime Pie

Crust:
1 c. graham cracker crumbs
½ c. butter, melted
⅓ c. sugar

Pie:
1 c. condensed milk
2 egg yolks
¼ c. Nellie & Joe's lime juice

Key Lime Pie (Cont.)

Combine crust ingredients in a bowl. Line 9" deep pie tin. Blend all ingredients for pie together and pour in graham cracker crust. Bake at 250° for 20 minutes. Let cool and refrigerate.

Serves 6-8

Flourless Chocolate Cake

12 oz. Bittersweet chocolate, chopped
½ c. unsalted butter
3 tbsp. Dutch process cocoa powder
10 large whole eggs, separated
½ c. granulated sugar
½ c. whipping cream
1 Tbsp. honey
½ tsp. lemon zest
mint sprig

Preheat oven to 350°. Select a 10" cake pan with straight sides. Prepare the pan by rubbing the bottom and sides of the pan with about ¼ teaspoon of butter. Add about ½ teaspoon of flour to the pan. Shake the pan to coat with an even layer of flour, discard excess flour. Line the bottom of the cake pan with a greased 10" parchment circle. Line the inner circles of the cake pan with a greased 4" wide strip of parchment paper, creating a "collar" that extends about 2" above the edge of the pan. Combine chocolate and ½ cup of butter in a double boiler and cook, stirring constantly, until melted. Using a wire whisk, stir in cocoa; keep warm. Combine egg whites and sugar and beat mixture until soft peaks form. Stir egg yolks into the chocolate mixture. Pour mixture into the cake pan and bake in center of oven for 40-45 minutes. The edges will appear cooked while the center will still be moist. Remove the cake from the oven and remove parchment "collar".

Flourless Chocolate Cake (Cont.)

Place a plate upside down on top of the cake pan; invert cake onto plate. Remove the parchment round. Let cool, but do not refrigerate. Combine cream, honey and lemon zest. Whip until soft peaks form. Slice cake and garnish with whipped cream and mint sprigs.

Serves 8

Planet Hollywood

Located inside:
Harrah's Casino
206 North Virginia Street
Reno, Nevada 89502
(775) 323-7837

Located Inside:
Caesar's Tahoe
55 Highway 50
South Lake Tahoe, Nevada
(775) 588-7828

Web site: www.planet hollywood.com
Reservations: Suggested for larger parties

Step into a fantasy world where you are the Star at Planet Hollywood. The setting is under a starlit, midnight blue sky at the Hollywood Bowl. Palm trees, unique movie memorabilia and five screens showing trailers from your favorite films, surround you. You will delight in a menu, which is mainly California Cuisine, accented with Mexican, Italian, and Oriental dishes that everyone will enjoy. A separate menu is devoted to specialty drinks, both creative and exotic. Leave room for dessert. The White Chocolate Bread Pudding and the Ghirardelli Double Chocolate Brownie are Oscar Winners. Planet Hollywood will also cater to your private party of 15 to 320 people, creating a memorable experience for that special event.

Specialties:
Hickory roasted chicken & pasta, exotic drinks, plus a "Planet Hollywood" merchandise shop

---

Hours:
11:30 AM - 10:00 PM, Sun. - Thurs.
11:30 AM - 11:00 PM, Fri.
11:30 AM - 12:00 PM, Sat.

Credit Cards Accepted:
All Major

Chopped Cobb Salad

4 c. chopped lettuce mix
¼ c. vinaigrette
¼ c. blue cheese, cubed
½ c. grilled chicken, diced
3 Tbsp. tomatoes, diced
1 Tbsp. bacon, cooked & diced
1 Tbsp. red onions, diced
1 Tbsp. Kalamata olives, pitted
1 Tbsp. egg, chopped (½ egg)

In a bowl, mix lettuce with all ingredients except egg. Toss well. Place into serving bowl. Sprinkle egg on top of salad.

Serves 1

Yaki Soba

1 Tbsp. vegetable oil
½ c. yellow onions, chopped
¼ c. green pepper, chopped
¼ c. red pepper, chopped
¼ c. cabbage, shredded
½ c. BBQ pork
8 oz. Japanese noodles
¼ c. Yaki Soba Sauce (available in oriental markets)

Heat oil in non-stick pan over high heat to near smoking point. Add onions, peppers, cabbage and pork. Cook for 1 minute. Add noodles, toss for 2 minutes on high heat. Add Yaki Soba Sauce and toss for 1 minute on high heat. Place in bowl, serve immediately.

Serves 1

Grilled Tuscan Chicken

salt & pepper to taste
7 oz. marinated chicken breast – in vinaigrette
1 slice proscuitto ham, thinly sliced
2 slices provolone cheese
4 slices ripe Roma tomato
1 ½ tsp. extra virgin olive oil
4 basil leaves
1 (6 ½ x 2 ¾") oblong focaccia bread, sliced

Sprinkle salt & pepper on each side of chicken breast. Place under broiler. Cook for 4 minutes on each side. Top chicken breast with proscuitto ham then provolone cheese. Toast foccacia. Cut in half. Place chicken on foccacia. Place 4 slices of Roma tomatoes across top of chicken, brush with extra virgin olive oil. Top tomato with whole basil leaves. Place top half of focaccia on sandwich.

Serves 1

Portobello Mushroom Burger

1 (5") portobello mushroom cap
2 Tbsp. vinaigrette dressing
salt & pepper to taste
1 slice mozzarella
4 slices Roma tomato

Brush mushroom completely in dressing and place under hot broiler. Sprinkle with salt & pepper. Cook for approximately 1 ½ minutes then turn. Cook for an additional 1 ½ minutes until tender, flip over and repeat. Toast bun. Place mozzarella on top of

43

Portobello Mushroom Burger (Cont.)

mushroom and grill until cheese is melted. Place on burger bun. Lay the tomatoes on top of cheese, cover with bun top.

Serves 1

Fire-Grilled Pizza

1 cracker bread (oval)
1 Tbsp. garlic oil
¼ c. mozzarella, shredded
1 Tbsp. Parmesan, shredded
¼ c. bruschetta

Place cracker bread in a hot broiler over medium heat. Lower heat. Flip the bread over and brush with garlic oil. Sprinkle with mozzarella cheese. Grill approximately 2 minutes,* until the cheese melts. Sprinkle with Parmesan cheese. Sprinkle evenly with drained bruschetta. Place the pizza onto a cutting board and cut into 4 pieces.

*some charring on the crust is common.

White Chocolate Bread Pudding with Whiskey Sauce

2 lbs. stale French bread
1⅛ c. milk
1 lb. + 1 c. granulated sugar
1 qt. heavy cream
1 Tbsp. vanilla extract
11 whole eggs (or 22 egg yolks)
1¼ lbs. white chocolate (broken or grated pieces)
6 oz. melted butter

Cut French bread into 1" cubes and set aside. Heat milk, one third of the sugar, heavy cream and vanilla over medium heat, mixing well with a wire whip. In a separate bowl, beat eggs with the remaining sugar until fully incorporated. As the milk/cream begins to boil and rise, quickly add a cup of the mixture to the eggs and whip to incorporate. Once fully blended, add the egg mixture to the milk/cream mixture, stirring constantly until the mixture reaches a thin custard consistency. Turn off heat. Add chocolate to the custard and mix until smooth. Pour the custard over the bread cubes and mix by hand using a folding motion, being careful not to smash the bread. Brush sides and bottom of a baking pan with melted butter. Equally distribute the custard/bread mixture into the pan and cover the pan with plastic wrap and foil. Fill a larger baking pan with water (one fourth full) and place the smaller pan inside. Bake in a 350° pre-heated oven for 2 hours. When fully cooked, a knife pushed into the center will come out clean. Remove foil and plastic wrap, brush with melted butter and cook 10 minutes more. Remove and cool. Serve with Whiskey Sauce.

Whiskey Sauce

1 lb. butter
1 qt. + ¼ c. granulated sugar
4 whole eggs
2 c. Jim Beam bourbon

Melt butter in heavy bottomed pan. Add sugar and mix well. Heat to simmering (do not allow to boil). Beat eggs with a whip, set aside. Carefully add bourbon to sugar mixture, stirring constantly. Continue cooking 2-3 minutes until bubbles begin forming around edge of pan. Add a small amount of bourbon mixture to eggs and whip to temper the mixture. Add egg mixture back to bourbon mixture, whipping constantly. When fully incorporated, strain through a sieve to remove any cooked egg. Store in plastic container and refrigerate until ready to use.

To serve, cut pudding into squares. Place a serving portion into a shallow bowl and ladle ¼ cup of sauce over the pudding and place in microwave for 30-40 seconds (depending on the microwave you have, it may take longer to heat) until warm. Serve with a scoop of white chocolate or vanilla ice cream on top. NOTE: Sauce will become very hot quickly. Be careful not to burn your mouth. This bread pudding will keep very well in the freezer (pre-cut before freezing).

Serves 8

La Vecchia

La Vecchia

3501 South Virginia Street
Reno, Nevada 89502
(775) 825-1113
Reservations: Strongly suggested

Lovely La Vecchia is the partnership of two of Reno's most talented chefs and Patricia, who flawlessly runs the restaurant, all Italian natives. It is romantic, comfortable and elegant. A large, lighted cabinet in the main dining room displays a fine selection of wines selected to compliment La Vecchia's fine food.

Look for a tempting selection of appetizers, imaginative salads, superb risottos and wonderful pasta dishes featuring homemade pasta. Veal is well represented, and you will also find dishes like baked pork chops topped with gorgonzola and sage in a red wine sauce, chicken Parmesan and fresh fish. Daily and seasonal specials may include such delights as ossobuco, roasted lamb shanks, venison ravioli, or roasted quail stuffed with sausage. Desserts keep to the same exacting high standards.

Specialties:
Eclectic Northern Italian cuisine

Hours:
11:00 AM - 2:00 PM, Mon. – Fri.
5:00 PM - 10:00 PM, Mon. – Sun.

Credit Cards Accepted:
All Major

Lentil Soup

1 lb. green lentils
1 carrot, diced
1 medium red onion, diced
2 celery stalks, diced
1 bunch fresh sage, minced (3 Tbsp.)
4 oz. panchetta, diced
½ c. olive oil
salt & pepper to taste
½ gal. chicken stock

Soak lentils in cold water, covered, for 3 hours. Drain. Sauté carrots, onion, celery, sage and panchetta in olive oil until tender. Add lentils, salt & pepper and chicken stock. Bring to a boil, reduce heat and simmer, uncovered, stirring occasionally, for 2 hours.

Serves 8

Fettuccine with Quail and Shiitake

Sauce:
2 Tbsp. butter
2 shallots, minced
½ lb. shiitake mushrooms, julienned
salt & pepper to taste
2 c. port wine
2 c. heavy cream

In melted butter, sauté shallots until golden. Add mushrooms and sauté until softened. Add salt & pepper and port. Reduce by half. Add cream and cook until thickened.

Fettuccine with Quail and Shiitake (Cont.)

Quail:
1 Tbsp. olive oil
2 Tbsp. butter
8 deboned quail

Heat olive oil and butter and sauté quail until browned on all sides. Bake in a preheated 350° oven for 15 minutes.

Stuffing:
1 Tbsp. olive oil
1 Tbsp. red onion, minced
1 tsp. fresh sage, minced
8 oz. Italian mild sausage
¼ c. fresh spinach, chopped
8 slices Italian proscuitto

Heat olive oil, add red onions, sage, sausage and spinach. Cook, breaking up sausage with wooden spoon, until sausage is browned. Let cool. Stuff quail with above mixture and wrap each in 1 slice of proscuitto.

Pasta:
1½ lb. fettuccine
1 c. grated Parmesan cheese

Cook fettuccine (in salted water) according to package directions. Drain pasta. Mix with prepared sauce and Parmesan cheese. Place on individual serving plates. Top with 1 quail on each plate and serve.

Serves 8

Venison Ravioli

Filling:
½ c. olive oil
1 carrot, chopped
1 onion, chopped
1 stalk celery, chopped
½ lb. venison shoulder stew meat
salt & pepper to taste
1 c. red wine
4 eggs
¼ c. Parmesan cheese, grated

Heat olive oil, sauté carrot, onion and celery until vegetables are softened. Add venison, salt & pepper and red wine. Cover and simmer for 25 minutes. Let cool. Grind filling mixture then add eggs and Parmesan.

Ravioli Dough:
1 lb. all purpose flour
6 eggs
1 c. water (more if needed)
1 egg plus 1 Tbsp. water

Mix flour with eggs and water until a firm dough forms (add more water if too dry). Roll as thin as possible. Cut into 1½" squares. Place 1 tablespoon of filling on each square and fold over to make triangle. Mix 1 egg and 1 tablespoon water together for egg wash. Close ravioli and spread egg wash on ends. Press edges with fork to close.

Venison Ravioli (Cont.)

Sauce:
2 Tbsp. butter
1 Tbsp. fresh thyme, minced fine
1 c. heavy cream
salt & pepper to taste
2 Tbsp. Parmesan cheese, grated

Melt butter. Add thyme, cream and salt & pepper. Cook until thickened.

Cook ravioli in boiling salted water for 5-7 minutes. Drain. Serve with sauce and sprinkle with Parmesan cheese.

Serves 8

Risotto Radicchio & Scallops

½ c. unsalted butter
1 shallot, minced fine
¼ lb. large scallops, quartered
1 whole radicchio, julienned
½ lb. riso, Arborio
½ gal. chicken stock, hot
½ c. Parmesan cheese

In 2 tablespoons butter, sauté shallots until golden. Add scallops and radicchio and sauté until softened. Add riso. Slowly add chicken broth, a little bit at a time, stirring until broth is absorbed, then repeat until all broth is used (this should take approximately 20 minutes). Remove from heat. Add Parmesan and remaining butter. Stir and serve.

Serves 8

Ossobuco

1 c. olive oil
8 (2") cut veal shanks (ossobuco)
2 carrots, diced
2 medium red onions, diced
2 stalks celery, diced
2 oz. porcini mushrooms, diced & soaked in water for 20 minutes
salt & pepper
2 c. white wine
16 oz. tomato sauce

Heat olive oil in large pan. Brown veal shanks on both sides.
Remove shanks from oil, place in baking pan and keep warm in
300° oven. In same hot oil sauté carrots, onions, celery, porcini
mushrooms, salt and pepper until vegetables are tender. Add wine
and reduce by ½ . Add tomato sauce and heat thoroughly. Pour
sauce over shanks in baking pan and cook at 250° for 2 hours.
Serve with polenta.

Serves 8

"**P**ANE **V**INO"
ITALIAN AMERICAN FOOD

Pane Vino

3446 Lakeside Drive
Reno, Nevada 89509
(775) 829-9449
Reservations: Suggested

Pane Vino (the name means bread/wine) was formerly Coco Pazzo. The name has changed, but it is still the same fine food and friendly staff. Pane Vino is a small, cheerful restaurant tucked into a popular strip mall. It's always busy, and it's easy to see why. The food is finely crafted Italian with specialties like Cioppino, Provini veal, fresh fish, and pastas. Try the mouth watering grilled polenta with crunchy slices of spicy sausage and tender grilled tomatoes, garnished with sliced garlic, pine nuts, fresh basil, and a grating of fresh Parmesan. It's available as an appetizer or entree. All dinners and lunches come with house salad and garlic bread. Portions are large, but you definitely should save room for their delightful desserts! Pane Vino has a good wine list, daily wine specials, and a small bar. It has the classic decor of red-and-white checked tablecloths with Chianti bottles hanging from the overhead "grape arbor". Big, comfortable brocade chairs look as though they have come from an Italian ducal palazzo. They will prepare your meal low fat upon request.

Specialties:
Italian and Daily Seafood

Hours:
11:30 AM - 2:00 PM, Mon. - Fri.
4:30 PM - 9:00 PM, Mon. - Sun.

Credit Cards Accepted:
American Express, MasterCard, Visa

53

Panevino Cioppino

¼ c. olive oil (for vegetables)
6 ribs celery, diced
2 medium carrots, diced
2 medium onions, diced
2 bulbs fennel, diced
2 Tbsp. garlic, pureed
2 Tbsp. Italian seasoning, dry
4 c. marinara or seasoned tomato puree
3 c. white wine
¼ Tbsp. red chili flakes, dry
1 gal. clam juice, fish stock or seafood base
1½ lb. cod or white fish, diced (no salmon, high oil)
1 Tbsp. olive oil (for shells)
½ lb. clams in shells
½ lb. mussels in shells
¼ lb. rock shrimp
¼ lb. large shrimp
¼ lb. scallops
¼ lb. cod or white fish, diced

In hot oil in 6 quart Dutch oven, sauté celery, carrots, onions, and fennel until tender. Add 1 tablespoon garlic and Italian seasoning. Sauté 5 more minutes. Add marinara, wine, chili flakes, clam juice and cod, cut in large chunks. Simmer, covered, for 1½ hours. Remove from heat. In a separate pan heat 1 tablespoon olive oil with remaining 1 tablespoon garlic. Add clams and mussels and cook until they start to open. Add to bouillabaisse and bring to boil. Add all remaining seafood and simmer for 2 minutes. NOTE: Do not overcook soft fish. May be served over linguini or your favorite pasta. Can be made 1 day ahead.

Serves 8-12

White Bean Minestrone

1 c. olive oil
2 medium onions, chopped
2 large potatoes, diced
2 carrots, chopped
2 fennel bulbs (sweet anise) chopped
4 ribs celery, chopped
1 red bell pepper, chopped
2 medium zucchini, diced
2 Tbsp. garlic puree
2 medium yellow squash, chopped
¼ c. total, equal parts fresh rosemary, oregano & thyme
⅛ c. "Herbs de Provence" (spice)
2 qt. chicken stock
1 qt. beef stock
1 c. Chianti
2 c. tomato puree
4 c. white beans, pre-cooked
salt & pepper to taste

Heat olive oil over medium heat. Sauté the onion and potato for 10 minutes. Add carrots, fennel, celery, red pepper, zucchini, garlic, squash and herbs. Simmer for 5 minutes. Add liquid stock and Chianti. Bring to a boil. Reduce heat and simmer for at least one hour. Add tomato puree, white beans, salt and pepper to taste. Cook for 10 minutes on medium heat. Let cool. Best served second day with peasant bread and fresh grated Parmesan.

Serves 8

Coco Chicken

½ c. pure olive oil, not extra-virgin
8-10 oz. chicken breast, diced, 1" cubes
1 lb. mild Italian sausage, cooked, cooled, sliced
2 Tbsp. garlic, chopped
1 Tbsp. fresh rosemary, chopped
1 Tbsp. fresh thyme, chopped
1 Tbsp. fresh basil, chopped
1 c. mushrooms, sliced
⅓ c. red bell pepper, roasted, julienne
⅔ c. red bell pepper, roasted, puree
1 Tbsp. kosher salt
½ Tbsp. cracked black pepper
½ lb. penne, rigatoni or bow-tie pasta, cooked
6 oz. Parmesan, grated
¼ c. parsley, chopped

In a hot skillet, add olive oil. Let heat and then add chicken breast. Cook 1 to 2 minutes. Add sausage then turn down heat. Add garlic and fresh herbs, cook an additional 3 minutes. Add mushrooms. Cook until mushrooms are tender. Add roasted pepper and roasted pepper puree. Salt and pepper to taste. Toss with al dente pasta. Serve with Parmesan and chopped parsley. Enjoy!

Serves 4

Cremosa Polenta Rosso

1 qt. chicken stock
1 qt. heavy cream
¼ lb. butter, melted
2 c. roasted red pepper, puree
¼ Tbsp. white pepper
3 c. Italian style polenta

In a saucepan, combine first 5 ingredients and bring to a boil. Slowly add polenta while stirring constantly with a wire whisk. Reduce heat to low. Stir frequently, for 25 minutes. Let cool 5 minutes. Serve warm.

Serves 8-12

Cioccolati Mousse

1 (1 lb.) chocolate (Callebau) or other high grade bar
2 Tbsp. dark rum
10 egg yolks
1½ c. powdered sugar
1½ Tbsp. vanilla
1½ c. heavy cream
10 egg whites

In top of double boiler, combine chocolate and dark rum. Cook over hot, not boiling water, stirring frequently until chocolate is melted. Whip egg yolks with ½ cup of the powdered sugar and the vanilla. Blend into chocolate mixture. Whip heavy cream, slowly adding ½ cup powdered sugar and whip into chocolate mixture. Whip egg whites with remaining ½ cup powdered sugar until soft peaks form. Fold into chocolate mixture.

Cioccolati Mousse (Cont.)

Refrigerate 4 hours. Keeps well. Serve with a dollop of kahlua whipped cream on top.

HELPFUL HINT: Work briskly so chocolate doesn't harden.

Serves 16

Cappuccino Cheesecake

Crust:
1½ c. graham cracker crumbs, chocolate cookie crumbs or chocolate graham cracker crumbs
3 Tbsp. butter, melted
¾ c. sugar

Filling:
1 lb. cream cheese
2 eggs
1 c. sugar
1½ tsp. vanilla
3 Tbsp. instant espresso, dissolved in small amount of hot water
2 c. sour cream

Combine crust ingredients with fork until well combined. Press mixture on bottom of 9" spring form pan. Combine all filling ingredients in food processor until smooth. Pour liquid over the back of a spoon into spring form pan so as not to disturb the crust. Bake at 375° for 50 minutes, until only the center portion "shakes". Let cool. Cover and refrigerate until firm and well chilled - at least 4 hours or overnight. Keeps well.

Serves 12

SEAFOOD STEAKHOUSE

Atlantis Seafood Steakhouse

Atlantis Casino Resort
3800 South Virginia Street
Reno, Nevada 89502
(775) 825-4700
Reservations: Suggested

Atlantis Seafood Steakhouse has an exotic atmosphere, with undulating fabric waves overhead to give an under-the-sea feeling. An illuminated pillar of water is filled with colorful, darting fish and flora. Around the room, plants in neon hues sway upward, reflected in the mirrored walls, giving the effect of sea-grottoes in a vast ocean.

The menu presents a fine selection of fish, shellfish, steaks, chops, chicken, veal, and imaginative pastas in addition to nightly specials. Desserts include spectacular table side preparation. The wine list includes a superb selection with plenty of affordable choices in every category. Each style of wine has a heading suggesting appropriate pairings. Wines by the glass present a comprehensive selection, too.

Specialties:
Fine dining in a uniquely beautiful setting

_____

Hours:
From 5 PM, Nightly

_____

Credit Cards Accepted:
All Major

Prawn Tropicale

Delicious sautéed prawns in a coconut, Grand Marnier and orange marmalade sauce

6 large or medium prawns
1 Tbsp. olive oil
1 Tbsp. butter
shallots and garlic to taste
1 Tbsp. Grand Marnier
1 tsp. marmalade
1 tsp. coconut flakes
1 Tbsp. fresh squeezed orange juice
⅓ c. whipping cream
¼ tsp. salt
¼ tsp. pepper
green onions to taste
2 Tbsp. melted butter

Clean prawns and drain on paper towel to dry. In hot sauté pan, melt olive oil and 1 tablespoon butter. Brown prawns. Add shallots and garlic, sauté until lightly browned. Add Grand Marnier and reduce. Add marmalade, coconut flakes, orange juice and cream. Simmer until thickened. Season to taste with salt and pepper. Add green onions and a touch of drawn butter. Serve hot.

Serves 1

Veal and Lobster Roulade

6 oz. veal medallion
salt & pepper
½ c. spinach, blanched
½ lobster tail
1 Tbsp. flour
Port Wine and Morel Mushroom Sauce (recipe follows)

Pound veal medallion to medium thickness. Season veal with salt and pepper. Put blanched spinach over seasoned veal, Poach lobster in salted water for 5-7 minutes, until done. Dice lobster finely and place over spinach. Roll veal as tight as possible. Sprinkle a little flour over finished roll. Cook over medium hot grill turning constantly to prevent burning until done. Slice veal roulade diagonally into about 1½" sections. Finish with Port Wine and Morel Mushroom Sauce.

Port Wine and Morel Mushroom Sauce

1 tsp. shallots, minced
1 tsp. garlic, minced
½ c. morel mushrooms, finely chopped
2 Tbsp. olive oil
½ c. port wine
1 tsp. beef stock base
demi glace
salt and pepper
4 Tbsp. butter

Sauté shallots, garlic and morel mushrooms in olive oil. Add port wine and reduce. Add beef base and demi glace to thicken. Add salt and pepper to flavor. Add butter.

Serves 1

Coral Reef Chicken

Chicken Breast stuffed with lobster, crab meat, and prawns finished with Tarragon Cream

1 c. prawns
1 c. lobster meat
½ c. crab meat
6 chicken breasts, boneless and skinless
½ c. tomato, diced
⅓ c. shallots, diced
⅓ c. green onions, diced
1 Tbsp. lemon juice
1 Tbsp. Dijon mustard
4 c. mayonnaise
dash of Cajun seasoning or Tabasco or cayenne to taste
¼ tsp. salt
¼ tsp. pepper
1 c. bread crumbs
Tarragon Cream Sauce (recipe follows)

Poach prawns and lobster 5-7 minutes, until done. Dice poached prawns and lobster finely and combine with crab meat. Pound chicken breast to medium size, covering with plastic wrap so chicken won't tear apart. Mix all seafood, tomato, shallots, green onion, lemon juice, Dijon mustard, mayonnaise and spices together. Put seafood spice filling into chicken and roll chicken tightly. Roll finished product into finely ground bread crumbs. Place chicken in pan and bake at 300° for 30 minutes. Finish with Tarragon Cream Sauce (recipe follows).

Tarragon Cream Sauce

1 Tbsp. shallots, minced
1 Tbsp. garlic, minced
3 Tbsp. butter
⅓ c. white wine
1 tsp. tarragon, dried or fresh
1 c. whipping cream
¼ tsp. salt
¼ tsp. pepper
2 Tbsp. butter

Sauté shallots and garlic in hot pan with butter. Add white wine and reduce. Add tarragon, whipping cream and salt and pepper. Simmer at low heat until cream thickens. Add 2 tablespoons butter, mix until melted and thoroughly combined. Upon serving, slice chicken diagonally in equal 1 to 1½" sections. Pour sauce over chicken.

Serves 6

Napa Sonoma Grocery Company

294 East Moana Lane (Independence Square)
Reno, Nevada 89502
(775) 826-0595
Reservations: Accepted

You might stop into Napa-Sonoma for one of their great sandwiches, salads, homemade soups, or grilled sandwiches. You can get lunch in a jiffy, but you're bound to linger over their tempting selection of gourmet foods, collection of unusual gift items, fine wines, and colorful cookbooks.

You can take a bit of Napa-Sonoma home with you, or send someone a very special gift of a Napa-Sonoma basket. There's even a "Made in Nevada" gift stuffed with gourmet items from the Silver State. There's a basket for everyone on your list! Napa-Sonoma's delightful, imaginative baskets are favorites for every gift occasion.

Napa-Sonoma will even come to you! Their catering menu has made them the choice for parties, receptions, and meetings. Stop in for a taste of inspiration.

Specialties:
Gift Baskets , catering, daily lunch, gourmet foods, great cookbooks, fine wines and a Unique Gift Shop

Hours:
9:00 AM - 5:30 PM, Mon. - Fri.
10:00 AM - 4:00 PM, Saturday
Closed Sunday

Credit Cards Accepted:
American Express, MasterCard, Visa

Butternut Squash Soup

½ c. white wine
3 tsp. ginger, minced
I large white onion, finely diced
3 large cloves garlic, finely diced
I large potato, peeled and diced
¼ c. celery, finely diced
3 tsp. olive oil
salt & pepper to taste
3 c. chicken stock
2½ lbs. butternut squash, peeled and cubed
½ c. heavy cream
½ c. fresh chopped chives to garnish

In a small saucepan cook white wine and ginger for 2 minutes, just until hot. Strain and discard ginger. Set wine aside. In a larger pan, sauté onions, garlic, potato and celery in olive oil along with salt and pepper to taste. Add chicken stock and butternut squash. Simmer until all vegetables are tender enough to puree (approximately 20-25 minutes). Puree soup in blender doing single cup portions at a time. When entire batch is pureed, place back into pot then add ginger/wine mixture and heavy cream. Simmer for 5 minutes, stirring occasionally. Garnish with fresh chives.

Serves 6

Tortellini Salad with Dijon Mustard Vinaigrette

4 Tbsp. olive oil
3 cloves garlic, minced
4 oz. Gouda cheese, julienne
1 lb. tortellini, cooked and drained
3 celery stalks, finely diced
1 small red onion, finely sliced
1 large green bell pepper, diced
¼ lb. bacon, cooked and coarsely chopped
½ tsp. thyme
salt & pepper to taste
Dijon Mustard Vinaigrette (recipe follows)
Romaine greens

Heat olive oil in skillet. Sauté garlic until browned. Remove from heat. In large bowl, mix garlic, cheese, tortellini, celery, onions, peppers, bacon and spices. Toss with dressing and place over bed of Romaine greens.

Dijon Mustard Vinaigrette

¾ c. olive oil
4 tsp. Dijon mustard
¾ c. red vinegar
¼ c. honey
½ tsp. garlic, minced
salt & pepper to taste
½ tsp. fresh basil

Combine all ingredients in a small bowl.

Serves 6

Grilled Medallions of Pork with Bourbon Apple Butter

2 lbs. pork tenderloin
4 tsp. lemon juice
4 Tbsp. olive oil
salt & pepper to taste
3 cloves garlic, minced
1 tsp. chipolte chili
2 tsp. Dijon mustard
½ tsp. thyme
½ tsp. oregano
Bourbon Apple Butter (recipe follows)

In shallow pan, marinate tenderloin in lemon juice and olive oil along with salt, pepper, garlic, chili, mustard, thyme and oregano for approximately 1-2 hours. Grill tenderloin for 15-20 minutes. Slice and set aside. Prepare Bourbon Apple Butter and pour over pork.

Bourbon Apple Butter

1 tsp. olive oil
1 shallot, finely chopped
1 tsp. sugar
4 apples, peeled and chopped
1 c. bourbon
2 tsp. ground cinnamon
1 pinch ground cloves
4 Tbsp. butter
1 c. beef stock
demi glaze

Bourbon Apple Butter (Cont.)

Heat oil over medium heat and sauté all ingredients with exception of demi glaze. Sauté for 5-10 minutes then add demi glaze. Simmer for an additional 10-15 minutes then pour over pork.

Serves 4-6

Lemon Herbed Breast of Chicken

6 split chicken breasts, skinned & boned
2 Tbsp. olive oil
2 Tbsp. butter
1 c. mushrooms, minced
1 shallot, minced
3 cloves garlic, minced
1 Tbsp. fresh basil, chopped
½ tsp. paprika
1 tsp. oregano
½ tsp. ground turmeric
½ tsp. cracked pepper
1 c. Chardonnay
¼ c. fresh lemon juice
zest of one lemon
3 dashes hot sauce
½ c. chicken broth

Sauté chicken in olive oil until golden and fully cooked (about 10 minutes). Set chicken aside. In same pan, melt butter, add mushrooms, shallots, garlic and all spices. Cook for 3 minutes. Add Chardonnay, lemon juice, lemon zest, hot sauce and chicken broth and simmer until mixture has reduced by a third. Transfer chicken to a heated serving platter and serve topped with herbed sauce.

Serves 6

Cafe Soleil

4796 Caughlin Parkway
Reno, Nevada 89509
(775) 828-6444
Reservations: Required on weekends, suggested otherwise

Cafe Soleil has a great view of Reno from almost any of the tables on two levels, but most diners focus on the open central kitchen. Copper-colored tubes radiate across the ceiling of the semicircular room drawing attention to the busy chefs, and the wood-burning, tile-faced oven. For a close-up view, there are seats at the counter whose arc separates the kitchen from the dining room. Entry is through the lively bar, but go slow as you pass the pastry case. You just might see a dessert you want to save room for!

Cafe Soleil's menu changes with the seasons, but the mainstay is on good, hearty fare prepared with imaginative flair. The menu leans a little towards Italian, but there is more than a taste of the Southwest, a touch of Pacific rim, and a generous helping of Americana. There are always a few vegetarian dishes, and a selection of pastas and pizzas. The pastas are so popular, that every Wednesday night is generally designated "pasta night" with its own special menu. Whatever you choose, you will be rightfully impressed with Café Soleil's presentation and mouth watering meals.

Specialties:
An eclectic menu with Asian, Moroccan and Mediterranean influence

---

Hours:
5:00 PM - 9:30 PM, Sun. & Mon.
5:00 PM - 10:00 PM, Tues. - Sat.
Sunday brunch 10:00 AM - 2:00 PM

Credit Cards Accepted:
American Express, MasterCard, Visa

Cafe Soleil Lamb Shanks Braised in Red Wine

¼ c. olive oil
4 lamb shanks
salt & fresh ground pepper to taste
2 Tbsp. Garlic, minced
1 c. onions, diced
2 c. red wine
3 c. beef stock
1 (28 oz. can) diced tomatoes
1 c. carrots, diced
1 c. celery, diced
2 Tbsp. fresh rosemary, minced
2 whole bay leaves

Heat olive oil over medium heat in a large heavy Dutch oven type casserole dish. Season lamb shanks with salt and pepper. Brown lamb shanks on both sides. Add garlic and sauté for 1 minute. Add onions and sauté for 3-5 minutes. Add red wine and beef stock and bring to a simmer. You may turn up the heat at this time. Add remaining ingredients and return to a simmer. Cover casserole and place in a preheated 325° oven and bake for 2½ to 3 hours or until shanks are very tender and meat comes easily off the bone.

Serves 4

Cafe Soleil Basic Polenta

10 c. cold water
2 Tbsp. salt
3 c. polenta
5 or 6 turns with peppermill
chili flakes (optional)
3-4 Tbsp. unsalted butter
1 c. freshly grated parmigiano cheese

Bring water to a boil in a large heavy saucepan over medium heat. Add salt and reduce heat to medium low. When water develops a gentle simmer, start pouring in the polenta by the cupful in a thin stream, very slowly, stirring constantly with a long wooden spoon or a sturdy wire whip to avoid lumps. When all the polenta has been added, you can relax a bit, then grind in your pepper and if you prefer the chili flakes. Keep the polenta at a steady low simmer and stir frequently. Cook the polenta 20-25 minutes. As it cooks, the polenta will thicken considerably. Keep stirring, crush any lumps that might form against the side of the pan. Polenta is done when it no longer tastes grainy and is smooth and creamy. At this time, add the butter and parmigiano cheese.

Serves 6

Grilled Salmon, Pot Au-Feu (Pot on the Fire)

1 Tbsp. Wesson oil
1 (2" piece) fresh ginger, peeled & cut in 1" julienne strips and blanched*
4 large garlic cloves, sliced thin lengthwise
1 jalapeno pepper, split in half lengthwise, seeds removed & finely julienned (optional)
2 ears corn, whole kernels sliced from the cob
2 large red bell peppers, 2" julienned
2 carrots, 2" fine julienned
½ c. white wine
1 Tbsp. rice wine vinegar
½ Napa cabbage, split lengthwise and cut in ¼ " slices
1 bunch scallions, ¼ " bias cut
2 c. chicken stock
4 (6-8 oz.) salmon filets, broiled or grilled
16-20 cilantro sprigs, washed thoroughly, chopped coarsely
2 limes, wedged

In a 4-6 quart large heavy-bottomed sauce pot, heat Wesson oil over medium heat. Add ginger, garlic and jalapenos and cook for 1 minute. Add corn, red bell pepper and carrots. Sauté for approximately 3 minutes. Add white wine and rice wine vinegar and reduce for 2 minutes. Add cabbage, scallions and chicken stock. Cook for approximately 3-4 minutes. Grill salmon on BBQ until just done. This will be approximately 3 minutes per side. You can also do this in the broiler. Ladle the vegetables and broth of the "Pot Au-Feu" evenly into 4 large bowls. Place a portion of grilled salmon on each and garnish with chopped cilantro and lime wedges.

*To blanch: put item in cold water, bring to a boil and then immediately immerse and shock in cold water. Drain on paper towels.   Serves 4

Cafe Soleil Roasted Bell Pepper Sauce

4 large red bell peppers
¼ c. red wine vinegar
¼ c. white wine
1 Tbsp. dried whole thyme or 1 Tbsp. fresh thyme
3 Tbsp. butter
3 Tbsp. Dijon mustard
½ c. heavy whipping cream
1 tsp. Salt
½ tsp. crushed red pepper chili flakes

Roast, peel an core red bell peppers. To roast peppers, preheat broiler and lay peppers on cookie sheet. Broil peppers on top rack of the oven until the skins blister and blacken, turning often for even roasting, about 10-12 minutes. Be sure to turn on your fan because the peppers may smoke. Place peppers in a paper bag, seal the top and let sit for 20 minutes. Meanwhile, in an enamel or stainless steel saucepan, reduce the vinegar, wine and thyme over medium high heat, until half the liquid is gone. Remove peppers and scrape off skins with a sharp knife. Remove the stem and seedy insides and puree peppers in a food processor to a very fine pulp. Strain the remaining wine/vinegar mixture and discard the thyme. Return liquid to saucepan. Add the bell peppers and the remaining ingredients. Cook over medium heat, whisking constantly until thoroughly hot.

Serve on top of grilled pork, halibut or pasta.

Serves 4

Cappuccino Panna Cotta

2 tsp. plain gelatin
2½ c. whipping cream
½ c. whole or 2% milk
½ c. granulated sugar
½ vanilla bean, split lengthwise
1 Tbsp. dark roast coffee beans, whole
1 Tbsp. kahlua (optional)
finely minced orange zest
mint sprigs
Fresh raspberries
Raspberry Sauce, (recipe follows)

Dissolve gelatin in 2 tablespoons water in a small dish. Let stand until softened, about 5-10 minutes. Heat cream, milk and sugar in a heavy-bottomed sauce pan to a simmer over medium heat. Scrape vanilla bean with a paring knife and put in cream mixture. Add coffee beans and kahlua. Add gelatin to cream mixture. Cook, stirring long enough to melt gelatin, approximately 5-7 minutes. Strain mixture into a stainless steel or glass bowl. Set in a larger bowl filled with ice. Add orange zest and cool, stirring occasionally. Lightly spray 4 custard cups with Pam spray to make it easier to unmold the panna cottas. Divide mixture in the custard cups. Refrigerate, covered, for at least 3 hours or preferably overnight. To serve, unmold custards onto dessert plates and garnish with mint sprigs and raspberries. Serve with raspberry sauce (recipe follows).

Raspberry Sauce

1 (8 oz. box or bag) frozen raspberries, defrosted
juice of ½ lemon
2 Tbsp. kirsch or triple sec
⅓ c. granulated sugar
1 tsp. cornstarch
2 Tbsp. water

Puree the raspberries and strain into a saucepan. Add lemon juice, Kirsch and sugar. Bring to a simmer. Mix the cornstarch with the water in a small bowl. Stir into raspberry puree. Cook over low heat until slightly thickened. May be served hot or cold.

Serves 4

Basic Bread Pudding with Praline Topping

Custard:
3 eggs
¾ c. sugar
1 ½ c. heavy cream
1 ½ c. half & half
1 tsp. nutmeg
1 tsp. cinnamon
½ stick butter, melted
1 tsp. Vanilla

Choice of: raspberries, strawberries, apples, etc. or dried fruits: raisins, cranberries, apricots,
½ Loaf French bread (sliced or cut into cubes - use more depending on size of baking dish)

Basic Bread Pudding with Praline Topping (Cont.)

Praline Topping:
½ c. sugar
¼ c. butter
¼ c. heavy cream
1 tsp. vanilla
1 c. nuts (to your liking - slivered almonds, pecan halves, walnut pieces)

Pudding: Mix all custard ingredients together. In a buttered baking dish, layer half of bread, sprinkle half of fruit on top, pour half of custard mixture over fruit and repeat. Bake in preheated 350° oven for 45 minutes. Prepare praline topping while pudding bakes.

Praline Topping: Combine ingredients in deep saucepan and cook over medium heat until all sugar is melted and caramelized and mixture is warm all the way through. Pour mixture over warm bread pudding and serve.

Serves 8

The New Hilltop
Bar & Eatery

Hilltop Bar & Eatery

4792 Caughlin Parkway
Reno, Nevada 89509
(775) 826-2665
Reservations: Accepted

One of the pleasures of the Hilltop Bar & Eatery is the great view of Reno below and to the east. A three-sided bar fills the center of the room, flanked by tables along the window side and booths on a raised platform opposite. On the wall above the entrance are 2 large black-and-white panels bearing caricatures of Reno-ites. The "San Francisco style" restaurant's menu is pleasingly eclectic with a variety of appetizers, burgers, pastas, and sandwiches in addition to the dinner entrees. There are nightly specials, too.

Live music is a feature at Hilltop, with different styles on Thursday, Friday, and Saturday nights when a nightclub atmosphere prevails. For sports fans, a trio of TVs above the bar lets you keep track of all the action.

Specialties:
Roast Chicken, New York Steak, Burgers & Sandwiches

Hours:
11:30 AM - 10:00 PM, daily
Closed Sundays & Major Holidays

Credit Cards Accepted:
All major

Hilltop Vegetable Soup

¼ green cabbage, shredded
2 medium carrots, peeled & diced
1 medium yellow onion, diced
2 medium zucchini, diced
1 stalk cauliflower, chopped
1 stalk broccoli, chopped
1 Tbsp. fresh garlic, chopped
4 c. tomato juice
4 c. chopped tomatoes in juice
8 c. water plus ¼ c. chicken broth
1 Tbsp. dry basil
1 Tbsp. dry oregano
1 Tbsp. black pepper
3 bay leaves
salt to taste

Mix all ingredients. Bring to boil and simmer 1 hour.

Yields: 1 gallon

Hilltop House Vinaigrette

4 c. Monazi Federzoni balsamic vinegar
2 c. extra virgin olive oil
2 c. orange juice
1 c. sugar
2 Tbsp. granulated garlic
2 Tbsp. ground black pepper

Mix all ingredients together. Shake to mix when needed.

Yields: ½ gallon

Chicken California Sandwich

1 Tbsp. Parmesan cheese, shredded
2 slices sourdough bread
2 slices Swiss cheese
1 (5 oz.) chicken breast, butterflied & grilled
½ avocado, sliced
2 slices tomato

In a non-stick sauté pan, sprinkle Parmesan cheese. Lay bread slices next to each other over the top of the Parmesan cheese. Put Swiss cheese on bread and heat. Grill the chicken breast. Put avocado and tomato slices on bread. Top with chicken to make a sandwich.

Serves 1

Fresco's Pizza

870 South Center Street
Reno, Nevada 89501
(775) 322-9210
Reservations: Not Accepted

Fresco's has pizzas, all your favorites from a 7-inch mini to an 18-inch extra large. They have all the toppings, of course, but there's a lot more. French bread pizzas, whole or half loaf, are available. In addition, there are chicken wings and chicken fingers with a choice of sauces from "mild" to "tongue-punishing" plus BBQ, honey mild, and Teriyaki.

Cold subs offer a variety of meats and cheeses, and "House Specials" are Chicken Parmesan, Meatball, Italian Sausage, Roast Beef, French Dip, and Cheese Steak sandwiches. Burgers, too.

Want more? How about Spaghetti? Ravioli? Lasagna? Manicotti? You can also get Calzones, salads, soup, chili, garlic bread, fried munchies, desserts, and beverages. Dine in or take out, and of course, they cater. Don't miss the Happy Hour Bar and Food Specials.

Specialties:
Pizza & Pasta. Friendly family atmosphere

Hours:
11 AM – 1 AM, Sun. – Thurs.
11 AM – 3 AM, Fri. & Sat.

Credit Cards Accepted:
American Express, MasterCard, Visa

Calzone

pizza dough
olive oil
oregano
garlic
mozzarella cheese, grated
tomato sauce (may substitute spicier pizza sauces)
choice of toppings

Start with either homemade or store bought pizza dough. Cut pizza dough into a circle 10" in diameter, ⅛" thick. Drizzle olive oil over "bottom" half (closest to you), leaving ½" space from the middle line (you will fold over below). Season with oregano and garlic. Top with tomato sauce and cheese. Top with favorite toppings such as sausage, pepperoni, mushrooms, etc. Fold top half over bottom half you just prepared and seal the edges with a fork. Be sure the seal is tight, to prevent the toppings from spilling out. Cut two small slits on the top for steam to escape. Place on a baking sheet and bake in preheated 450° oven for 10 minutes. Remove from oven and top with more tomato sauce and cheese. Return to oven just until cheese melts.

Serves 2

PIZZA

Stromboli

pizza dough
olive oil oregano
basil
parmesan cheese
garlic
1 ½ c. mozzarella cheese, grated
choice of toppings

Start with either homemade or store bought pizza dough. Cut pizza dough into a circle 16" in diameter, ⅛" thick (called a pizza skin). Drizzle olive oil in a 3" wide circle in the center of the pizza skin. Season with oregano, basil, parmesan cheese and garlic just over the olive oil. Top with mozzarella cheese, placed on the middle and spread in a line to the edges. Top with favorite toppings such as sausage, pepperoni, mushrooms, etc., again in a line. Roll the skin like a cigar, folding the ends in as you go. When finished rolling, bend into a horseshoe shape. Drizzle more olive oil on top and season with more herbs as above. Place on a baking sheet and bake in a preheated 450° oven for 10 to 15 minutes.

Serves 3

Elegant Party Catering

705 Trademark, Suite 103
Reno, Nevada 89511
(775) 851-8080
Reservations: Essential

If you can dream it, Elegant Party Catering and Rentals can make it happen. They can provide music and the floor to dance on plus flowers, tents, and champagne fountains. From lavish weddings to business meetings, bar mitzvahs to birthdays, parties to picnics-they do it all. And they do it just the way you want it.

Elegant Party Rentals can customize their menus to match your theme. Sushi bars are a cinch. Tostada tables are terrific. Mexican is marvelous. Italian is ideal. Prime rib is perfect. Buffet or sit-down, Elegant Party Catering can do it all-and that includes the clean-up, too!

Specialties:
Catering & complete event co-ordinating

Hours:
9 AM to 5 PM, Mon. – Fri.
10 AM to 1 PM, Saturday

Credit Cards Accepted:
Visa, MasterCard, Discover

Grandma Dot's Easy Stir Fry Vegetables

4 Tbsp. sesame oil
4-6 c. bean sprouts
1 small Napa cabbage, diced
1 bunch green onions, in ½" slices
4 Tbsp. sesame seeds
¼ -½ c. Kikkoman soy sauce

Heat sesame oil on medium high heat in wok. Stir fry sprouts and cabbage until softened. Add green onion, sesame seeds and sprinkle with soy sauce. Turn down heat and let simmer for 5 minutes.

Serves 4

Chicken Eggplant Parmesan Casserole

4 chicken breasts, split, boneless & skinless, sliced in half lengthwise between the counter and small cutting board while mostly thawed (so now you have 8 thin pieces of chicken)
garlic salt & pepper to taste
½-1 c. olive oil for frying
2 eggs, beaten
½ c. milk or half-and-half
6 cloves garlic, crushed
1 large round eggplant with skin on, cut in slices about ½" thick
1 c. Italian seasoned bread crumbs mixed with ½ c. flour
1 c. onions, diced
12 oz. fresh mushrooms, sliced
1 Tbsp. Italian seasoning
1 Tbsp. garlic salt
pepper to taste

Chicken Eggplant Parmesan Casserole (Cont.)

1 c. sliced black olives
1 c. grated Mozzarella cheese
1 c. grated cheddar cheese
1 (26 oz. jar) spaghetti sauce

Season chicken breasts with garlic salt and pepper to taste. Heat 3 tablespoons olive oil in pan on medium high heat. Add chicken and cook until browned on both sides (about 4-5 minutes each side). Drain on paper towel. Whisk eggs and milk together with half of the crushed garlic. Dip sliced eggplant in egg/milk mixture and then dredge in bread crumb/flour mixture. Heat remaining olive oil and fry eggplant until golden (about 5 minutes each side). Remove and drain on paper towel. In same pan, sauté onions, mushrooms, Italian seasoning, garlic salt, pepper and remaining crushed garlic on medium high heat, until browned and all liquid has evaporated. Add olives. Oil large casserole dish and place chicken in bottom. Then layer cheese, fried eggplant, spaghetti sauce, and top with onion/mushroom/olive mixture. Season to taste with salt & pepper. Bake at 350° for 55-75 minutes or until bubbly in middle and golden on top.

Serves 4

Bambi's Macaroni and Cheese

4 c. macaroni noodles, uncooked
2-3 c. shredded cheese (hard cheddar, mozzarella or Jack is preferred)
salt, pepper & garlic salt to taste
milk
1 lb. fried bacon or sausage, crumbled
1 (4 oz. can) sliced black olives
2 Tbsp. chopped onions

Boil macaroni noodles in salted water in large pot until tender approximately 7-10 minutes. Rinse in cool water in colander and drain. Layer macaroni, cheese and seasonings. Pour milk ¾ top of casserole and bake at 375° until golden and bubbly in middle, about 1 hour. Top with crumbled bacon or sausage, olives and onions.

Serves 4

Seafood Stuffed Croissants

2 (8½ oz. cans) real crab meat
2 (8½ oz. cans) imitation crab
1 c. boiled bay shrimp
1 c. mayonnaise
1 c. celery, sliced
½ c. sliced black olives
1 tsp. fresh parsley, chopped
1 tsp. mustard
salt, pepper & Mrs. Dash to taste
4 croissants
chopped parsley
lemon slices

Seafood Stuffed Croissants (Cont.)

Combine real crab with imitation crab, shrimp and mayonnaise. Mix in celery, olives, parsley and mustard. Season with salt, pepper and Mrs. Dash. Cut croissants in half lengthwise and make seafood sandwiches with filling. Serve on an elegant platter garnished with parsley and sliced lemon.

Serves 4

Summer Tortellini Salad

1 lb. tortellini
½ c. green pepper, diced
½ c. red pepper, diced
½ c. celery, diced
½ c. sliced black olives
½ c. string cheese, diced
¾ c. light vinaigrette dressing
8 garlic marinated mushrooms, sliced
8 marinated artichoke hearts, sliced
tossed greens

Boil tortellini in large amount salted water until tender. Drain in colander and rinse with cold water. Mix in green pepper, red pepper, celery, olives, string cheese, mushrooms and artichoke hearts. Toss with dressing and serve over a bed of tossed greens.

Serves 4

Yogurt Berry Pie

1 c. plain yogurt
1 c. Cool Whip
1 c. fresh or frozen berries (of your choice) with ¼ c. sugar sprinkled over
1 graham cracker crust

Mix yogurt and Cool Whip until just smooth. Add berries. Stir gently just until mixed. Pour over crust cover with saran wrap. Freeze overnight. Defrost 15-30 minutes. Cut and serve.

Serves 6-8

Bavarian World

595 Valley Road (6th & Valley)
Reno, Nevada 89512
(775) 323-7646
Reservations: Suggested

Bavarian World provides a taste of Alpine Germany that goes beyond the authentic cuisine. They have a gift shop with items from cuckoo clocks to clothing, a deli with a comprehensive selection of cold cuts, sausages, hams, and more. A bakery provides fresh breads, rolls, and pastries. Home cooks can find Swiss and German packaged foods, too. Beautiful party trays are a specialty.

The restaurant, which serves breakfast, lunch and dinner, surrounds a large dance floor with a mirrored disco ball. There's a wide podium for the musician at the far end, backed by panoramic alpine scenes and a picture of mad Ludwig's castle. Overhead lights are covered by delicate brass and glass shades hand painted with pretty blue flowers. What better place to enjoy Wiener schnitzel, beef rouladen, spaetzle, and lots of juicy sausages (not to mention the breads and pastries)! Enjoy live music on weekend evenings.

Specialties:
Bavarian Alpine Cuisine

Hours:
8:00 AM - 9:00 PM, Mon. – Sat.
Closed Sundays

Credit Cards Accepted:
American Express, MasterCard, Visa

Potato Cabbage Soup

5 medium potatoes
1 medium head of cabbage
1 carrot
1 small onion
1 gallon water
4 oz. chicken bouillon
parsley
pepper
all spice seasoning
maggi liquid*
2 slices bacon
2 heaping Tbsp. flour

Chop potatoes, cabbage, carrot and onion into small pieces and boil with water and the bouillon. Add parsley, pepper, seasoning and maggi to taste. Chop bacon and fry with a little oil to a golden brown. Add flour into the bacon pan and stir to absorb all the fat. Add to the soup.

*Available in supermarkets and specialty stores.

Serves 8-12

Rouladen

4 top round slices, 12 oz. each
Dijon mustard
4 lean slices of bacon
1 slightly sweet pickle, cut in 4 quarter wedges
2 medium onions
salt & pepper to taste
water
pickle juice
cornstarch, dissolved in water

For a good slice of beef, ask your butcher to cut you ¼ inch thick slices of top round beef. Lay slice flat on table, very thinly spread the mustard over entire area. Add one slice of bacon, one wedge of the pickle. Note: It is important to get the right pickles. They should be slightly sweet and sour. Slice onions very thin and add one half of the onion to each rouladen. Salt and pepper to taste. Roll the beef into a roll. Heat a sauce pan with oil and brown the rouladen. When slightly browned, add some water and some pickle juice to roughly one third of the height of the rouladen. Place rouladen with the seam side down so it cannot open up and make sure the pan is small enough so that the meat cannot roll open. Roast in oven at 350° for approximately 1 hour and 20 minutes. Turn once during roasting. Take out rouladen and add water to drippings to make gravy. Bring drippings to a boil and add dissolved cornstarch to desired thickness of gravy. You can add some au jus to get a more intense roast taste. Return rouladen to sauce until ready for serving. Serve with pasta or mashed potatoes and your favorite vegetable.

Serves 4

Pork Roast in Beer Sauce

3 lbs. pork shoulder with the fat
salt & pepper
2 tsp. caraway seeds
¼ c. oil
1 c. + 2 Tbsp. vegetable bouillon
1¼ c. dark beer
1 Tbsp. cornstarch

Season the meat with salt, pepper and 1 tsp. of caraway seeds. Roll up, making sure the fat is on the outside. Tie it up. Put oil in roasting pan and heat on top of stove. Brown meat all around in the hot oil. Add remaining caraway seeds. Put roasting pan in hot oven at 425° for 30 minutes. Add vegetable bouillon and further roast meat at 325° for 70 to 80 minutes. In steps, add the beer and baste roast several times during roasting. Remove roast and carve. Add a little water to the drippings. Bring to a boil. Dissolve cornstarch in water and add to drippings. Season with salt and pepper to taste.

Serves 6-8

MonteVigna

ITALIAN RISTORANTÉ

MonteVigna

Atlantis Casino Resort
3800 South Virginia Street
Reno, Nevada 89502
(775) 825-4700
Reservations: Suggested

MonteVigna was envisioned as a truly Tuscan restaurant with Tuscan wood-grilled meats, poultry, and fish, rotisserie slow-roasting, artisanal breads made from old-world starters, and handmade pastas. In the center of the restaurant is a free-standing wine room with space for 4,000 bottles cellared at proper temperature, and private dining facilities. From its 400-year-old tile floor to its gorgeous Venetian-style chandeliers suspended from domes painted with blue skies, MonteVigna is an experience for all the senses.

The extensive menu presents a variety of dishes including pastas, risottos, fish, meats, and poultry. Attention is paid to every detail from the water poured at the start of the meal - a choice of bottled Italian still or sparking - to the delectable desserts. Try a flambé dessert, prepared tableside, They are delicious! In fine weather, there is outdoor dining (and cigar smoking) on the patio with its herb garden.

Specialties:
Tuscany-style Italian Cuisine, Extensive Wine Collection

Hours:
5:00 PM - 10:00 PM, Sun. – Thurs.
5:00 PM – 11:00 PM, Fri. & Sat.

Credit Cards Accepted:
All Major

97

Salmone Ai Carcioffi

Grilled Salmon finished with sautéed artichoke hearts, garlic, extra virgin olive oil, and a light Chardonnay Butter Sauce

2 tsp. olive oil
¼ tsp. garlic, finely diced
7-8 oz. salmon filet
Chardonnay Butter Sauce (recipe follows)

Heat oil in pan. Add garlic and sauté quickly. Add salmon and sauté for 2 minutes on each side over medium heat. Place salmon in a baking pan. Bake at 350° for 3 to 7 minutes.

Chardonnay Butter Sauce

¼ c. artichoke hearts, diced
⅛ tsp. salt
4 tsp. white wine
¼ c. heavy cream
1 tsp. lemon juice
1 tsp. butter
1 tsp. parsley, chopped

Cook above ingredients over medium heat until slightly thickened. Serve over salmon.

Serves 1

Linguini Pescatora

Tuscany home recipe linguini pasta sautéed with fresh scallops, shrimp, clams, mussels, and calamari in a light tomato herb sauce

1 lb. linguini
¼ c. plus 1 Tbsp. olive oil
2 tsp. garlic, sliced

fresh seafood:
1 lb. mussels
1 lb. clams
½ lb. shrimp
½ lb. calamari
½ lb. scallops

¼ c. white wine
2 c. cored Roma plum tomatoes with juice
1 tsp. salt
1 tsp. black pepper
2 tsp. parsley, chopped

Boil linguini to al dente. Remove from water and drain. Stir in 1 tablespoon olive oil to prevent pasta from sticking together. Set aside. Lightly brown garlic in remaining olive oil. Add mussels and clams, allowing clams and mussels to open. Add remaining seafood. Add white wine and reduce. Add tomatoes with juices, salt, pepper and parsley. Add pasta and simmer thoroughly. Drizzle pasta with olive oil and serve hot.

Serves 6

Anatra al Balsamico

Sonoma duck slow-roasted in our rotisserie oven and finished with a Balsamic Peppercorn Sauce

whole Sonoma duck
Tuscany herbs:
rosemary
sage
garlic
basil
thyme
mint
salt & pepper
olive oil
Balsamic Peppercorn Sauce (recipe follows)

Sprinkle duck with Tuscany herbs. Rub olive oil into meat and marinate for several hours. Preheat oven to 375°. Bake duck in an oven pan, uncovered, for 1½ to 1¾ hours until golden brown. Cut duck in half, removing backbone from breast and separate thighs. Finish with Balsamic Peppercorn Sauce.

Balsamic Peppercorn Sauce

4 c. balsamic vinegar
1 c. honey
2 tsp. whole peppercorns
⅛ tsp. salt
⅛ tsp. white pepper
1 tsp. butter

Heat sauce pan to medium heat. Add vinegar to pan and reduce to about ¼ of original quantity, to a glazed syrup consistency. Add remaining ingredients. Cook until sauce gets to a nice firm glaze. Remove from heat. Pour sauce over top of duck.

Serves 2

The Grill at Wolf Run

1400 Wolf Run Road
Reno, Nevada 89511
(775) 851-3304
Reservations: Not accepted

The Grill at Wolf Run opens for breakfast for golfers (and anyone else) wanting an early start. They have all the expected options including New York steak and eggs, corned beef hash, eggs Benedict and more. Lunch and dinner options include everybody's favorites... sandwiches, burgers, salads, home made chili and soups. There's a nice array of appetizers and delicious entrees, including pastas, salmon and steak, plus daily specials and yummy desserts. Vegetarian meals are available upon request.

There are spacious sunny patios for outdoor dining in fine weather, with a non-stop view of the Sierras and golf course. Indoors you will find a vaulted ceiling and a large brick fireplace. A full-service sports bar is well-stocked with friendly folks. The Grille at Wolf Run is also available for private parties and events.

Specialties:
Grilled steaks, seafood, sandwiches and burgers

Hours:
7:30 AM - 9:00 PM, Daily, winter
6:30 AM - 9:00 PM, Daily, summer

Credit Cards Accepted:
MasterCard, Visa

Caesar Salad

6 eggs
4 c. olive oil
juice of 1 lemon
1 c. red wine vinegar
5 large cloves garlic, finely minced
6 anchovy filets
½ c. Dijon mustard
black pepper to taste
2 heads romaine lettuce
½ c. Parmesan cheese, grated
2 c. croutons

Whip eggs in food processor until fluffy. Slowly add oil, whip until emulsified. Add lemon juice, vinegar, garlic, anchovies, mustard and pepper. Mix until well blended. Chop lettuce and place in a bowl. Pour dressing over lettuce. Add cheese and croutons. Toss well.

Serves 6

Shrimp Scampi

1 c. flour
salt & pepper to taste
10 large shrimp, peeled & de-veined
2 Tbsp. olive oil
1 Tbsp. garlic, minced
1 c. white wine
juice of ½ lemon
¼ c. butter
1 tsp. parsley, chopped

Combine flour with salt and pepper to taste. Dip shrimp in flour mixture. Shake off excess flour. Heat oil in sauté pan on medium heat. Add shrimp and garlic. Cook to medium done. Add white wine and lemon juice. Let reduce by ¼. Add butter and parsley. Cover and heat slowly, until butter is melted and shrimp are completely cooked. Place shrimp on a heated serving platter and pour sauce over top. Serve with fettuccine noodles.

Serves 2

Rickshaw Paddy

4944 South Virginia Street
Reno, Nevada 89502
(775) 828-2335
Website: www.rickshawpaddy.com
Reservations: Not accepted

Swags of cloth swaying from the ceiling give a feeling of gentle seas as Rickshaw Paddy takes you on a tour of Pacific Rim and Indian cuisine that ranges from Seoul to Singapore and Mysore to Mandalay. There are plenty of favorite dishes to tempt the adventurous. Feast on Asian Bistro Bouillabaisse, Chicken Marsala, Grilled Steak Teriyaki, Bulgogi, Thai Spicy Shrimp, Curry Roast Duck and Grilled Mongolian Lamb Chops - to name just a few. Appetizers provide a similar pan-Asian sampling, as do the soups and salads. There's a fine assortment of noodles, rice dishes and vegetable sides plus, delicious innovative desserts. In a hurry? Rickshaw Paddy has "Express Luncheons". Take-out is available, too.

Specialties:
An Asian Bistro

Hours:
11:30 AM - 2:30 PM
5:00 PM - 10:00 PM
Closed Sundays

Credit Cards Accepted:
American Express, MasterCard, Visa

Asian Bistro Bouillabaisse

1 gallon water
¾ lb. prawns, (21-25 size), peeled and de-veined
½ lb. scallops
½ lb. fresh tuna
12 whole clams
12 snow crab claws
4 c. fish stock
2 tsp. fresh lemon grass, chopped
1 tsp. fresh ginger, peeled & chopped
4 baby bok choy
16 tomato wedges
½ c. celery, sliced
½ c. yellow onion, sliced
24 snow pea pods
2 tsp. fish sauce
3 Tbsp. white wine
2 tsp. lemon juice
2 tsp. sugar
salt & pepper to taste
4 sprigs cilantro (for garnish)

Bring water to a boil. Add all the seafood. Boil until the seafood is cooked, 8-10 minutes. Drain and set seafood aside. Heat the fish stock. Add vegetables, seasoning and spices. Stir well until the stock boils. Add the cooked seafood and mix well. Put in a soup bowl and garnish with cilantro.

Serves 4

Szechwan Duck Breast Salad

4 Indian non bread (available in gourmet or oriental grocery)
1 c. yellow onion, sliced
¼ c. peanut oil
1 lb. duck breast, sliced
½ c. soy sauce
¼ c. sesame oil
¼ c. sherry wine
1 Tbsp. dry red chili peppers
½ c. salad oil
¼ c. garlic, chopped
2 c. mixed green salad
1 c. Italian dressing
½ c. toasted cashew nuts
½ c. Lychee fruit, canned
½ c. pickled ginger
½ c. bean sprouts
2 Tbsp. carrots, shredded
2 Tbsp. green onion, julienne

Toast Indian bread (1 at a time) in a sauté pan without oil. Place on 4 individual plates. Sauté onion in peanut oil until caramelized. Spread the onion on the Indian bread. Marinate duck slices with soy sauce, sesame oil, wine and chili pepper for 15 minutes. Heat the wok. Place the salad oil, garlic and duck in the wok. Stir fry until the meat is done. Put mixed greens in a mixing bowl. Add dressing, cashews, Lychee, ginger and cooked duck and toss well. Place salad mixture, in 4 portions, on top of the onion bread. Garnish with bean sprouts, shredded carrots and green onion.

Serves 4

Tiger Prawns and Swordfish

½ c. black bean paste
½ c. fresh cream
½ c. sweet butter
¾ c. white wine
1 Tbsp. white pepper
4 baby bok choy, cut in ¼" pieces
½ c. salad oil
1 lb. swordfish steak
salt & pepper
1 lb. prawns (16-20 size), peeled & de-veined
¼ c. red bell pepper, julienne
¼ c. green onion, julienne

In a saucepan, heat black bean paste, cream, butter, ¼ cup of the wine and white pepper. Stir well until the sauce thickens. Keep sauce warm. Blanch the baby bok choy in boiling water for 1 minute, then plunge into cold water and drain. Add oil and heat. Add swordfish steak and salt and pepper. Cook until fish is almost done. Add shrimp and cook for 4 minutes. Add remaining white wine, heat and remove. Place sauce in heated serving platter. Place the fish on the sauce, then shrimp. Place the bok choy around the seafood and garnish with red peppers and green onion.

Serves 4

Spicy Basil Chicken

1 lb. chicken breast, boneless and skinless, sliced
salad oil
¾ c. yellow onion, shredded
1 green chili pepper, sliced
½ tsp. garlic, chopped
2 tsp. fresh basil, chopped
2 tsp. fish sauce
1 tsp. sugar
1 Tbsp. soy sauce
1 Tbsp. cornstarch, mixed with ⅔ c. water
1 tsp. green onion, shredded

Place the chicken in a deep fryer with enough hot oil to cover and cook until well done. Drain on paper towels. Place onion, chili pepper, garlic, basil, fish sauce, sugar and soy sauce in heated wok. Stir well.   Reduce and add chicken. Thicken with cornstarch water mixture. Garnish with green onion and serve.

Serves 2

Nik-N-Willies Pizza

1485 Geiger Grade on the
Virginia City Hwy.
Reno, Nevada 89511
(775) 851-4400

Comstock Pizza Company

120 Highway 50 East
Dayton, Nevada 89403
(775)246-7300

Reservations: Accepted

Both Nik-N-Willies in South Reno and Comstock Pizza Co. in Dayton are family owned and operated and offer a clean, comfortable, friendly environment for your dining pleasure. Pizzas are available to take-n-bake, hot to go, or to enjoy in the restaurants. There are over 20 different pizza toppings for your selection and 5 distinctive sauces. You can create your own masterpiece or try one of theirs. They have everything from a traditional pepperoni pizza to the outrageous "Comstock Load". The cream cheese white sauce is unlike any other white sauce, and is highly recommended. The hand tossed dough and savory sauces are homemade and the selected cheeses are grated daily. Their unique blend of the freshest ingredients and abundant toppings will assure you of the finest pizza available in the territory.

The Garlic Chicken Dijon and the Gold Pan are two of the several gourmet style pizzas available at Nik-N-Willies and Comstock Pizza Co. With an enticing cuisine like this, it is no surprise that the Reno Gazette Journal rated Nik-N-Willies "BEST TAKE & BAKE PIZZA IN RENO".

For a refreshing alternative to the ordinary, a vast selection of hot or cold sandwiches, salads and made to order calzones round out the menu and will please most any taste or appetite. Call ahead and your order will be ready when you are.

Specialties:
Hand Tossed Gourmet Pizzas

Hours:
11:00 AM - 9:00 PM "eight days a week"

Credit Cards Accepted:
MasterCard, Visa

113

Garlic Bread

8 Tbsp. butter
2 tsp. Parmesan cheese
1½ Tbsp. granulated garlic
2 tsp. basil flakes
2 Tbsp. Olive oil
1 (18" piece) French bread

Slowly melt butter over low heat or in double boiler. Add Parmesan, garlic, basil and olive oil. Cut fresh French bread in half and split again in half to get 4 pieces. Using a pastry brush apply mixture to the open bread pieces. Be sure to get the brush to the bottom of the mixture each time you dip. Broil lightly until the edges sizzle, about 1-2 minutes. Cut and serve.

Serves 2-4

Garlic Chicken Dijon Pizza

1 (12") pizza crust
2 Tbsp. Dijon mustard
1¼ c. mozzarella cheese, shredded
1 c. cooked chicken, diced about ½" cubes
2-3 cloves garlic, minced
½ c. red onions, chopped
10-12 fresh basil leaves, finely chopped
½ tomato, diced about ½" cubes
2 Tbsp. Parmesan cheese, grated

It may sound strange, but it tastes great! Preheat oven to 400°. Pick up a fresh piece of 12" dough from us or a pre-packaged one from the grocery store. Spread Dijon evenly on the crust, leaving a

Garlic Chicken Dijon Pizza (Cont.)

1" edge. Add mozzarella cheese. Top with chunked chicken. Spread evenly, minced garlic, onion, basil and tomatoes. Sprinkle liberally with Parmesan cheese. Place on parchment paper or pizza stone (no cookie sheet!) on middle or top rack in oven. Bake 9-13 minutes until the cheese is fully melted and the crust is golden. Cool a few minutes, cut and enjoy!

Serves 2-4

Gold Pan Pizza

1 (12") pizza crust
2 Tbsp. olive oil
1¼ c. mozzarella cheese, shredded
½ c. BBQ sauce (Bullseye works well)
1 c. cooked chicken, diced about ½" cubes
½ c. red onions, chopped
2 Tbsp. fresh cilantro, chopped medium

A favorite of many customers! Pick up a fresh piece of 12" dough from us or one from the grocery store. Lightly spread olive oil on the crust leaving about a 1" edge. Add mozzarella cheese. Mix the BBQ sauce and chicken - allow to marinate a few minutes or up to a day. Evenly add the BBQ chicken on top of the cheese. Top with onions and garnish with cilantro. Bake on middle or top rack in pre-heated 400° oven on parchment paper or a pizza stone (no cookie sheet!). Bake 9-13 minutes until the cheese is fully melted and the crust is golden. Remove from oven. Cool a few minutes and serve.

Serves 2-4

TEXAS LONGHORN
BAR & GRILL

Texas Longhorn

2325 Kietzke Lane, (Inside Franktown Corners)
Reno, Nevada 89502
(775) 828-3927; (82-TEXAS)
Website: mcollins@powernet.net
Reservations: Suggested, especially on weekends

Texas Longhorn Bar & Grill is a fun place to go for real "Texas roadhouse" atmosphere and hearty cowboy food. The barn-like structure has a rustic interior with checkered tablecloths, and rodeo paraphernalia decorating the walls. It's a casual, laid-back, but very fun place where they speak "friendly" and invite you to "just throw your peanut shells on the floor". Savory- Smoked barbecued meats are the house specialty. "Maui Wowie" ribs are a winner in the "Best in the West" Rib Cookoff sponsored by John Ascauga's Nugget in Sparks. The ribs are rubbed with a secret spice and herb blend, smoked, slathered with their "Maui Wowie" sauce, then grilled for a mouth-watering treat.

Texas Longhorn serves up blackened ribeye, chicken fried steak, smoked turkey, rotisserie chicken, and Tex-Mex fajitas. They have sandwiches, salads, and a catch of the day. There's a "Buckaroo Menu" for kids under 8. Texas Longhorn has banquet facilities, and a covered wagon for catered affairs. Beverages include microbrews, as well as domestic and imported beers, wine, and a full-service bar.

Specialties:
Ribs, Rotisserie chicken and a very fun atmosphere

Hours:
11:00 AM - 9:00 PM, Mon. - Sat.
Closed Sunday

Credit Cards Accepted:
American Express, MasterCard, Visa, Discovery

117

Texans don't mess around with a lot of sugary sauces. Instead, they favor dry rubs - full-flavored mixtures of paprika, black pepper and cayenne, with just a touch of sugar for sweetness. The rubs are massaged into the meat the night before cooking, by way of a marinade, then sprinkled on the ribs at the end of cooking. This double application of spices creates incredible character and depth of flavor, while preserving the natural taste of the pork. Sometimes a vinegar-and-mustard-based sauce - aptly called a "mop" sauce - is swabbed over the ribs during cooking. There is one included here for you to use if you like.

Texas-Style Ribs

6 racks pork ribs (4-6 lbs. baby back or 6-8 lbs. spareribs)

Dry Rub Seasoning:
¾ c. paprika
1½ Tbsp. freshly ground black pepper
1½ Tbsp. firmly packed dark brown sugar
1 Tbsp. salt
1½ tsp. celery salt
1½ tsp. cayenne pepper
1½ tsp. garlic powder
1½ tsp. dry mustard
1½ tsp. ground cumin

Mop Sauce: (optional)
1 c. yellow mustard
2 c. cider vinegar
2 tsp. salt

Remove the thin, papery skin from the back of each rack of ribs by pulling it off in a sheet with your fingers, using the corner of a kitchen towel to gain a secure grip or with pliers. Combine the ingredients for the rub in a small bowl and whisk to mix. Rub two-

Texas-Style Ribs (Cont.)

thirds of this mixture over the ribs on both sides, then transfer the ribs to a roasting pan. Cover and let marinate in the refrigerator 4-

8 hours. If using a charcoal grill, preheat to medium and place a drip pan in the center. If using a gas grill, place the wood chips in the smoker box and preheat the grill to high. When smoke appears, reduce heat to medium. When ready to cook, if using charcoal, toss half the wood chips on the coals. Oil the grill grate and arrange ribs on the hot grate over the drip pan. Cover the grill and smoke-cook the ribs for 1 hour. Meanwhile, prepare the mop sauce (if using). Mix together the mustard, vinegar and salt in a bowl and set aside. When ribs have cooked for an hour, uncover the grill and brush the ribs with the mop sauce. If using a charcoal grill, toss the remaining wood chips on the fire. Continue cooking the ribs until tender and almost done, one-half to one hour longer for baby back ribs, somewhat longer for spareribs. If using charcoal, after one hour add 10 to 12 fresh coals per side to the grill. The ribs are done when the meat is very tender and it has shrunk back from the ends of the bones. Fifteen minutes before the end, season the ribs with the remaining rub, sprinkling it on. To serve, cut the racks in half or for plate-burying effect, just leave them whole.

Serves 6

Rasta Ribs

4 racks baby back pork ribs (3-4 lbs.)

Dry Jerk Seasoning:
2 tsp. to 2 Tbsp. scotch bonnet or habanero chili powder
2 Tbsp. dried chives
1 Tbsp. dried onion flakes
1 Tbsp. dried garlic flakes
1 Tbsp. coarse (kosher or sea) salt
2 tsp. ground coriander
2 tsp. ground ginger
1 tsp. freshly ground black pepper
1 tsp. ground allspice
½ tsp. ground cinnamon
¼ tsp. ground cloves
¼ tsp. freshly grated nutmeg

Follow the same directions for Texas-Style Ribs (previous page). Substitute Dry Jerk Seasoning for Dry Rub Seasoning and omit the Mop Sauce.

Texas-Style Pulled Pork

For the Rub:
1 Tbsp. mild paprika
2 tsp. firmly packed light brown sugar
1½ tsp. hot paprika
¾ tsp. celery salt
½ tsp. garlic salt
½ tsp. dry mustard
½ tsp. freshly ground black pepper
½ tsp. onion powder
¼ tsp. Salt

For the Barbecue:
1 Boston butt (bone-in pork shoulder roast, 5-6 lbs., covered with a layer ½-1" thick of fat)

For the Rub: combine all the ingredients in a bowl and toss with your fingers to mix. Wearing rubber or plastic gloves, rub this mixture into the pork shoulder on all sides, then wrap in plastic and refrigerate for at least 3 hours, preferably 8. If using a gas grill, place all the wood chips in the smoker box and preheat the grill to high. When smoke appears, lower the heat to medium-low. If using a charcoal grill, preheat to medium-low and adjust the vents to obtain a temperature of 325°. When ready to cook, if using a charcoal grill, toss 1 cup wood chips on the coals. Place the pork shoulder, fat side up, on the hot grate over the drip pan. Cover the grill and smoke-cook the pork shoulder until fall-off-the-bone tender. The cooking time will depend on the size of the piece of meat and heat of the grill. If using charcoal, add 10 to 12 fresh coals per side every hour and toss more chips on the fresh coals, adding about 1 cup chips (½ cup per side) every time you replenish the coals. With gas, all you need to do is be sure that you start with a full tank of gas. Transfer the cooked pork roast to a cutting board, tent with aluminum foil and let rest for 15 minutes. After

Texas-Style Pulled Pork (Cont.)

the resting period, wearing heavy-duty rubber gloves, pull off and discard any skin from the meat, then pull the pork into pieces, discarding any bones or fat. Using your fingertips or a fork, pull each piece of pork into shreds 1 to 2 inches long and ⅛ to ¼ inch wide. This requires time and patience, but a human touch is needed to achieve the perfect texture. If patience isn't one of your virtues, you can finely chop the pork with a cleaver.

Serves 10 to 12

Texas-Style Barbecued Brisket

1 beef brisket (5-6 lbs.), with a layer of fat at least ½" thick
1 Tbsp. coarse (kosher or sea) salt
1 Tbsp. chili powder
2 tsp. sugar
1¼ tsp. freshly ground black pepper
1 tsp. ground cumin

Rinse the brisket under cold running water and blot dry with paper towels. Combine the remaining ingredients in a bowl and toss with your fingers to mix. Rub this mixture into the brisket on all sides. If you have time, wrap the brisket in plastic and let marinate 8 hours (or even overnight), but don't worry if you don't have time for this - it will be plenty flavorful, even if you cook it right away. Set the grill up for indirect cooking. No drip pan is necessary for this recipe. If using a charcoal grill, preheat to low. If using a gas grill, place as many wood chips as you can in the smoker box and preheat the grill to high. When smoke appears, lower the heat to medium-low. When ready to cook, if using a charcoal grill, toss one-quarter of the wood chips on the coals. Place the brisket, fat side up, in an aluminum foil pan (or make a pan with a double sheet of heavy duty aluminum foil). Place the pan in the center of the hot grate,

Texas-Style Barbecued Brisket (Cont.)

away from heat. Cover the grill. Smoke-cook the brisket, using the indirect method, until tender enough to shred with your fingers, 5-8 hours. The cooking time will depend on the size of the brisket and heat of the grill. Baste the brisket form time to time with the fat and juices that accumulate in the pan. If using charcoal, add 10 to 12 fresh coals per side every hour and toss more wood chips on the fresh coals. (Add about ½ cup chips per side every time you replenish the coals.) With gas, all you need to do is be sure that you start with a full tank of gas. Remove the brisket pan from the grill and let cool for 15 minutes. Transfer the brisket to a cutting board and thinly slice across the grain, using a sharp knife, electric knife or cleaver. Transfer the sliced meat to a platter pour the pan juices on top and serve immediately.

Serves 10-12

Jamaican Jerk Marinade

4 to 15 scotch bonnet chilies, seeded (for hotter marinade, leave the seeds in)
1 bunch scallions, both white and green parts, trimmed and coarsely chopped
2 shallots, halved
1 small onion, quartered
2 cloves garlic, peeled
1 Tbsp. grated fresh ginger
2 tsp. chopped fresh thyme (or 1 tsp. dried)
2 tsp. ground allspice
3 Tbsp. canola oil
3 Tbsp. soy sauce
3 Tbsp. fresh lime juice
2 Tbsp. firmly packed dark brown sugar
1 Tbsp. Salt

Jamaican Jerk Marinade (Cont.)

1 tsp. freshly ground black pepper
1 c. water

Combine all ingredients in a blender. Blend until smooth. Correct seasoning, adding more salt and lime juice as necessary. Store tightly covered in the refrigerator for up to 2 weeks.

Yields 2 cups (enough to marinate 4 lbs. meat, chicken or seafood)

Quick Garam Marsala

2 Tbsp. ground cumin
2 Tbsp. ground coriander
2 tsp. freshly ground black pepper
1 tsp. ground cardamom
1 tsp. ground ginger
¼ tsp. ground cinnamon
¼ tsp. ground cloves
¼ tsp. ground nutmeg

Combine all the ingredients in a jar, twist the lid on airtight, and shake to mix. Store away from heat and light for up to 6 months. Yields ⅓ cup (enough for 3 lbs. Meat, poultry or seafood)

Nothing to it Culinary Center

225 Crummer Lane
Reno, Nevada 89502
(775) 826-2628

"Nothing to It" may describe Jennifer Bushman's informed approach to fine cooking, but her culinary center has a great deal to it. Her cooking school offers a variety of courses with everything from a techniques series, and breadmaking, to regional cuisines, menu planning, entertaining, and a series of guest-hosted "Master Chef" classes by well-known experts. There are also children's classes, culinary tours, and a Friday night gourmet club.

In addition, "Nothing to It" sells tools, kitchenware and cookbooks, they also have house brand oils, vinegars and spices. The NTI Gourmet Deli serves soups, salads, and sandwiches for lunch, and a variety of delicious entrees and desserts for gourmet take-out dinners. Wm. Ohs Cabinets by Design has designed the magnificent cooking class kitchen. "Nothing to It" has something for everyone.

Hours:
10:00 AM - 6:00 PM, Mon. – Fri.
10:00 AM - 4:00 PM, Sat.
Closed Sunday

Credit Cards Accepted:
Visa, MasterCard

Nothing to it!!! Salads

In America today, we no longer think of eating as we did long ago. Many Americans used to eat what their mothers prepared for them: meat, potatoes and vegetables. Salad usually consisted of iceberg lettuce and tomato wedges drowning in commercially prepared bottled dressing. Salad was something that we ate because it was "good for us".

In our current way of looking at food and how we eat, salads have taken on a new importance. Salads have become an essential first course, sometimes even a main course. Instead of being tacked onto our menu, salads are now one of the starring attractions.

The difference between an average salad and a truly wonderful salad are the ingredients that you use.   There are special preparations for some of the ingredients and how you combine those ingredients will make or break your salad. Preparing a great salad is just like any other recipe - you cannot take short cuts. They compromise quality.

Start every salad by preparing your ingredients. Read the recipe carefully and check to see if all the ingredients are readily available.   Substitute other ingredients if necessary and make sure that all of the ingredients that you have picked are fresh.

Seasonality will be the key to your success in salad making. A tasteless tomato in the middle of winter has no place in a good winter salad. Using the correct ingredients at the correct time of year will ease your salad making task. The food production chain is really quite simple. We grow it, we gather it, we prepare it, we eat it. If our food is treated this way, with a minimum amount of interference, your salad will be perfect every time.

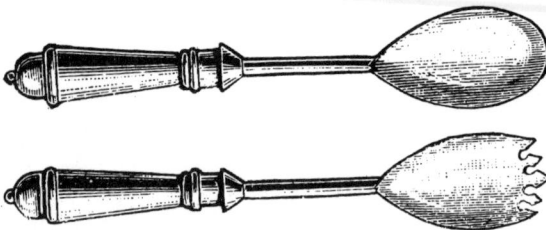

Baby Greens with Strawberries and Sugared Almonds

3 Tbsp. sugar
½ c. slivered almonds

Dressing:
2 Tbsp. sugar
1 Tbsp. Italian parsley, chopped
2 Tbsp. white wine vinegar
½ tsp. sea salt
dash of pepper
dash of tabasco
¼ c. olive oil
1 1b. baby greens, cleaned
1 c. celery, finely chopped
2 whole green onions, finely chopped
1 pint strawberries, cleaned, hulled and sliced

In a small skillet, heat the sugar over medium heat until it begins to melt. Add the almonds to the pan and toss rapidly until the sugar coats all of the almonds and the almonds are lightly browned. Pour them out onto a Pyrex dish and separate the almonds with a fork. Cool until hardened and break into pieces. In a small bowl, combine all of the dressing ingredients except for the olive oil. Add the oil in a slow stream, whisking as you add the oil until the dressing thickens. Place the greens, celery, green onions and strawberries in a large bowl. Toss them with the dressing. Add the almonds, toss lightly and serve.

Serves 8

Classic Caesar Salad*

Dressing:
½ c. olive oil
1 can anchovies, chopped to a paste
3 cloves garlic, minced
1 Tbsp. Dijon mustard
1 tsp. Worcestershire sauce
1 large cold egg
juice of 1 ½ lemons

Salad:
2 heads romaine lettuce, cleaned and torn
one recipe of Homemade Garlic Croutons (recipe follows)
¼ c. Parmigiano Reggiano cheese, grated
freshly ground black pepper

Put olive oil, anchovies, garlic, mustard and Worcestershire sauce in a bowl. Crack the egg on top of the ingredients. Squeeze the lemon juice over the egg. Mix with a fork until thick. In a large bowl, toss the dressing with the romaine lettuce then add the croutons, Parmesan cheese and fresh ground pepper. Toss lightly and serve.

*Remember that a real Caesar salad is made with a raw egg. If you aren't comfortable eating a raw egg, or if you are pregnant, omit the egg.

Serves 8

Homemade Garlic Croutons

⅓ c. olive oil
4 cloves garlic, sliced lengthwise
4 thick slices coarse sourdough bread, crust removed and cut into ¾" cubes

In a frying pan, over medium heat, combine the oil and the garlic and fry the garlic until brown, about 4 minutes. Remove the garlic from the oil and discard. Add the bread cubes to the pan and fry over high heat, stirring often, until browned. Transfer to paper towels and drain.

Roasted Red Potato Salad

Salad:
5 lbs. baby red potatoes
2 Tbsp. olive oil
6 slices bacon, diced
6 green onions, trim the tops and cut off all but 2" of the green
2 celery stalks, trimmed, finely chopped
1 green bell pepper, seeded, de-veined and finely chopped
½ c. pecan pieces, toasted
5 large eggs, hard boiled

Dressing:
2 Tbsp. whole grained mustard
¼ c. red wine vinegar
⅓ c. fruity olive oil
⅓ c. mayonnaise
½ tsp. sea salt
¼ tsp. pepper
2 tsp. fresh thyme, chopped

Roasted Red Potato Salad (Cont.)

Preheat oven to 425°. Wash and dry the red potatoes. Place them on a cookie sheet and toss them with the olive oil. Season them with salt and pepper. Roast the potatoes until tender, about 30 minutes. Meanwhile, in a medium skillet, fry the diced bacon until crispy. You may need to pour off the fat as you fry it to add some crispness to the bacon. Drain on a paper towel and cool. Place the green onion, celery, bell pepper, bacon and pecan pieces in a large bowl. Separate the hard boiled egg whites from the yolks. Place the hard boiled yolks into a separate medium sized bowl. Chop the egg whites and add them to the salad ingredients. To make the dressing: Mash the mustard and the egg yolks together with a fork until it forms a smooth paste. Whisk in the red wine vinegar and then, in a slow stream, add the olive oil. Finally, whisk in the mayonnaise, salt, pepper and chopped thyme. When the potatoes are tender, remove them from the oven and cool 15 minutes. Quarter the potatoes into bite sized pieces and add them to the bowl. Toss with the dressing. You can make the salad a day ahead, but bring it to room temperature before serving.

Serves 8

Chicken and Grape Pasta Salad

3 c. chicken breast, poached and cubed
sea salt & pepper
dry white wine
8 oz. Rotelle Pasta
1 (8 oz. can) pineapple slices, drained and chopped (reserve juice for the dressing)
½ c. celery, chopped
⅔ c. red or yellow bell pepper, seeded, de-veined and chopped
¼ c. green onions, trimmed and chopped
½ c. sliced almonds, toasted

Chicken and Grape Pasta Salad (Cont.)

1 c. seedless white grapes
½ c. seedless red grapes
½ c. Granny Smith apple, peeled and chopped

Dressing:
1 c. mayonnaise
¼ c. reserved pineapple juice
1 ½ tsp. fresh lemon juice
1 tsp. cumin
½ tsp. sea salt
¼ tsp. freshly ground pepper
½ c. Italian parsley, chopped

Poach the chicken by preheating your oven to 350°. Lay the chicken breasts on a jellyroll pan. Sprinkle them with sea salt and pepper and then pour enough dry white wine over them to cover half way. Cover the pan with aluminum foil and place in the oven. Poach about 30 minutes or until cooked through. In a large pot, bring 4 quarts of water to a boil. Season the water with salt and add the rotelle. Cook until just tender and drain. Meanwhile, place the pineapple, chicken, celery, bell pepper, onion, almonds, grapes and apple in a large bowl. In a small bowl, combine all of the dressing ingredients with a fork until smooth. Add the drained pasta to the large bowl. Pour the dressing into the large bowl. Toss to mix. Season with salt and pepper if necessary and refrigerate 30 minutes before serving.

Serves 8

OPEN
24
HOURS

Longneck's Bar & Grill

200 Lake Street
Corner of Lake & Second, behind Harrah's, downtown Reno
Reno, Nevada 89501
(775) 323-6004
Reservations: Not accepted

Longneck's Bar & Grill boasts "the best sandwiches in Reno". These include goodies like turkey and Swiss cheese on a Dutch crunch roll with cranberry horseradish mayo, a blackened chicken club sandwich with bacon, Swiss cheese, lettuce, tomato and cilantro mayo, plus hearty, hot Italian sandwiches. All are served with Parmesan-seasoned French fries. Hamburgers are on the menu, too.

There's more! Longneck's has a nibblers delight array of appetizers, of course. But they also serve homemade soup, chili, salads, pizzas, pastas, and specialties like fish and chips, and fried chicken. They cater, as well. And if you're in your jammies and you suddenly get the munchies, it's nice to know they deliver until 3 AM.

Specialties:
Great sandwiches, Takeout, Delivery (until 3:00 AM), House special drinks

---

Hours:
Open 24 hours

Credit Cards Accepted:
American Express, MasterCard, Visa, Discover

Longneck's Italian Dip Sandwich

4 bread rolls
1 lb. roast beef, thinly sliced
2 c. au jus
Marinated Mushroom Salad (recipe follows)
8 slices provolone cheese

Cut French roll in half for sandwiches. Boil roast beef in au jus. Place roast beef on bottom half of roll. Place Marinated Mushroom Salad over meat. Place cheese over mushroom salad. Toast in oven until cheese is melted and slightly brown. Remove and cut diagonally.

Marinated Mushroom Salad

2 c. sliced mushrooms
olive oil
1 small tomato, diced fine
¼ c. green onions, diced
3 Tbsp. red wine vinegar
6 Tbsp. olive oil
1 heaping Tbsp. grated Parmesan cheese
1 small pinch fresh rosemary, chopped fine
1 small pinch fresh thyme, chopped fine
1 small pinch fresh basil, chopped fine
salt & pepper to taste

Sauté mushrooms in small amount of olive oil until water in pan is evaporated. Dice tomatoes and onions, add to cooled mushrooms. Add remaining ingredients and mix thoroughly. Salt & pepper to taste. Cover and refrigerate.

Serves 4

Longneck's Turkey and Swiss Cheese Sandwich

4 Dutch crunch rolls
Cranberry Horseradish Mayo (recipe follows)
4 slices tomato
4 thick slices onion
lettuce
1 lb. sliced turkey breast
8 slices Swiss cheese

Cut Dutch crunch roll in half for sandwiches. Spread Cranberry Horseradish Mayo on roll (top and bottom). Place garnish on bottom half of roll. Place turkey and cheese on top of garnish. Cut diagonally.

Cranberry Horseradish Mayo

1 c. mayonnaise*
3 Tbsp. whole berry cranberry sauce
1 Tbsp. horseradish (or more to taste)
½ tsp. lemon juice
salt & pepper to taste
honey (optional)

Mix together thoroughly the first 4 ingredients. Add salt, pepper and honey (if desired) and mix. Cover and refrigerate.

*You may substitute cream cheese or sour cream for mayonnaise in a party dip

Serves 4

Longneck's Blackened Chicken Club Sandwich

blackened seasoning to taste
4 chicken breast filets
oil for sautéing
4 Dutch crunch rolls
Citrus Cilantro Mayo (recipe follows)
8 slices Swiss cheese
12 strips cooked bacon
4 slices tomato
4 thick slices onion
lettuce for 4 sandwiches

Season breast filets with blackened seasoning and sauté in oil in cast iron pan. Cut Dutch crunch roll in half for sandwiches and toast. Spread Citrus Cilantro Mayo on roll. When chicken is cooked (both sides), melt cheese and place bacon on top. Place garnish (tomato, onion, lettuce) on bottom half of roll. Place chicken on top of garnish on the roll and cut diagonally.

Citrus Cilantro Mayo

1 Tbsp. orange juice
1 Tbsp. lemon juice
1 Tbsp. lime juice
½ tsp. grated zest* of orange
½ tsp. grated zest of lemon
½ tsp. grated zest of lime
1 c. mayonnaise
honey to taste
salt & pepper to taste
2 pinches fresh cilantro, chopped fine

In a small sauce pot, reduce juice and grated zest to a syrup consistency. Cool. Once cool, add mayonnaise and mix well. Add honey and salt & pepper to taste. Add cilantro and mix. Cover and refrigerate.

*Zest is a finely chopped peel with no white under the skin. Use the fine side of cheese grater.

Serves 4

Toucan Charlie's Buffet and Grille

Atlantis Casino Resort
3800 South Virginia Street
Reno, Nevada 89502
(775) 825-4700
Reservations: Not required

Toucan Charlie's is repeatedly voted "Reno's Best Buffet" by Reno restaurant goers and was recently voted "Best of the Millenium" by Casino Players Magazine. The lush, tropical setting is an oasis of exotic greenery in the heart of the casino. An extensive selection of buffet choices includes unique features like the Chinese Wok and Exhibition Kitchen, the Southwest and Fajita Station, Fresh Salsa Bar, and Wood-Fired Grill and Rotisserie. There is also the popular Made-to-Order Salad Station plus an Elaborate Salad Bar, Action Mongolian BBQ Grille, All-American Favorites, and Famous Dessert Pantry and Sundae Bar. Breakfast features cooked-to-order omelets.

Weekends are very special with the Friday night Seafood Buffet, Saturday night's Steak and Seafood buffet, and Sunday's Champagne Brunch. You will also find special brunches for holidays such as Mother's Day, New Years, Christmas, and Easter.

Specialties:
Friday night seafood buffet, Saturday night steak and seafood buffet. Special brunches on holidays throughout the year.

Hours:
7:30 AM - 10:30 AM, Monday-Saturday
8:00 AM – 3:00 PM, Sunday Brunch
11:00 AM - 3:30 PM, daily
4:30 PM – 10:00 PM, nightly

Credit Cards Accepted:
All Major

139

Spicy Crab Salad

3 lb. crab flakes
4 green onions, chopped
4 stalks celery, chopped
2 c. mayonnaise
1 c. cocktail sauce
1 Tbsp. lemon juice
½ tsp. black pepper
¼ tsp. cayenne pepper

Mix together crab, green onions, and celery in a large container. In a separate bowl, combine mayonnaise, cocktail sauce, lemon juice, black pepper and cayenne pepper. Combine crab mixture ingredients with dressing just before serving.

Serves 6-8

Antipasto Salad

1 c. artichoke hearts
½ c. whole black olives
¾ c. red cherry peppers
¾ c. yellow wax peppers
1 c. cherry tomatoes
1 lb. pepperoni, sliced
2 lb. provolone, rectangle cut ⅜" by 1"
2 lb. salami, rectangle cut ⅜" by 1"
1 Tbsp. basil, chopped fine
¾ c. LaFlora dressing (or your favorite vinaigrette)
⅓ c. canola salad oil
1 c. red wine vinegar
½ tsp. salt
½ tsp. black pepper

Antipasto Salad (Cont.)

2 tsp. granulated garlic
½ tsp. ground oregano
½ tsp. sugar

Drain vegetables and rinse. Place in large container with cherry tomatoes, pepperoni, provolone, and salami. Make dressing: In separate bowl mix remaining ingredients together. Pour dressing mixture over salad contents. Mix and refrigerate until ready to serve.

Serves 6

Garlic Chicken

2 (2½ lb.) frying chicken, cut into serving pieces
1 c. sour cream
2 Tbsp. lemon juice
¼ tsp. Worcestershire sauce
1 clove garlic, chopped
½ tsp. salt
½ tsp. celery salt
¼ tsp. pepper
¼ tsp. paprika
flour
vegetable oil for frying

Wipe chicken pieces with damp cloth and put into refrigerator in pan covered with saran wrap. Mix all other ingredients together and pour over chicken, covering well. Let stand, covered, overnight in refrigerator. When ready to fry, drain, dredge in flour and fry in hot vegetable oil until thoroughly cooked and golden.

Serves 6-8

Salsa

2 c. tomatoes, seeded and coarsely chopped
2 green onions with tops, sliced
1 clove garlic, minced
2 tsp. jalapeno or serrano chili, seeded and minced
1 Tbsp. vegetable oil
3 tsp. lime juice
10 sprigs cilantro, minced
salt to taste
½ tsp. sugar
¼ tsp. pepper

Combine all ingredients in a bowl. Refrigerate for several hours before serving.

SPARKS

B. J.'s Bar-B-Que

754 North McCarran Boulevard
Sparks, Nevada 89431
(775) 355-1010
Reservations: Not accepted

B.J.'s Barbecue consistently wins just about every Rib Cook-Off and Barbecue Prize to be had. One taste will tell you why. Actually, you get the idea the moment you walk in the door, because B.J.'s meats are slow-smoked over "smoldering oak" for up to twelve hours. You can choose your (award-winning) barbecue sauce in hot, medium, or mild. The menu features lots of ribs, plus pork, chicken, beef brisket and homemade hot links. Sandwiches and salads are also available.

At this no-frills restaurant, all half-orders, dinners, and combos are served with beans, and your choice of potato salad, coleslaw or French fries, and cornbread or roll. All are freshly made and very good. Take-out is available, and catering is a specialty. You can even buy a jar of their good barbecue sauce to take home. This is real, down-home, finger-lickin' good!

Specialties:
Prize winning Barbecued Ribs

Hours:
11:00 AM - 9:00 PM, Mon. - Sat.
Closed Sundays

Credit Cards Accepted:
American Express, MasterCard, Visa, Discover

Grilled Pork Tenderloin

1 pork tenderloin
2 cloves garlic, sliced
B. J.'s BBQ spice rub (or other meat spice rub)

Make small cuts in tenderloin and insert sliced pieces of garlic. Generously sprinkle spice rub on all sides of tenderloin. Grill until internal temperature is 165°. (Option - put some flavored wood chips in the grill with some water for added flavor).

Serves 4

B. J.'s BBQ'd Beans

1 (1 lb.) bag dry pinto beans
½ c. packed brown sugar
1¼ c. B. J.'s BBQ Sauce (or store bought BBQ sauce)
2 Tbsp. mustard
1 heaping Tbsp. chili powder

Cover dry beans with water. Boil until tender (approximately 3-4 hours). Drain. Combine all other ingredients, pour over beans. Mix thoroughly and heat through.

Serves 4-6

Sweet Potato Tarts

2 c. cooked, mashed sweet potatoes
½ c. butter, softened
2 eggs, separated
½ c. milk
1 c. packed brown sugar
¼ tsp. salt
½ tsp. cinnamon
½ tsp. nutmeg
½ tsp. ginger
¼ c. sugar
20 frozen unbaked tart shells

Combine potatoes, butter, egg yolks, milk, brown sugar and spices. Beat egg whites at room temperature for 1 minute. Gradually add sugar until stiff peaks form. Fold egg white mixture into sweet potato mixture. Fill unbaked tart shells. Bake at 400° for 10 minutes, reduce to 350° for 30 minutes. Serve with whipped cream.

Yields: 20 tarts

Sparks, Nevada

Great Basin Brewing Company

846 Victorian Avenue
Sparks, Nevada 89432
(775) 355-7711
Reservations: For parties of 8 or more

This 6-time winner of the Great American Beer Festival is a no-frills, comfortable, laid-back kind of place where you can dine indoors or out and watch the passing parade on Sparks' Victorian Square. Inside, there's a congenial bar along one wall. On a raised platform are rows of tables and bentwood chairs. Beside the entrance, T-shirts with the Great Basin logo hang from the ceiling like colorful flags. Live entertainment is often part of the fun at this lively pub.

The menu is a fun collection of pub favorites including burgers, wraps, sandwiches, and fish and chips plus all the things that go well with beer. Salads, pastas, pizzas, and hearty entrees are on tap, as well. Great Basin offers a variety of brews rated as some of the best beers in America. Nevada's most award winning brewery features ten beers on tap, including the four regulars; Nevada Gold, Wild Horse Ale, Jackpot Porter, and Ichthyosaur India Pale Ale, fondly known as "Icky". There are Brewmaster's seasonal specials that rotate with the seasons also.

Specialties:
Parties, Local Events, Beer brewed on premises

Hours:
11:30 AM - 10 PM, daily

Credit Cards Accepted:
All major

149

Wisconsin Style Beer Cheese Soup

Wisconsin was once the U.S. brewing hub as well as the center of dairy and cheese production. Food and beverage from the heartland is a paradise for the hearty eater. This soup combines some of the best of this cuisine blending beer, cheese, and sausage. The soup is a meal in itself as long as it is accompanied by a glass of fine beer. This soup is delicious with a malty lager such as Great Basin's seasonal brew Oktoberfest or the brewery staple, the award winning altbier, Wild Horse Ale.

Soup Base:
½ c. carrot, chopped
½ c. onion, chopped
½ c. celery, chopped
1 bratwurst sausage, thinly sliced
2 Tbsp. olive oil
1½ c. Nevada Gold (Kolsch style beer, available only at Great Basin Brewing Company) or other crisp pilsner style lager
1½ c. Wild Horse Ale (German "Alt-Style" beer, available only at Great Basin Brewing Company) or any fine amber German style lager, such as Marzen or Oktoberfest
2 c. chicken stock
1 tsp. paprika
1 tsp. ground thyme
1 Tbsp. Worcestershire sauce
1 c. heavy cream or half and half (milk can be substituted but the soup will not have the rich texture for maximum enjoyment)
2 Tbsp. butter & 2 Tbsp. flour, for roux
1 c. shredded Wisconsin medium cheddar cheese

Sauté the carrots, onion, celery and sausage in oil in a saucepan until the onions are translucent. Add the beer, chicken stock, paprika, thyme and Worcestershire sauce. Stir occasionally and bring to a boil. Turn the burner to low and add the cream. Next,

Wisconsin Style Beer Cheese Soup (Cont.)

thicken the soup by adding the roux: Melt 2 Tbsp. butter or margarine. Add about 2 Tbsp. flour to make a thick paste. Stir constantly over medium heat until the mixture turns light brown and has a nut-like aroma. Add roux one teaspoon at a time, stirring continuously, until the soup has the consistency of a chowder. Finally, add the cheese a little at a time, stirring until it is dissolved.

Serves 4

Wild Horse Ale Cinnamon Bread

Archeologists have discovered evidence of an ancient brewery in Mesopotamia dating over 5,000 years old. No earlier evidence of an ancient bakery has been discovered meaning that beer might well have been produced well before bread was conceived. So, when did the description of beer as "bread in a glass" come into vogue?

1¼ c. Wild Horse Ale (German "Alt-Style" beer, available only at Great Basin Brewing Company) or substitute any fine amber German style lager, such as Marzen, Oktoberfest or Dunkel. A pale ale can be used but increase the brown sugar to 1 cup.
1 beaten egg
4 Tbsp. vegetable oil
1 tsp. vanilla
2 ⅛ c. flour
⅓ c. powdered milk
½ c. brown sugar
1 c. white sugar
1 Tbsp. cinnamon
1 tsp. baking powder
¼ tsp. baking soda

Wild Horse Ale Cinnamon Bread (Cont.)

Mix beer, egg, oil and vanilla together. Set aside. In a medium-sized mixing bowl, mix flour, powdered milk, brown and white sugar, cinnamon, baking powder and baking soda. Add liquid slowly, stirring constantly until mixed and consistent. Pour into well greased 5½ x 9½" standard bread pan. Bake in 375° oven for 40 minutes or until a toothpick inserted in the middle comes out clean. Let the bread cool for 10 minutes in the pan. Remove, and slice. This bread is particularly delicious when served warm.

When cooking with beer where the liquid or water and alcohol portion are evaporated as would happen in baking, the spicy bitterness from the hops is balanced by adding sugar. Another way to make this bread moist and sweet is to add fruit. At the brewery we often change the spice mix and add fruits. It is rare that you will visit and find the same bread twice. Our beer bread always appears with raspberries whenever we are brewing our St. Valentine's Day special berry ale, Lip Lock Lager or our summer favorite Rail City Raspberry. Add about ¾ to 1 cup of fruit. Also try nuts, raisins or dates. Enjoy as an appetizer or complement to a salad or soup. This bread goes very well with the Wisconsin-Style Beer Cheese Soup.

Makes 1 loaf

Nevada Gold Cucumber Salad

At Great Basin Brewing Company, we serve our Nevada Gold Cucumber Salad with our always-popular Fish and Chips and with our sausage selections. This is a light and tasty, "fat-free" side dish that will complement many entrees that might lean a bit to the "heavy" side, such as fried foods, stews or casseroles.

2 Tbsp. Nevada Gold (a Kolsch style beer available at the brewery in ½ gallon bottles and 5 and 15.5 gallon kegs) If unavailable, substitute: Continental or Bohemian Pilsner, Marzen or Vienna style lager.
2 tsp. olive oil
2 Tbsp. white vinegar
2 to 3 tsp. white sugar (to taste)
¼ tsp. salt
1 ½ cucumbers, thinly sliced
2 Tbsp. onion, chopped
1 Tbsp. carrots, shredded

Combine beer, oil and vinegar in a medium mixing bowl. Stir in sugar and salt until dissolved. Add cucumber, onion and carrot. Marinate in refrigerator for at least one hour.

Serves 4

Jamaican Jerk-Style Pork Medallions

A Great Basin Brewery tip of ye old "pint" goes to Chef Alex Angelo from Genoa for guiding us through the spectacular joys and wonders of spicy cuisine. Alex first offered this dish as one of our nightly specials serving the sauce over marinated chicken. It was instantly popular and we now serve this fascinating and delectable sauce every night with tender pork tenderloin medallions.

No one really knows the true origin of Jamaican "Jerk" sauces. It is believed to be derived from the spice blend created by Carib-Arawak Indians who would cook cleaned and gutted large game animals over fires built in deep pits lined with stones. The game was elevated over the hot fire on green logs and sticks. The Indians would "jerk" the carcass over the green wood to pierce the skin and let the smoke flavor of the green wood permeate the meat. They would then fill the voids with spices for a superb island delicacy. Although we welcome you to try the "jerk" procedure the next time you bring home some wild game, as a worthy alternative, we offer an easier way to enjoy this exotic blend of spices and bring a bit of the Caribbean home to Nevada.

This dish offers an aggressive blend of flavors that is beautifully balanced with fine beer. Try this with a refreshing Great Basin Brewing Company's Wheeler Peak Wheat (Hefe-Weizen) or with a malty German Altbier like Wild Horse Ale.

Jamaican "Jammin" Jerk Sauce:
1 Tbsp. ground allspice
1 Tbsp. dried thyme
1 ½ tsp. ground cayenne pepper
1 ½ tsp. ground sage
2 Tbsp. ground nutmeg
2 tsp. ground cinnamon
3 Tbsp. salt
10 cloves fresh garlic, chopped

Jamaican Jerk-Style Pork Medallions (Cont.)

2 Tbsp. white sugar
⅓ c. olive oil
½ c. soy sauce
½ c. white vinegar
½ c. orange juice

2 lbs. pork tenderloin strips

Mix all ingredients, except pork tenderloins, to make Jamaican "Jammin" Jerk Sauce. The recipe above will result in "medium" spiciness. In Jamaica, jerk sauce is generally significantly hotter than you will find with this recipe, although most would consider this level "hot". If you dare, you can double the cayenne pepper, but make sure that you have plenty of Great Basin beer on hand to tame the fire. Place the tenderloins individually on foil that is shaped into the form of a dish. Pour just enough of the "Jammin" Jerk Sauce on the pork to cover the meat, approximately 3 to 4 tablespoons for each strip. Wrap with foil and marinate for at least 2 hours. At the restaurant, we cook the wrapped medallions on the char-broiler until the internal temperature reaches 165°. This method demands more attention than you might want to give. We think it is important to engage in some pre-dinner discussion with your guests as you enjoy a glass of one of our award winning ales and ponder the world's joys and spirit. Slaving over a hot broiler is a serious interruption to this endeavor. The results will be nearly as satisfying if you bake the wrapped strips in a 350° oven for 35 to 45 minutes or until the internal temperature reaches 165°. By baking the strips, most of the work can be accomplished well before dinner. When the entree and you are ready, unwrap the tenderloins and slice into ¾" thick medallions. Arrange them by feathering the medallions on a plate. Spoon some of the jerk sauce onto the hot medallions and offer a side cup of the sauce to your guests for dipping. We recommend serving the "jerk" pork medallions with garlic mashed potatoes (mash the potatoes in the

Jamaican Jerk-Style Pork Medallions (Cont.)

usual way and add one chopped clove of fresh garlic per medium-sized potato).

Serves 4

Salmon Tacos with fresh Mango Salsa

We love to cross cultural cuisine boundaries at the brewery. These tacos blend some of the best: Northwestern salmon, Cajun influenced blackening, Northern Mexico persuasion with the use of the container or "taco", and Central American influenced Mango Salsa. They were invented at Great Basin Brewing Company when someone double ordered mangos and we had to figure out a way to use them up. The combination was a summertime hit as a special and now they are on our menu year-round. The components, blackened salmon, mango salsa and lettuce can be prepared separately for custom self-assembly.

Mango Salsa

1 large or 2 small mangos, peeled and chopped
¾ c. jicama (one small or medium), peeled and chopped
½ cucumber, chopped
1 nectarine, peeled and chopped (depending upon season, substitute fresh pineapple, plums or peaches)
15 sprigs cilantro, remove stems and chop very finely
2 Tbsp. white vinegar
2 tsp. white sugar (add more or less to taste)
¼ tsp. salt
1 Tbsp. olive oil

Salmon Tacos:
1 Tbsp. oil

Salmon Tacos with fresh Mango Salsa (Cont.)

2 Tbsp. blackening seasoning (a commercially prepared product available in spice sections of any grocery is effective and simple for home use. If you are interested in making it from scratch, just ask us and we will provide you with a recipe for our mix of 10 spices).
1 ½ lb. fresh king salmon fillet
8 (10") flour tortillas
1 ½ c. chopped green leaf lettuce

Mix all ingredients for Mango Salsa and set aside in the refrigerator. The amount is more than enough for the tacos, but, based on our experience, you won't have any leftovers. It is nearly irresistible. It goes well on other light meat, such as charbroiled chicken. (Don't be afraid to put it out with a spoon and watch your family or guests sneak spoons of it onto anything they can find, such as bread rounds or crackers.) Put 1 tablespoon of oil in frying pan (a cast iron pan works best for blackening). Sprinkle about 2 tablespoons of the blackening seasoning to cover the bottom of a shallow pan. A pie plate works just fine. Slice the salmon fillet(s) into ½" strips. Cook, turning once, for about 4 minutes. Distribute the blackened salmon into 8 (10") tortillas. Top each with 1 or 2 tablespoons of Mango Salsa and finish the filling with chopped green leaf lettuce. These unique tacos go very well with Spanish rice and black beans. Enjoy them with an aggressive ale such as Great Basin Brewing Company's Ichthyosaur India-Style Pale Ale (often asked for affectionately as "Gimme an Icky").

Serves 4

CARSON CITY

Glen Eagles

3700 North Carson Street
Carson City, Nevada 89706
(775) 884-4414
Reservations: Suggested

Perhaps because the setting suggests a sprawling ranch house, Glen Eagles has the feel of a house party. The lively bar and restaurant is a favorite with locals and visitors. There are rooms with views of the Sierras, outdoor dining, and rooms for private parties. An eclectic menu offers enticing dishes from Mexico, Italy, Thailand, and the good old U.S.A. Choose from a variety of Angus beef selections, chicken, and seafood. Create a "custom" meal by choosing a pasta sauce, matching it with your favorite style of pasta, and ordering it as an entree or side dish.

Glen Eagles has such a lovely assortment of desserts, that they offer a chef's selection dessert sampler for two or four people. There's even a children's menu.

Specialties:
Steaks, Seafood & Pasta

Hours:
11:00 AM - 11:00 PM, Mon. – Fri.
12:00 PM – 11:00 PM, Sat. & Sun.

Credit Cards Accepted:
American Express, MasterCard, Visa, Discover

Vicky Shrimp

1 bottle nut brown ale
2 c. flour
1 whole egg
1 tsp. salt
1 tsp. paprika
½ tsp. white pepper
6 jumbo prawns
2 c. Panko breadcrumbs (available in Oriental markets)

Mix together first 6 ingredients. Dip prawns in batter. Coat with Panko. Deep fry until crisp and prawns are cooked through, about 5 minutes.

Serves 1

Neptune Sauce

1 Tbsp. butter
1 Tbsp. garlic, crushed
1 Tbsp. shallot, diced
½ c. white wine
1 tsp. fresh oregano, chopped
1 tsp. fresh basil, chopped
1 Tbsp. lime juice
½ lb. cooked linguine

Heat medium sauté pan. Add butter, garlic and shallot. Cook until translucent. Add white wine, oregano, basil and lime juice. Toss with pasta.

Serves 2

Creme Brulée

1 vanilla bean
1½ c. milk
2½ c. heavy cream
6 egg yolks
2 whole eggs
¾ c. granulated sugar
½ tsp. salt

Scrape out insides of the vanilla bean. Put bean and insides of the bean into a medium sauce pan with the milk and cream and heat to scald. Remove from heat. Cover and let steep for 20 minutes. In medium bowl, whisk together the egg yolks, eggs, sugar and salt. Scald the cream mixture again and slowly whisk it into the egg mixture. Strain into a clean bowl and refrigerate 1 hour. Preheat oven to 325°. Pour custard into 4 ounce ramekins. Place ramekins into a large baking pan. Fill pan half way up the ramekins with water. Cover with foil and bake about 50 minutes or until all but the very center is firm. Refrigerate 4 hours. Place 1 tablespoon granulated sugar on top of custard and place under preheated broiler until sugar is browned.

Serves 6

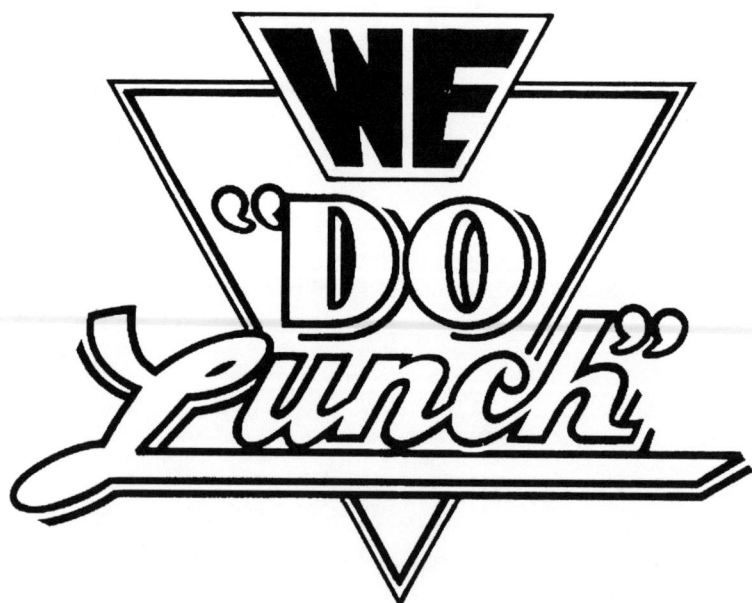

WE "DO Lunch"

Adele's
Restaurant & Lounge

Adele's Restaurant & Lounge
1112 North Carson Street
Carson City, Nevada 89701
(775) 882-3353
Reservations: Suggested

Chef/owner Charlie Abowd continues a 20-year family tradition of culinary excellence at Adele's. The historic house retains its Victorian charm, newly refurbished by co-owner Karen Abowd. A lively, friendly bar, attractive rooms and an outdoor verandah provide a variety of dining choices. Charlie's exceptional wine list is a consistent award-winner.

The menu draws inspiration from all corners of the globe. Adele's is known for daily specials including fresh fish, seasonal meats and produce. Tuscan-style pan-searing produces unbelievably juicy, flavorful steaks, chops, and chicken, and lifts herb-crusted fresh fish to new heights. Appetizers include fresh oysters, Maryland crab cakes, and soft-shelled crabs. Every item is individually prepared to order. Home-made soups and desserts, too.

Specialties:
Extensive menu featuring eclectic cuisine, prepared to order. A pastry chef is on the premises

---

Hours:
Lunch - 11:00 AM - 2:30 PM, Mon. - Fri.
11:30 AM - 2:00 PM, Sat.
Dinner - 4:30 PM - 10:00 PM weekdays, until 11:00 PM on weekends
Closed Sundays and Holidays

Credit Cards Accepted:
American Express, MasterCard, Visa

Louisiana Oyster Fritter Salad

When Charlie and Karen travel, they always look for new ideas and new recipes. This was obviously inspired by a recent trip to New Orleans. Warm, crisply-breaded oysters are a delightful contrast to the cool, creamy spinach salad.

fresh baby spinach leaves, about 3 cups loosely packed

Caesar Dressing (recipe follows)
¼ c. Pickled Onions (recipe follows)
¼ c. homemade garlic croutons
6 freshly shucked oysters (medium-size Fanny Bay)
flour
2 eggs, well beaten , in a shallow bowl
homemade sourdough bread crumbs
oil for deep frying
cayenne pepper
kosher salt
2 slices thick-cut smoked bacon, cooked crisp, cut in 1 inch pieces
½ hard-cooked egg, chopped

Toss the spinach leaves with Caesar Dressing. Toss with the Pickled Onions and croutons and arrange on a serving plate. Dip the oysters in flour. Shake off the excess. Dip the floured oysters into the beaten egg, then into the bread crumbs to coat lightly. Deep-fry the oysters in oil at 350 degrees for about 3 minutes or until breading is just lightly golden. Dust lightly with cayenne pepper and kosher salt and arrange around the spinach salad. Top the salad with the smoked bacon and chopped egg. Serve immediately.

Caesar Dressing

3 cloves garlic
¼ tsp. kosher salt
2 anchovies, rinsed (optional)
1 tsp. Dijon mustard
1 tsp. whole-grain Pommery mustard
2 Tbsp. fresh lemon juice
½ tsp. Tabasco sauce
½ c. extra-virgin olive oil
1 egg, coddled*

Peel and chop the garlic. Mash it with the kosher salt and anchovies to make a fairly smooth paste. Blend in the mustards, lemon juice, Tabasco and olive oil. Whisk in the egg until well blended. Use immediately or keep in refrigerator, tightly covered.

*Carefully lower an unshelled egg into boiling water. Cover the pan and remove from heat. Let stand 6-8 minutes.

Pickled Onions

1 onion, peeled and sliced
1 Tbsp. pickling spice
½ tsp. red pepper flakes
white wine vinegar

Place the onion in a small saucepan with the pickling spice and pepper flakes. Add white wine vinegar to cover. Bring to a boil. As soon as the mixture comes to a boil, remove from heat and let cool. Store in refrigerator. Drain onions to use.

Serves 1

Seared Salmon Salad

2-3 c. mesclun or mixed salad greens
2 Roma tomatoes
1 small bunch seedless flame grapes
1 tart apple
2 large strawberries
1 clove garlic, peeled
6 oz. fresh king salmon
1 tsp. kosher salt
1 tsp. freshly ground pepper
2 Tbsp. fresh tarragon leaves, chopped (or 2 tsp. dried)
¼ c. chopped fresh Italian (flat leaf) parsley
4-5 Tbsp. extra-virgin olive oil (we prefer B.R. Cohn)
3-4 tsp. balsamic vinegar
¼ c. chopped macadamia nuts

Put the mesclun in a large bowl. Dice one tomato and add to the mesclun. Cut the other tomato in wedges and arrange them on a serving platter. Halve 6-8 grapes and add to the mesclun. Use the rest to garnish the serving platter. Peel, core and seed the apple. Slice it and cut the slices into matchsticks. Set aside about one third of the matchsticks. Cut the remaining two-thirds into dice and add to the mesclun. Hull and slice the strawberries. Add one to the mesclun. Set the other aside. Crush the garlic with a press to puree. Rub the puree on one side of the salmon. Over it, sprinkle kosher salt, freshly ground pepper, 1 tablespoon of fresh tarragon and 2 tablespoons of parsley. On a medium-high setting, heat a few tablespoons of olive oil in a skillet. When it is very hot, add the salmon, seasoned side down, to sear. After about a minute, turn it over, sprinkle on a teaspoon or two of the balsamic vinegar. Remove the pan to an oven with the broiler on, about 4 inches from the broiler. On a medium-high setting, heat a teaspoon or two of olive oil in a second skillet so that the oil is "dancing" on the skillet. Add the macadamia nuts, a pinch of tarragon and a few grinds of pepper. Stir in 2 tablespoons olive oil and 2 teaspoons

Seared Salmon Salad (Cont.)

balsamic vinegar. Cook, stirring, until nuts are just beginning to color. Pour the macadamia mixture over the mesclun, reserving a tablespoon or so of the macadamias. Toss the mesclun mixture to mix well, arrange on the prepared serving platter and sprinkle with ½ teaspoon kosher salt. Place the salmon, seasoned side up, on top of the mesclun. Top it with the remaining macadamias, apple matchsticks, sliced strawberry, parsley, tarragon and a few grinds of fresh pepper.

Serves 2-3

Salmon Fusilli

6 oz. dried fusilli pasta
8 oz. fresh salmon, sliced in ½ inch pieces
all-purpose flour
1 Tbsp. butter
1 Tbsp. vegetable oil
salt and freshly ground pepper to taste
4 large mushrooms, sliced
2 large shallots, peeled and minced (2 Tbsp.)
¼ c. dry white wine
3 Tbsp. Pernod, divided*
2 Tbsp. fresh lemon juice
2 tsp. fresh tarragon (or 1 tsp. dried)
1 tsp. drained capers
½ c. chicken stock
3 Tbsp. sour cream (or low-fat substitute)
dash white Worcestershire sauce
lemon wedges to garnish

Salmon Fusilli (Cont.)

*Pernod is an anise-flavored liqueur that does marvelous things to fish dishes.

Cook fusilli in boiling salted water according to package directions. Drain and set aside. On a medium-high setting, heat a non-stick skillet. Toss the salmon in the flour to coat very lightly. Heat the butter and oil in the skillet. When the butter melts, add the salmon and stir to coat with butter. Add the mushrooms and shallots to the pan. Toss gently. Sprinkle with salt and pepper. Add the white wine, 2 tablespoons of Pernod, the lemon juice, tarragon, capers and stock. Cook, stirring gently until well blended. Stir in the sour cream, white Worcestershire sauce and remaining tablespoon of Pernod. Adjust seasoning. Add fusilli and toss gently. Garnish with lemon wedges and serve immediately.

Serves 2

Moroccan Lamb

In Charlie and Karen's large family, get-togethers always involve food. Charlie can still remember the invitingly spicy aroma of lamb roasting in his grandmother's kitchen. That warmth, exuberance and abundance inspired this lamb dish. This recipe, adapted from one of Adele's most popular entrees, can be prepared in less than 10 minutes. We've specified brand names, when necessary, so you can easily duplicate our delicious results.

¼ c. California sherry
¼ c. Hiram Walker Apricot Brandy
¼ c. balsamic vinegar
⅓ c. Kern's Apricot Nectar
3 Tbsp. Smucker's Apricot Strictly Fruit

Moroccan Lamb (Cont.)

1 ½ tsp. Moroccan Spice Mixture (recipe below)
4 inch-thick loin lamb chops
flour for dusting (about ¼ c.)
2 Tbsp. olive oil
1 Tbsp. unsalted butter
2 Tbsp. dried cherries
5 dried apricot halves, slivered
4 whole dried apricot halves
2 pitted prunes
¼ c. chicken stock
6-8 seedless green grapes
sesame seeds to garnish

Mix the sherry and brandy together. Set aside. Mix the balsamic vinegar, apricot nectar and apricot Strictly Fruit together. Stir in the Moroccan Spice Mixture. Set aside. Dip the chops in flour to cover all sides and shake off the excess flour so that only a light coating remains. Place a non-stick pan large enough to hold the chops in one layer over high heat. Add the olive oil. When the oil is hot, add the chops and brown them on both sides, about 2 minutes per side. Pour off and discard any fat in the pan and stir in the unsalted butter. Reduce heat to moderately high. Add the sherry and brandy mixture. When it is warm, touch it with a lighted match to flambé (you may omit the flambé, but let the mixture cook for a minute to cook off some of the alcohol). Stir in the vinegar-apricot nectar mixture. Stir in the dried cherries and apricot slivers. Cook, stirring until the meat is almost done (it will begin to feel resistant when pressed with the back of a wooden spoon). Add the apricot halves and prunes. Remove the lamb to a warm serving dish. Stir the chicken stock into the sauce in the pan and cook, stirring, until it is thickened to taste, or about the consistency of maple syrup. Add the green grapes.

Moroccan Lamb (Cont.)

Spoon the sauce over the chops, topping each chop with an apricot half and each pair of chops with a prune. Sprinkle with sesame seeds.

NOTE: this is very good with hot, cooked rice and makes enough sauce to flavor the rice too.   Serves 2

Moroccan Spice Mixture

½ tsp. crumbled saffron
¾ tsp. ground cardamom
1 tsp. cinnamon
½ tsp. ground ginger
pinch ground clove

Mix the spices together and store in a tightly covered jar in a dark, cool place.

Yields: enough for 4 servings

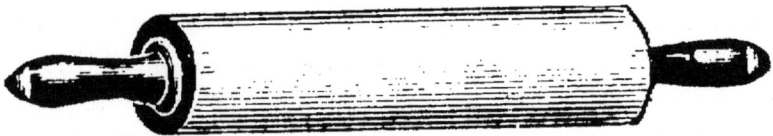

Veal Joshua

This is one of our most popular veal dishes and exemplifies Adele's "signature" combination of sweet fruits and savories.

3 veal medallions (4 oz. total) - use strip loin
⅝ oz. prosciutto ham, sliced paper thin (3 slices)
2 oz. goat cheese
1 Tbsp. ½ oz. coarsely chopped pistachio nuts
flour for dusting
¼ c. canola oil
2 Tbsp. unsalted butter
1½ Tbsp. dry sherry
1½ Tbsp. apricot brandy
3 oz. rich veal stock
¾ oz. demi-glaze
2 halves dried apricots, sliced thin
1 Tbsp. sour cherry preserves
1½ tsp. whole, shelled pistachio nuts
1 fresh plum, peeled and sliced thin
whole, shelled pistachios to garnish

Pound the veal slices very thin. Lay a slice of prosciutto on each of the veal slices. Pound lightly to make the prosciutto adhere to the veal. Divide the goat cheese into three equal portions. Pat each portion into an oval about the shape of the veal and place on the veal slices. Divide the chopped pistachio nuts evenly onto the veal slices. Starting at the narrowest end, roll the veal slices into cylinders roughly one and one-half inch in diameter. Dust with flour and shake off excess. On a medium-high setting, heat a skillet. Add the canola oil. Add the veal rolls, seam side down, and brown lightly and evenly on all sides. Drain and discard excess oil. Add one and one-half tablespoons of the butter to the skillet. Add the sherry and brandy. When the sherry and brandy are warm, touch with a lighted match to flambé. When the flame subsides, add the

Veal Joshua (Cont.)

veal stock, bring to a boil, lower heat and simmer for 1 minute. Remove the veal rolls to a warm dish and keep warm. To the liquid in the skillet, add the demi-glaze, apricot slices and sour cherry preserves. Stir over high heat for about one-half minute to reduce and slightly thicken the sauce. Return veal rolls to the skillet. Cook for about one-half minute more. Add the whole pistachios, the plum slices and the remaining half-tablespoon of butter. Cook for one-half minute. Place a portion of sauce on a warm serving dish. Arrange the veal rolls in the center of the sauce and top with remaining sauce. Sprinkle with a few pistachios to garnish. Serve immediately.

Serves 1

Molly's Catering

Molly's Catering

2198 Courtside Circle
Carson City, Nevada 89703
(775) 885-2804
(775) 885-8388 - Fax

Molly Gingell graduated from the Cordon Bleu in London and has worked in all facets of the food and beverage industry. She worked for major catering companies before starting her own gourmet catering business.

Molly specializes in unique, delicious food for any event from box lunches to elaborate weddings. She works closely with clients, and can develop a menu to suit any budget. Part of Molly's expertise is her artistic ability to present and display food beautifully. Molly makes beautiful moments happen.

Specialties:
Everything from soup to nuts, with imaginative, attractive presentation

Credit Cards Accepted:
None

Seafood Stuffed Mushrooms

4 oz. cream cheese
4 oz. Rondele Cheese
1 Tbsp. sweet onion, chopped
1 Tbsp. Anaheim green chili
1 tsp. garlic, minced
4 oz. Gruyere cheese (reserve 2 oz.)
dash hot sauce
salt & pepper to taste
10 oz. canned crab meat & chopped shrimp
40 medium mushroom caps
⅓ c. butter, melted

Mix cream cheese and Rondele. Add next 6 ingredients and mix well. Fold in seafood slowly to maintain texture. Adjust seasoning to taste. Remove mushroom stems and discard. Place mushrooms in a shallow baking dish, brush with butter. Stuff mushrooms with seafood mixture. Top with remaining Gruyere. Bake for 15 minutes at 350° until bubbly.

Serves 12-15 as an appetizer

Chicken & Shrimp Won Tons with Chili Sweet & Sour Sauce

Filling:
¾ lb. raw chicken, diced
¾ lb. prawns, diced
2 Tbsp. green onion, diced
1 Tbsp. cilantro, minced
1 tsp. garlic, minced
1 tsp. ginger, minced
1 serrano chili, minced

Chicken & Shrimp Won Tons with Chili Sweet & Sour Sauce (Cont.)

1 ½ Tbsp. soy sauce
1 Tbsp. sherry
1 tsp. cornstarch
1 tsp. sesame oil
1 tsp. flaked red chili (crushed red chili)
dash salt & pepper
pinch sugar
2 packages won ton wrappers (square)
oil for deep frying
Chili Sweet & Sour Sauce (recipe follows)

Mix together all filling ingredients. Refrigerate at least 1 hour or overnight. Place 1 heaping teaspoon of filling in the center of a won ton wrapper. Tuck in sides to seal in filling. Place on lined baking tray. Refrigerate 1 hour. Deep fat fry in oil until golden and serve with Chili Sweet & Sour Sauce.

Chili Sweet & Sour Sauce

½ c. ketchup
½ c. water
¼ c. distilled vinegar
¼ c. sugar
1 Tbsp. chili garlic sauce
dash soy
½ tsp. sesame oil
1 tsp. garlic, minced
1 tsp. ginger, minced

Puree all ingredients. Place in a heavy saucepan and bring to a boil, stirring constantly until thickened. Serve with won tons as a dipping sauce.   Serves 12-15 as an appetizer

Crab & Shrimp Cocktail Lahvosh

16 oz. Philly cream cheese, softened
6 oz. dungeness crab meat
6 oz. coarsely chopped shrimp meat
1 packet Hidden Valley Ranch "buttermilk" dried dressing
2-4 dashes hot sauce
salt & pepper to taste
1 piece (round) rye roller bread/lahvosh, softened (sprinkle with water to soften)

Mix 8 oz. cream cheese with crab, shrimp, Ranch dressing, hot sauce and season to taste with salt and pepper. Spread remaining 8 oz. cream cheese evenly over softened lahvosh. Place crab & shrimp mixture on front half of lahvosh. Roll lahvosh tight and thin. Wrap in plastic wrap and refrigerate at least 2 hours or overnight. Slice into mini rounds and arrange creatively on a platter.

Yields 24 pieces

Brie Wrapped in Puff Pastry Stuffed with Wild Mushroom & Maui Sweet Onion Filling

2 Tbsp. unsalted butter
1 Tbsp. olive oil
1 tsp. garlic, minced
1 medium sweet onion (Maui onion preferred), sliced thin
8 oz. shittake mushrooms, de-stemmed and sliced thin
1 oz. porcini mushrooms, soaked & minced
8 oz. white mushrooms, sliced thin, stems okay
¼ c. sherry
salt & pepper to taste
1 wheel of brie
1 pkg. puff pastry (2 sheets), thawed

Brie Wrapped in Puff Pastry Stuffed with Wild Mushroom & Maui Sweet Onion Filling (Cont.)

Heat skillet. Add butter, olive oil, garlic and onions. Cook until onions are softened. Add mushrooms and sherry. Season with salt & pepper. Cook until liquid is incorporated. Let cool. Slice brie into 2 rounds. Fill with mushroom mixture and put back together. Lightly roll out puff pastry. Place stuffed brie on 1 sheet of the pastry. Fold pastry around brie. Place partially wrapped brie onto second puff pastry sheet, unwrapped side down on the new sheet of pastry. Cover completely. Mark sides of wrapped brie with vertical fork lines. Chill or freeze. To cook, bring brie to room temperature. Bake at 450° for 10 minutes on a lightly greased baking sheet. Turn down to 400° until golden brown. Watch closely. If overcooked, brie will leak. Remove from oven. Let cool 15-30 minutes before serving. Serve with slices of baguette.

Serves 12-15 as an appetizer

Garlic Chili Beef with Parmesan Baguette Croute

1½ lbs. beef tri tip, grilled and thinly sliced against the grain
½ c. soy sauce
1 Tbsp. sesame oil
1 Tbsp. garlic, finely chopped
1 Tbsp. ginger, finely chopped
2 Tbsp. cilantro, chopped
½-1 tsp. red chili flakes
2 Tbsp. distilled vinegar
3 Tbsp. olive oil
salt & pepper to taste
Parmesan Baguette Croutes (recipe follows)

Marinate cooked beef in next 9 ingredients for 1-2 hours. Arrange marinated beef in a circular fashion on a platter. Serve with Parmesan Baguette Croutes.

Serves 4-6

Parmesan Baguette Croutes

¼ lb. unsalted butter
¼ c. olive oil
4 cloves garlic, minced
1 sourdough baguette, sliced into 30-35 pieces (rounds or diagonals)
¼ c. Parmesan, asiago or romano cheese

Combine butter, oil and garlic. Brush sourdough rounds with butter/oil mix and sprinkle with chosen cheese. Bake at 350° for 12-15 minutes until golden. Cool. Place in basket and serve alongside beef slices.

Serves 12-15 as an appetizer

Spicy Thai Chicken Bites

2 lb. chicken breast or thigh (boneless & skinless)
½ c. soy sauce
2 Tbsp. sesame oil
1 tsp. distilled vinegar
2 Tbsp. red wine vinegar
1 Tbsp. hot chili oil
4 cloves garlic, minced
1 (1" piece) ginger, minced
2 Tbsp. cilantro, coarsely chopped
1 tsp. red chili, crushed
2 Tbsp. sugar
½ c. scallions, finely chopped
2 Tbsp. sesame seeds

Remove all fat from chicken. Cut chicken into large bite size pieces. Mix all liquid ingredients in a large bowl and add garlic, ginger, cilantro, chili and sugar. Mix well. Add chicken pieces and refrigerate overnight. To cook, remove chicken from marinade and place in a baking pan with sides. Cook at 350° for 12-15 minutes until firm. Serve hot or at room temperature. Sprinkle with green onions and sesame seeds.

Serves 6

Café

Shortbread

1 lb. flour
1 lb. butter, softened
½ lb. sugar
½ lb. cornstarch
Additional sugar for sprinkling

Mix all ingredients in a large bowl. Incorporate into a dough that holds together. Press into a 9 x 13" pan. Prick with fork. Bake for 1 hour at 325°. Check for firm, flaky center. Sprinkle with sugar and bake until done in center. Upon removal from oven, cut into desired pieces immediately. Let cool. Serve. To keep: Wrap tightly in saran wrap.

Yields 27 pieces

B'Sghetti's

318 North Carson Street (One block north of the Capitol)
Carson City, Nevada 89701
(775) 887-8879
Reservations: Suggested for parties of 8 or more

B'Sghetti's name tells you that the fare is Italian. It's Southern Italian which means slow-simmered red sauces and generous portions of pasta. Personal Pizzas have their menu niche, and there are special dishes just for kids. B'Sghetti's Platters provide an opportunity for sampling two or more of the entrees. They are more than generous. Vegetarian appetites are satisfied by dishes like Cheese-filled Ravioli, Eggplant Parmigiana, and Fettuccini with Creamy Mushroom Sauce. Hearty soups and salads round out the bill of fare. The wine list is mostly California's with a few Chiantis.

The Curry Street entrance to B'Sghetti's leads to the lively bar where Happy Hour happens every Monday through Friday from 4 to 6 PM. Drinks and appetizers are available at bargain prices. The bar is adjacent to the "party room" which accommodates up to 40 people. B'Sghetti's provides banquets and catering services, too.

Specialties:
Classic Italian "family style"

Hours:
11:00 AM - 9:00 PM, Mon. - Fri.
4:00 PM - 9:00 PM, Saturdays
4:00 PM - 8:00 PM, Sundays

Credit Cards Accepted:
MasterCard, Visa

Pasta E. Fagioli

¼ lb. ground beef
¼ lb. mild Italian sausage
6 stalks celery, diced
1 large carrot, diced
1 medium onion, diced
2 cloves garlic, minced
4 c. water
2 c. tomato sauce
2 Tbsp. beef bouillon
½ tsp. Tabasco
1 Tbsp. basil
1 Tbsp. oregano
1 c. garbanzo beans
1 c. kidney beans
½ lb. shell pasta, pre-cooked and cooled
garlic butter croutons for garnish
Grated Parmesan cheese for garnish

In a large sauce pan, brown beef and sausage. Add celery, carrots, onions and garlic. Cook until onions are translucent. Add water, tomato sauce, bouillon, tabasco and spices. Bring to a boil. Add beans and simmer for 10 minutes. Fill bottom of serving bowl with generous amounts of shell pasta and spoon soup over the top. Sprinkle with garlic butter croutons and Parmesan cheese.

Serves 4-8

Fresh Basil Bruschetta

2 lbs. Roma tomatoes
1 large bunch basil
½ c. olive oil
3 cloves garlic, minced
1 Tbsp. Balsamic vinegar
1 tsp. salt
½ tsp. white pepper
¼ c. garlic infused olive oil
1 loaf French bread
1 c. Grated Parmesan cheese

Dice tomatoes into ¼ inch pieces and put into mixing bowl. Separate basil leaves from stems and shred leaves. Add olive oil, minced garlic, vinegar, salt and pepper. Combine well; cover and refrigerate overnight. Slice French bread into ½ inch slices. Brush with garlic-infused olive oil. Grill each side until golden brown. Arrange in single layer on large serving platter. Top each slice with approximately 1 Tbsp. of the marinated tomatoes (drain thoroughly). Sprinkle with grated Parmesan cheese.

Serves 8

Ravioli Fritta

1 large zucchini
2 small yellow squash
2 c. broccoli florets
1 small red onion, julienned
¼ c. olive oil
24 large cheese filled ravioli
1 c. butter
1 c. white wine
splash lemon juice
salt & pepper to taste

Dice or slice vegetables. In a large skillet, heat olive oil. Place ravioli in oil and sauté until crisp and golden brown. Drain oil, remove ravioli and pat dry. Place in warm oven. Add butter to skillet on high heat (careful not to brown). Add all vegetables and sauté until the onions are translucent. Add wine and lemon juice to deglaze. Add salt and pepper. Reduce by half. Arrange 6 raviolis on each plate and lightly spoon sautéed vegetables and sauce over the top.

Serves 4

Lemon Basil Chicken

½ lb. mushrooms, sliced
1 bunch fresh basil
4-5 oz. boneless skinless chicken breasts
1 medium carrot, grated
1 c. unsalted butter
1 c. white wine
2 tsp. fresh squeezed lemon juice
Salt & pepper to taste
8 oz. Capellini pasta, cooked al dente

Choose assorted mushrooms (preferably mild in flavor) and slice. Remove basil leaves from stems, discard stems. Mince basil coarsely. Tenderize chicken with kitchen mallet. In a large skillet, melt butter on high heat (careful not to brown butter). Add tenderized chicken breasts and cook approximately 2 minutes. Turn breasts and add mushrooms, basil and carrots. Continue cooking until mushrooms become tender. Add white wine, lemon juice, salt and pepper. Reduce by half. Serve over capellini pasta.

Serves 4

Tiramisu

Espresso mixture:
¼ c. sugar
¾ c. coffee
¾ c. espresso
¼ c. kahlua

Filling:
4 egg yolks
6 Tbsp. sugar
¼ c. kahlua
1 c. marscapone cheese, softened
1 c. whipped cream
3 doz. lady fingers
¼ c. cocoa powder
¼ c. chocolate syrup

Combine sugar, coffee, espresso, and kahlua. Set aside and cool. Combine egg yolks, sugar and kahlua. Beat in stainless steel bowl over hot water bath until thickened. Beat yolk mixture in bowl until cooled. Fold in softened marscapone and whipped cream. Dunk lady fingers in espresso mixture quickly and place in pan. Alternate lady fingers, marscapone mixture, lady fingers, and marscapone mixture. Top with cocoa powder and refrigerate overnight. Slice and put a dollop of sweetened whipped cream on top. Drizzle with chocolate syrup and serve.

Serves 4-6

Carson Valley

River Bend Grille at Genoa Lakes Golf Club

1 Genoa Lakes Drive
Genoa, Nevada 89411
(775) 782-6644
Website: www.genoalakes.com
Reservations: Not accepted

Looking out on the rolling green grounds of the Genoa Lakes Golf Course, the Grille at River Bend caters (naturally) to the hearty appetites and discerning tastes of golfers. Bread for sandwiches is baked in house daily. Find a variety of brick oven pizzas, soup and salad bar, and a tempting assortment of yummy appetizers, as well as a variety of pasta dishes. Daily specials really are exceptional as they give Riverbend's talented chef the opportunity to take advantage of the freshest ingredients available.

River Bend Grille has a full bar and a variety of attractive rooms for private parties. From business luncheons to dinner parties, banquets, receptions, reunions, and an exceptional setting for weddings indoors or out. Spectacular Sierra views at no additional charge.

Hours:
11:00 AM - 3:00 PM, Year round, depending on season, daily
Dinner, 4 PM – 9 PM (Fridays only, June through September)
Limited menu off season

Credit Cards Accepted:
American Express, MasterCard, Visa

191

Italian Sausage Stuffed Mushrooms

½ c. marinara sauce
4 lbs. mushroom caps
½ lb. raw Italian sausage (hot or mild)
Mozzarella or Parmesan cheese

Put ½ c. marinara sauce in bottom of baking dish. Stuff mushroom caps with sausage and place on top of marinara sauce. Bake at 350° for 10-15 minutes. Top with mozzarella or Parmesan cheese and put under broiler until cheese melts.

Serves 12

Pasta Al Boro

1 Tbsp. butter
1 Tbsp. olive oil
1 tsp. garlic
pinch red pepper flakes
pinch parsley, chopped
10 oz. cooked spaghetti
2 Tbsp. Parmesan

Combine first five ingredients in sauté pan over medium heat. Do not over cook! Add cooked pasta that has been dipped in warm water. Toss in Parmesan.

Serves 2

Shrimp BLT with a Lemon Caper Dill Mayo

Lemon Caper Dill Mayo:
mayonnaise
½ tsp. lemon juice
capers
pinch dill
2 slices grilled sourdough bread
4 shrimp, butterflied & grilled (1 minute per side)
4 slices cooked bacon
lettuce
tomato

Combine ingredients for Lemon Caper dill Mayo in small bowl and mix well. Assemble sandwich and serve.

Serves 1

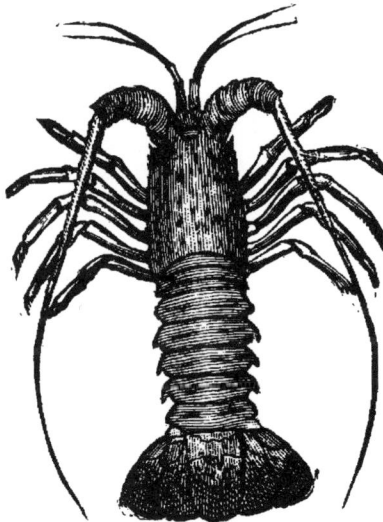

Tequila Lime Marinade

1 c. tequila (gold), any brand
1 c. lime juice
2 Tbsp. chopped garlic
½ onion, chopped
2 Tbsp. cumin
2 tsp. salt
1 Tbsp. black pepper
2 cups salad oil

Combine and blend smooth. Great for shrimp or chicken. Determine the amount of meat or fish to be marinated. If using chicken, cut into 1½" pieces. Put shrimp or chicken into a container or large ziplock bag and pour marinade over until covered. Marinate shrimp for at least 1 hour, rotating container several times. Skewer and barbecue with or without veggies. Do not re-use the used marinade. Refrigerate the unused marinade.

Papaya Cilantro Salsa

4 papayas, diced
1 (20 oz. can) pineapple chunks, diced
½ red onion, minced
½ c. cilantro, minced
½ Tbsp. white wine vinegar
¼ tsp. crushed red chiles
¼ tsp. salt
1 Tbsp. sugar

Combine and mix well. Great as a topping for fish and poultry.

Chocolate Mousse

1 lb. cream cheese, softened
2 c. sugar
2½ tsp. vanilla
½ c. Hershey cocoa
3 c. heavy whipping cream

Beat together cream cheese, sugar and vanilla until light and fluffy and the sugar is completely dissolved. Beat in cocoa until blended and the chocolate is dissolved. Set aside. Whip heavy cream until soft peaks form. Add half the whipping cream to the chocolate mixture. Fold together until completely blended. Fold in other half of the whipping cream. Divide chocolate mousse into six individual serving glasses. Mixture should be firm enough to hold shape. If not, refrigerate until set, at least 30 minutes. Keep chilled until ready to serve.

Serves 6

D. W.'s Restaurant

2001 Foothill Road
Genoa, Nevada 89441
(775) 782-8155
Reservations: Suggested

DW's is the restaurant at historic David Walley's Hot Springs and Spa in Nevada's oldest town, Genoa. Mark Twain loved the place, which takes you back to the glory days of the Comstock in a beautiful country-like setting of lush Nevada marsh and meadow, nestled against the mountains. The spacious dining room sparkles with beveled glass dividers. Ice buckets and white tablecloths provide an elegant air.

Prime rib of Black Angus beef is slow-roasted and served with Twain heart salad, rosemary garlic mashed potatoes, and green beans tossed with crisp smokehouse bacon. Other choices include filet and New York steaks, daily fresh fish specials, shrimp, grilled salmon, lobster Victoria, chicken, lamb, and veal, in addition to nightly specials.

Sunday brunch always adds a chef's special dish to such delights as eggs Benedict, chicken and spinach crepes, seafood Newburg, fresh corned beef hash, and exceptional French toast and that's in addition to the omelet station, the fajita station, fresh fruits, pastas, and salads.

Specialties:
Eclectic, elegant dining

Hours:
5:00 PM - 9:00 PM, Wed. - Sat.
10:00 AM - 2:00 PM, Sundays

Credit Cards Accepted:
American Express, Visa, MasterCard, Discover, Diners

General Grant's Pepper Steak

4 (10 oz.) New York steaks
1½ c. cracked black pepper
1 Tbsp. oil
2 Tbsp. shallots
½ c. Jack Daniels
2 c. veal stock or canned demi glace
1 Tbsp. cornstarch

Roll New York steaks in cracked black pepper. Press firmly to meat (Note: The more peppercorns you use, the hotter the steak). For sauce: in a sauce pan add oil and shallots. Cook slightly. Add Jack Daniels and flambé, reducing slightly. Add veal stock or demi glace and bring to a boil. Thicken with cornstarch. If thicker consistency is required, add more cornstarch. Cook steak in a very hot sauté pan, searing to your taste.

Serves 4

Roasted Red Bell Pepper Chicken

4 (8 oz.) chicken breasts
Vegetable oil
salt & white pepper
1 red bell pepper
2 Tbsp. shallots, chopped
½ c. white wine
2 Tbsp. lemon juice
3 pints heavy whipping cream
1 ½ c. unsalted butter
¼ tsp. white pepper
½ tsp. salt

Coat chicken with oil. Season with salt and pepper and broil or bake. For sauce: take bell pepper and place under broiler. Cook until black. Place in ziplock bag and rub with hands under cold water to peel black and skin off pepper. Thinly slice. In a sauce pan, add shallots, white wine, lemon juice and red bell peppers. Bring to a boil and reduce three quarters. Add whipping cream and bring to a simmer for 15 to 20 minutes, watching pot so that it does not boil over. Add butter and cook another 10 minutes on slow simmer (do not boil). Season with salt and pepper. Take off heat and blend with a hand held food processor until creamy. Strain and serve or hold in a water bath. Note: If sauce breaks, bring to a boil. Add a little rue (flour and butter) and mix until sauce thickens.

Serves 4

The Wild Rose Inn

The Wild Rose Inn Bed & Breakfast

2332 Main Street (P.O. Box 605)
Genoa, Nevada 89411
(775) 782-5697
Reservations: Required

Sue Haugnes is the Innkeeper of the charming Victorian style Wild Rose Inn Bed & Breakfast nestled in the serene Sierra foothills in historic Genoa. The Wild Rose Inn pampers you with antique furnishings, queen-size beds, private baths, a full buffet breakfast, and afternoon tea, plus lovely views of Carson Valley and the Sierras.

The romantic Wild Rose Inn is close to skiing, golf, tennis, cycling, biking, soaring, and horseback riding. There's a hot springs and spa close by (Inn guests get a discount), historical sites and museums for sightseers, antiques, and bookstores. The area also boasts a variety of fine dining choices. Arrangements can be made for retreats, weddings, reunions, or conferences.

Credit Cards Accepted:
American Express, Visa, MasterCard

Currant Scones

2½ c. all-purpose flour
1 Tbsp. baking powder
½ tsp. salt
¼ c. sugar
¼ c. butter, cut into small pieces
½ c. Zante currants
1 Tbsp. grated lemon peel
⅔ c. buttermilk
Lemon Curd (recipe follows)

Mix first three dry ingredients together in a bowl. Work butter into flour mixture with fingers until granular consistency is obtained. Stir in sugar, currants and lemon peel. Stir in buttermilk to form a soft dough. Turn out onto floured surface and knead about 10 times. Form one big bun and place on ungreased baking sheet. Score into 8 wedges. Bake at 375° for 12-15 minutes until golden brown. Serve warm with Lemon Curd or strawberry jam and clotted cream. Individual scones can be made by rolling dough into a ½" slab and cutting round scones with a 2" cookie cutter. Baking time would be reduced to approximately 6-8 minutes.

Lemon Curd

¼ c. unsalted butter
3 large fresh eggs
1 c. granulated sugar
grated zest of 3 large lemons
½ c. fresh lemon juice

Melt butter slowly in saucepan (do not brown). In a bowl, whisk together eggs, sugar, zest and lemon juice. Pour into saucepan and stir constantly until the mixture thickens. Pour into sterilized jars. Store in refrigerator. Best used within four weeks. Serve with scones.

Serves 8

Wild Rose Morning Casserole

4 eggs
1 c. milk
½ c. baking mix (Trader Joes)
½ tsp. garlic powder
salt and pepper to taste
2 c. fresh, frozen or canned corn, drained
1 can quartered artichoke hearts, drained and chopped
1 (4 oz. can) mild green chilies, diced
1½ c. extra sharp cheddar cheese, shredded (can be varied by using Monterey Jack cheese)

Beat together first five ingredients. Fold in remaining ingredients and pour into a greased 9 x 13" pan. Sprinkle with paprika. Bake at 350° for 45 minutes or until top is bubbly and golden. Serve warm with salsa. Note: This can also be cut into 1 inch squares and served as an hors d'oeuvre! Serves 10

Toad in the Hole

3-4 Aidell's Chicken Apple Sausages, sliced ¼" thick
1 tsp. olive oil
3 eggs
½ c. all purpose flour
½ c. milk
1 Tbsp. grated Parmesan cheese (optional)
dash of salt

Sauté apple sausages in olive oil until lightly browned. Spread over the bottom of a glass or ceramic pie plate. Mix together remaining ingredients and pour over sausages. Bake for 20 minutes at 450° degrees until lightly browned. Serve immediately.

Serves 4

Seafood Lasagne

Red Sauce:
2 Tbsp. olive oil
1 onion, finely chopped
1 garlic clove, minced
1 (28 oz. can) crushed tomatoes
¼ c. chopped fresh basil (or 1 tsp. dried)
¼ tsp. crushed hot red pepper (optional)

Heat olive oil in pan. Sauté onions, add garlic. Stir in other ingredients and simmer until thickened, about 45 minutes.

White Sauce:
5 Tbsp. unsalted butter or olive oil
2 shallots or green onions, minced
⅓ c. all-purpose flour
1 c. milk

Seafood Lasagne (Cont.)

½ c. bottled clam juice
½ c. dry white wine
¼ tsp. salt
⅛ tsp. ground white pepper
pinch of grated nutmeg
½ c. grated Parmesan cheese

Melt butter in saucepan, add shallots and cook for about 2 minutes. Add flour, stirring constantly until bubbly. Whisk in other ingredients, except cheese, and cook for about 10 minutes. Remove from heat and stir in the Parmesan cheese.

Seafood Mushroom filling:
2 Tbsp. olive oil
10 oz. fresh mushrooms, sliced
1 lb. medium or large shrimp (peeled and deveined)
1 lb. bay scallops or chopped sea scallops
½ tsp. salt
⅛ tsp. ground white pepper

Heat oil in pan, add mushrooms and brown. Add shrimp, scallops, salt and pepper. Stir and cook until shrimp have turned pink, approximately 1-2 minutes. Drain and return juices to the pan. Boil until reduced to about 2 tablespoons. Stir the reduced juices and white sauce into the seafood mixture.

12 oz. fresh or 9 oz. dried lasagna noodles, cooked al dente, drained and rinsed with 1 Tbsp. oil added to prevent sticking
1 c. Swiss or Gruyere, freshly grated
fresh basil, finely chopped

To assemble, lightly grease a 9 x 13" deep lasagne pan. Spread one third of the red sauce on the bottom of the pan. Arrange 4

Seafood Lasagne (Cont.)

overlapping strips of noodles lengthwise over the red sauce. Spread half the seafood filling over the noodles and cover with another layer of noodles. Repeat the process and spread the remaining red sauce over the top layer of noodles. Sprinkle 1 cup of freshly grated Swiss or Gruyere on top. Bake at 375° for 30 minutes. Let stand for 10 minutes. Before serving sprinkle with finely chopped fresh basil.

Serves 12

Carson Valley Country Club

1029 Riverview
Gardnerville, Nevada 89410
(775) 265-3715
Reservations: Suggested for large groups

Co-owners Jesus Rey (who is also the chef) and Carlos Iribarren have created a little corner of the Basque homeland in a lovely golf-course setting. The atmosphere is laid-back casual and country friendly. The dark-paneled bar is decorated with trophy game heads and birds. Dining rooms are light and airy with tables that can be rearranged to suit groups of any size. Basque dinners include all the soup, salad, and bread you could want, plus a vegetable dish, French fries, and wine. These are in addition to your entree choice. Ice cream and coffee are also included. There is no printed dinner menu, your server tells you the entree choices such as steak, shrimp, salmon or lamb chops. It's very good and the portions are for the truly hungry.

Lunch provides a good selection of hot and cold sandwiches, plus some of Rey's daily specials like lamb shanks, lemon chicken, or red snapper. Since 1974, The Carson Valley Country Club has been pleasing customers. Banquet facilities can accommodate up to 150 people.

Specialties:
Family Style Basque

Hours:
11:30 AM - 2:30 PM, Mon., Wed. - Sat.
5:30 PM - 9:00 PM, Mon., Wed. – Sat.
5:30 PM – 8:30 PM, Sun.
Closed Tuesday

Credit Cards Accepted:
None (ATM Machine)

Oxtail Stew in Brown Gravy

8 lb. oxtails, cut in 2" long pieces
1 tsp. cayenne pepper
1 tsp. black pepper
salt to taste

Brown Gravy:
1 medium size yellow onion
7 cloves garlic
½ c. vegetable oil
¾ c. flour
6 c. water
1 (8 oz. can) tomato puree
1 Tbsp. Kitchen Bouquet
1 tsp. beef base
salt to taste
1 lb. carrots, cut in ½" slices

Place oxtails in a roasting pan. Season with cayenne, black pepper and salt. Bake uncovered at 450° for 1 hour, turning occasionally so they brown evenly.
Brown Gravy: Combine onion, garlic and oil in a blender. Process until smooth, pour into a 2 gallon casserole. Cook over medium heat until translucent. Add flour, whisk for a few seconds, add water and whisk until flour dissolves. Add tomato puree, Kitchen Bouquet, beef base and salt. Bring to a slow boil. Add the baked oxtails and carrots and simmer for about 2 hours or until the meat separates from the bone. Serve hot. Accompany with sour dough bread and a good red wine.

Serves 6

Grilled Lamb Chops

3 lb. lamb chops, cut 1" thick
1 tsp. salt
1 tsp. pepper
6 garlic cloves, peeled
½ c. oil & vinegar (2 parts oil, 1 part vinegar)
¼ c. olive oil
1 tsp. parsley, finely chopped

On a platter, arrange lamb chops and season with salt & pepper. In a food processor, combine garlic, oil and vinegar. Process the mixture until creamy and pour on top of lamb chops, making sure both sides are covered. Let sit for approximately 4 hours. Heat olive oil in large cast iron skillet. Cook lamb chops for about 4 minutes on each side for medium rare, 6 minutes for medium. Garnish with parsley. Accompany with fresh vegetables and homemade French fries.

Serves 6-8

Chicken and Rice

4 lb. chicken, cut in pieces
salt & pepper to taste
½ c. olive oil
1 medium yellow onion, chopped
4 cloves garlic, chopped
1 large green bell pepper, chopped
1 c. carrots, chopped
1 c. tomatoes, chopped
2 c. cooked rice
1 Tbsp. chicken base bouillon
5 c. hot water

Chicken and Rice (Cont.)

Season chicken with salt & pepper. In a large pot, fry chicken in oil over medium heat until brown. Add onion, garlic, green pepper, carrots and tomatoes. Cook for about 10 minutes, stirring often. Add rice, chicken bouillon and hot water. Cook for about 20 minutes. Turn off heat and let sit for about 15 minutes.

Serves 8

Basque Beans

2 lb. dry pinto beans
2 lb. pork ribs or ham hocks
1 lb. can crushed tomatoes
salt to taste
½ tsp. black pepper
½ lb. bacon, cut in ½" pieces
½ lb. chorizo, cut into ½" slices
3 cloves garlic, minced

Soak beans overnight in 2 gallons of water. The next day, drain, add ribs or ham hocks, tomatoes and salt and pepper. Add water to 2" above ingredients. Bring to a boil. Remove any foam or particles that come to the top and cook on medium heat for about 2 hours. Sauté bacon, chorizo and garlic in a pan until crisp. Add to beans. Remove ribs or ham from beans. Pull meat off bones and add to beans. Discard bones. Cook for another ½ hour.

Serves 12

Incline Village

212

Lone Eagle Grille

Lone Eagle Grille

Hyatt Regency Lake Tahoe
Country Club Drive at Lakeshore
Incline Village, Nevada 89450
(775) 832-3205
Reservations: Accepted

Vaulted beam ceilings, wrought-iron chandeliers, and two-story tall rock fireplaces give The Lone Eagle Grille the look of a rustic hunting lodge. Tall picture windows frame views of Lake Tahoe. This beachfront restaurant sits just across the street from the Hyatt at Incline Village. As its name indicates, mesquite grilling is a specialty here, with a selection of grilled seafood, steaks, and poultry. Certified aged Black Angus beef is offered in a variety of cuts and sizes.

Also on the menu are pasta dishes, a Vegetable Napoleon, Roast Duck, and more. Appetizers include such gems as Crabcakes, Steamed Clams, and Shrimp Tortilla. The Lone Eagle Grille's wine list is well chosen, mostly California's with prices beginning at the moderate range. There is also a featured "wine of the quarter", by the bottle or glass. Wines are helpfully grouped according to style.

Specialties:
New American Cuisine

Hours:
11:30 AM - 2:30 PM, daily
6:00 PM - 10:00 PM, nightly

Credit Cards Accepted:
All Major

213

Caesar Salad

1 bunch, hearts of romaine
½ c. Asiago cheese, ¼ c. grated and ¼ c. shaved
⅓ c. Caesar dressing (recipe follows)
4 croutons
2 anchovies
black pepper to taste

Wash lettuce and tear into bite sized pieces. Toss lettuce first with grated cheese, then with dressing. Arrange on plate and garnish with fresh shaved cheese, croutons, anchovies and pepper. Serve with sourdough baguette which has been cut on the bias, brushed with olive oil and sprinkled with Asiago cheese, parsley, oregano and basil and baked until light brown.

Caesar Salad Dressing

7 egg yolks
¼ c. warm water
2 c. salad oil
2 c. olive oil
3 Tbsp. Dijon mustard
¼ c. garlic cloves
6 anchovy filets
¼ c. lemon juice
¼ c. red wine vinegar
1 tsp. black pepper
3 oz. Asiago cheese, finely grated
1 tsp. salt & pepper to taste

Start in mixer with yolks and water. With mixer remaining on, slowly add half the oil. Add Dijon and remaining oil. Add remaining ingredients and adjust flavors.   Serves 2

Braised Lamb Shanks

1 bunch thyme, chopped
1 bunch rosemary, chopped
1 bunch sage, chopped
½ c. flour
salt & pepper to taste
olive oil for browning
6 Frenched lamb shanks
3 onions, roughly chopped
6 carrots, roughly chopped
1 bunch celery, roughly chopped
⅓ c. garlic, chopped
⅓ c. shallots, chopped
1 bottle red Zinfandel or red wine
4 pkgs. prepared Knorr demi glaze or brown gravy
2 turnips, peeled & diced
2 parsnips, peeled & diced

Mix half the herbs with flour, salt and pepper. In large pan heat olive oil. Roll shanks in flour mixture. Brown shanks in hot oil, turning frequently to get all sides. Remove shanks from pan and place in a deep braising pan or other ovenproof pan. In same pan on stove, add half of the chopped onions, carrots and celery and all of the garlic and shallots. Brown until they release aroma and crust forms on pan. Add the wine and deglaze. Let wine reduce by half. Add the prepared Knorr gravy or demi glaze. Bring to a boil, season with salt and pepper and pour over shanks. Cover and cook in oven at 250° for 3 hours. During that time, sauté turnips and parsnips with remaining carrots, onions and celery In olive oil in a separate pan. Once shanks have been removed from oven, place each one in a bowl to serve. Strain sauce from pan into sautéed vegetables and bring to boil. Season again, adding the rest of the chopped herbs and salt and pepper, if needed. Ladle sauce over the shanks and serve. Serves 6

Yellow Tomato Tomatillo Salsa

½ lb. tomatillo, diced
1½ lb. yellow tomato, diced
1 c. red onion, diced
½ c. cilantro, chopped
⅛ c. mint, chopped
⅛ c. basil, chopped
2 Tbsp. lemon juice
2 Tbsp. olive oil

Combine tomatillos, tomatoes and red onions. Add herbs and remaining ingredients. Mix well.

Yields: approximately 1 quart

Root Beer Float Pie with Pastry Cream

Pastry Cream (recipe follows)
¾ c. bottled root beer
¾ c. root beer syrup
1 Tbsp. cornstarch & 3 Tbsp. Water, mixed together
1 graham cracker crust
1½ c. heavy cream
1 tsp. vanilla
½ c. powdered sugar

Make Pastry Cream and cool. Stir bottled root beer into pastry cream for flavor. Heat root beer syrup and thicken with cornstarch and water. This will make the root beer sauce. Cool and set aside. Layer the graham cracker crust with half the root beer sauce, all of the Pastry Cream and then the remaining root beer sauce. Whip heavy cream with vanilla and powdered sugar until stiff peaks form.

Root Beer Float Pie with Pastry Cream (Cont.)

Spread or use pastry bag to cover top of pie with whipped cream. Refrigerate until ready to serve.

Pastry Cream

Group 1:
3½ c. milk
½ c. sugar
¼ c. butter

Group 2:
½ c. milk
2 eggs
6 Tbsp. cornstarch
½ tsp. lemon juice
1 Tbsp. vanilla

Group 3:
¼ c. sugar
2 tsp. gelatin

Mix all three groups separately and set aside. Put Group 1 in a pot and heat until bubbles form around the edges. Remove from heat. Temper by adding small amounts of Group 1 into Group 2, slowly raising the temperature of Group 2. Continue until it is all incorporated. Slowly stir in Group 3, stirring constantly. Place back on burner, stirring constantly, until thick. Place in a shallow pan to cool. Cover with plastic wrap to prevent a skin from forming.

Serves 6-8

COCKTAILS

ciao mein
T R A T T O R I A

Ciao Mein Trattoria

Hyatt Regency Lake Tahoe
Country Club Drive at Lakeshore
Incline Village, Nevada 89450
(775) 832-1234
Reservations: Suggested

Tucked away on the main floor of the Hyatt at Incline Village, Ciao Mein Trattoria is a quietly stylish venue for an intimate dinner. The menu blends Pacific Rim recipes and Italian dishes in a marriage that would have made Marco Polo envious. How do you choose between Veal Picatta with Fettuccine Alfredo, and Stir-fry Lemon Chicken with Vegetables and Strawberries? Barbecued Char Siu Duck vies for attention with Garlic Rubbed Lamb Chops. New York Steak or Mongolian Beef? Mushroom Ravioli or Shrimp Pad Thai Noodles?

Appetizers have the same two-continent appeal including Dungeness Crab Fritters with Pineapple dipping sauce, Lobster Spring Rolls, Roasted Portobello Mushrooms, and Kung Pao Calamari.

Specialties:
Pacific Rim & Northern Italian

_____

Hours:
6:00 PM - 10:00 PM, Wed. - Sun.
Closed Mon. & Tues.

_____

Credit Cards Accepted:
All Major

Roasted Portobello Mushrooms with Balsamic Reduction

4 large Portobello mushrooms, stems removed
¼ c. extra virgin olive oil
salt & pepper to taste
½ lb. spring lettuce blend
½ c. extra virgin olive oil
2 Tbsp. balsamic vinegar
salt & pepper to taste
8 cherry tomatoes, halved
2 c. balsamic vinegar, reduced to ⅓ c.

Place mushrooms, rib side down, on a baking sheet. Brush olive oil over tops of mushrooms, using all of the ¼ c. oil. Sprinkle lightly with salt and pepper. Bake at 350° until mushrooms are tender, 10-12 minutes. Toss spring mix with remaining ½ c. olive oil, 2 Tbsp. balsamic vinegar, and salt & pepper to coat. Place a mound of spring lettuce mixture on center of 4 individual plates. Top with a mushroom. Place cherry tomato halves around mushroom and drizzle balsamic reduction over all.

Serves 4

220

Tempura Prawns

Tempura Batter:
1 c. cornstarch
3 c. flour
1 Tbsp. sugar
2 tsp. salt
1 tsp. white pepper
2 c. white wine
enough water to make a pancake batter consistency (approximately 1-2 cups)
1 Tbsp. oil
Lemon Grass- Jalapeno Ponzu Sauce (recipe follows)

24 prawns (16-20 size), peeled and deveined
1-2 yams, sliced ¼" thick, 12 slices total
12 green onions, 4" long
24 button mushrooms
12 asparagus spears, 6" long (as thin as possible)
canola oil for frying

Mix first six ingredients together, adding water a little at a time to proper consistency. Mix in oil. To fry: Dip prawns and vegetables into batter, then put into deep fryer (or a pot) of canola oil at 375° a few at a time, cooking until deep golden brown. Drain on paper towels. While continuing to fry prawn and vegetables, put first batches on a plate in a low (200°) oven to keep warm. Serve with Lemon grass-Jalapeno Ponzu Sauce (recipe follows).

Lemon grass-Jalapeno Ponzu Sauce

1 qt. mirin (sweet Japanese rice wine) reduced by ½
1 c. soy sauce
½ c. lemon juice
1 jalapeno, cut into thin rings
1 stalk Lemon grass, seam end trimmed to remove core, top trimmed to produce 6" piece, finely diced

Mix all ingredients together. Serve as dipping sauce for Tempura Prawns.

Serves 4

Mongolian Beef

2 lbs. flank steak
¼ c Soy Sauce
3 cubes beef bouillon
2 egg whites
1 Tbsp. Beef soup mix
⅓ c. cornstarch
2 c. green onions, cut 2" long
2 c. bamboo shoots, sliced
1 red bell pepper, julienne
2 small or 1 large red onion, julienne
3 Tbsp. chili-garlic paste
½ c. hoisin sauce
¼ c. beef stock
2 Tbsp. distilled vinegar
1 Tbsp. sesame oil
canola or peanut oil for deep frying
crispy noodles

Trim fat from flank steak. Cut in half lengthwise, and then slice thinly (⅛") crosswise. In a bowl, mix soy sauce with beef bouillon

Mongolian Beef (Cont.)

and crush to a paste. Mix egg whites, soup mix, cornstarch and meat together with your hands until well incorporated. Set aside. Fill a hot wok one-third full with oil for frying. Heat until it just begins to smoke. Add flank steak, carefully stirring to separate meat. Cook until meat begins to brown slightly. Remove meat and set aside (you can reuse the oil). Return wok to heat, add vegetables and chili-garlic paste. Stir fry until vegetables start to wilt, about 5 minutes. Return meat to wok, toss to mix vegetables and meat. Add hoisin sauce and stock, stir-frying to coat. Add vinegar and sesame oil, tossing to incorporate all ingredients. Serve over crispy noodles.

Serves 4

Pollo Ripieno

Filling:
1 c. ricotta cheese
1 c. mozzarella cheese, grated
2 Tbsp. pine nuts, toasted
3 thin slices prosciutto, cut in half lengthwise, then julienne crosswise ⅛"
2 Tbsp. basil leaves, julienned
½ c. spinach leaves, julienned
¼ c. plain bread crumbs
salt & pepper to taste

4 (8 oz.) chicken breasts, boneless, skin on
sun-dried tomato marinara
toasted pine nuts
sun-dried tomatoes
chopped parsley

Pollo Ripieno (Cont.)

Mix cheeses, pine nuts, prosciutto, basil, spinach, bread crumbs, salt and pepper together until well blended. Lay out chicken breasts, skin side down. Place a mound of filling on one side of breast and roll breast around filling. Place seam side down on greased baking sheet. Continue with remaining breasts and stuffing. Bake at 350° for approximately 25 to 35 minutes until skin is golden and chicken is fully cooked. To serve, slice breast crosswise into four pieces and place on a pool of sun-dried tomato marinara. Garnish with a few toasted pine nuts, julienne sun-dried tomatoes and chopped parsley.

Serves 4

Crab Topped Swordfish with Sesame Cilantro

Crab topping:
1 c. ricotta cheese
1 c. crabmeat
1 tsp. sesame seeds, toasted
1 tsp. black sesame seeds
½ c. mayonnaise, more if necessary
2 tsp. chopped parsley
1 tsp. garlic powder
¼ c. plain bread crumbs
salt & pepper to taste
4 (8 oz.) swordfish steaks, seared
Sesame-Cilantro Aioli (recipe follows)

Mix all ingredients (except swordfish) together until blended well enough to bind together. If too dry, add a little more mayonnaise; if too wet, add a little more bread crumbs. Divide mixture into fourths and press onto top of each swordfish steak. Place steaks onto a baking sheet sprayed with canola or olive oil spray. Bake at 400° until steaks are cooked through and top is golden, 10 to 20 minutes, depending on the thickness of the fish. Serve over stir-fried vegetables and topped with Sesame-Cilantro Aioli (recipe follows).

Sesame-Cilantro Aioli

1 c. mayonnaise
1 tbsp. cilantro
1 tsp. sesame seeds, toasted
1 tsp. black sesame seeds
1 tbsp. red bell pepper, finely diced
2 tsp. garlic, minced
2 tsp. mirin Japanese rice wine
1 tsp. sesame oil
1 tsp. lemon juice
white pepper to taste

Mix all ingredients together. Let stand in refrigerator at least one hour before use.

Serves 4

SIERRA CAFE

Sierra Cafe

Hyatt Regency Hotel & Casino
111 Country Club Drive
Incline Village, Nevada 89451
(775) 832-1234
Website: www.laketahoehyatt.com
Reservations: Not accepted

The Sierra Cafe has a 24-hour menu with some tasty pluses and tempting choices. There's a Grand Breakfast Buffet starting at 7 AM every morning with all the traditional breakfast favorites, or choices from a menu filled with yummy dishes. The Sierra Cafe has "Cuisine Naturelle" dishes available for every meal, too, featuring health-conscious dishes that are low in calories and fat, high in fiber, and nutritionally balanced. Lunch also offers a wide variety of burgers, sandwiches, pizzas, and pastas as well as a salad bar with features like a pasta bar, taco bar, chili bar, assorted desserts and a frozen soft-yogurt machine.

For dinner, you'll find a full menu, including Cuisine Naturelle dishes, plus an exciting dinner buffet with Prime Rib carved to order, Peel-and-Eat Shrimp, and a selection of hot entrees in addition to all the goodies found on the lunch time salad bar. The Friday seafood buffet is everybody's favorite. Sierra Cafe has an affordable selection of wines, with all available as by-the-glass options, plus non-alcoholic wines, beers and bottled waters.

Specialties:
Casual meals from a 24-hour menu; the North Shore's largest salad, taco, pasta and dessert bar, plus Friday night's famous seafood buffet

Hours:
Open 24 hours

Credit Cards Accepted:
All major

Fajita Wrap

3 lbs. chicken tenderloins (approx. 6 oz. per serving)

Marinade:
1 Tbsp. fresh garlic, minced
2 tsp. cayenne pepper, ground
2 oz. cumin powder
2 Tbsp. onion powder
1 Tbsp. cumin seeds
1 c. olive oil
2 tsp. salt
pepper to taste

Fajita Mix:
¼ c. olive oil
4 green bell peppers, seeded & julienned
4 white onions, quartered & sliced

8 slices Monterrey Jack cheese
8 flour tortillas
2 c. guacamole
2 c. Pico de Gallo
16 leaves ornamental lettuce
16 leaves savoy lettuce
1 bunch fresh cilantro
1 lb. tortilla chips

Rinse chicken tenderloins in cold running water and drain. Combine all marinade ingredients. Mix well with chicken. Refrigerate for approximately 4 hours. Make Fajita Mix. Heat oil in skillet and cook chicken on both sides. Add peppers and onions and cook until chicken is done and peppers and onions are crispy. Divide fajita mix into 8 portions.

Fajita Wrap (Cont.)

Add Monterrey Jack cheese to top of fajita mix and barely melt. In a non-stick skillet, warm each tortilla on both sides. Stuff warmed tortillas with fajita mix. Roll like burrito and cut in half. Repeat the process until all wraps are made. Garnish with remaining ingredients and serve with tortilla chips.

Serves 8

Coconut Shrimp

40 large shrimp (5 lbs.), rinsed and de-veined
4 c. flour
8 c. egg wash
1 lb. Panko (Chinese bread crumbs)
1 box shredded philo dough
3 c. coconut flakes
Oil (for deep frying)

Vegetable Medley:
2 carrots, julienned
1 bunch broccoli, separated in florets
1 head cauliflower, separated in florets
2 zucchini, julienned
4 yellow squash, julienned

2 Tbsp. olive oil
2 Tbsp. garlic, minced
1 c. white wine
salt & pepper to taste
4 c. basmati rice
Sweet & Sour Dipping Sauce (recipe follows)
parsley for garnish

Coconut Shrimp (Cont.)

Rinse shrimp, pat dry and dredge in flour. Dip floured shrimp in egg wash. Combine bread crumbs, shredded philo and coconut flakes together. Coat the shrimp with bread crumb mixture. Fry shrimp in hot oil, 350°, in deep fryer until crispy and set aside. Steam vegetable medley until al dente. Heat olive oil in sauté pan, stir in garlic. Add vegetable medley and cook. Deglaze with white wine, season with salt & pepper to taste. Rinse basmati rice 3 times in cold water and add 8 cups water. Bring to boil, cover, and reduce heat and cook rice until done, approximately 20 to 25 minutes. Arrange shrimp on dinner plate with vegetables, steamed rice and Sweet & Sour Dipping Sauce. Garnish with parsley.

Sweet & Sour Dipping Sauce

1 c. water
6 Tbsp. granulated sugar
2 Tbsp. ginger, crushed
1 quarter lemon
zest of 1 orange
3 Tbsp. catsup
¼ c. white vinegar
1 tsp. red food coloring
1 tsp. yellow food coloring
2 Tbsp. cornstarch

In sauce pot, mix water and sugar until dissolved. Add ginger, lemon and orange zest. Bring to a boil for 10 minutes. Add catsup, white vinegar and food coloring and simmer on low heat for ½ hour. Dissolve cornstarch in cool water and add to sauce. Let it cook for 15 minutes until thick. Drain, keep sauce refrigerated and serve cold as a dipping sauce.   Serves 8

Austin's

120 Country club Drive, #24
(Across from the Hyatt)
Incline Village, Nevada 89451
(775) 832-7778

7671 South Virginia Street
Reno, Nevada 889511
(775) 852-1600

Although Austin's now has two locations, both have the same warm hospitality and western mountain atmosphere. It's a family operation for owners Doug and Gloria Brimm. At the new Reno Restaurant, son John manages the bar, while son Tom oversees the dining room. The original Tahoe restaurant is run by son Andy and daughter-in-law Andrea. Andy and wife also own the Incline Village General Store and Pie Shoppe, the source of Austin's famous pies and unique game lasagna.

The ambiance is High Sierra log cabin. Food is All-American melting pot. Everything from Chinese Chicken Salad to Chicken Fried Steak with homemade country gravy. You'll find favorites like Chicken Fried Chicken, homemade meatloaf and liver and onions, as well as pan poached salmon with tangy herbs, all served up with delectable corn bread (home-made too, of course). Whatever you choose, save room for a slice of their delicious pie!

Specialties:
Mountain Country food and spirits

Hours:
11:00 AM - 10:00 PM, Sun. – Thurs.
11:00 AM – 11:00 PM, Fri. & Sat.

Credit Cards Accepted:
American Express, MasterCard, Visa

Chicken Fried Steak

1 small top round roast
1 c. flour
½ c. bread crumbs
½ Tbsp. garlic powder
½ Tbsp. paprika
½ tsp. cayenne
¾ Tbsp. salt
1 tsp. pepper
2 eggs, whipped
canola oil

Cut top round against the grain into several small cutlets about ¼" thick. Pound each cutlet so that it grows to nearly twice its original circumference. Mix flour and seasonings together thoroughly. Dip meat into whipped eggs then place into seasoned flour and, with your fingers, press flour into meat. Fry quickly in a cast iron skillet with canola oil, for best results, using ¼" oil in pan.

Serves 10

Sierra Chicken Stew

Roux:
1 ½ c. margarine
1 c. flour

Stew:
1 gallon water
½ c. parsley
1 tsp. salt
1 tsp. pepper
1 tsp. Worcestershire sauce
2 Tbsp. "Minor's" brand chicken base
1 potato, cubed
1 green bell pepper, chopped
1 white onion, chopped
3 ribs celery, chopped
2 dashes Tabasco sauce
4 c. cooked chicken chunks
1 (1-lb. Box) frozen mixed vegetables

For the roux: Make a quick and easy roux by melting the margarine in the microwave and slowly mixing in the flour until you develop a thick paste.

For the stew: Bring water to a boil. Add all ingredients except chicken, frozen vegetables and roux. Cook until potato is firm but done (approximately 15 minutes). Take off heat and let stand for 10 minutes. Add roux and mix slowly to thicken to desired consistency. Add newly thawed mixed vegetables and cooked chicken. Bring entire stew back to a slow boil for a few minutes and serve.

Serves 10-12

Texas Taco Salad

4 c. mixed greens
1 c. chili meat
¼ c. sliced olives
1 c. tortilla chips
¼ c. chopped tomatoes
½ c. shredded cheddar cheese
½ c. sour cream
¼ c. chives
Ranch dressing

Place the mixed greens in a large salad bowl. Add warmed chili meat, sliced olives, tortilla chips, tomatoes and shredded cheddar cheese. Add a dollop of sour cream and chives on top. To serve, add ranch dressing and mix thoroughly. Divide among 4 small salad plates. Place a dollop of sour cream and chives on each plate and serve.

Serves 4

Mountain Pinto Beans

3 c. pinto beans (dry)
3 slices raw bacon, cut in small strips
1 yellow onion, diced
1½ tsp. salt
½ tsp. pepper
2 dashes hot sauce
2 dashes Worcestershire sauce
1 tsp. garlic powder

Mountain Pinto Beans (Cont.)

Cover beans with cold water in large pan or pot to depth of 3" or 4" over beans. Soak beans in water overnight. Next day, pour off water and rinse beans. Add fresh water (same amount) and all other ingredients. Bring to boil and cover with loose fitting lid. Cook until tender, approximately 1½-2 hours.

Serves 8-10

Andy's Incredible Apple Pie

Crust:
1½ c. flour
½ tsp. Salt
½ c. shortening
3-5 Tbsp. cold water

Apple Mixture:
⅔-1 c. sugar
3 Tbsp. all purpose flour
½ tsp. cinnamon
¼ tsp. nutmeg
1-2 tsp. lemon juice
7-8 apples, peeled, cored and thinly sliced
(for best results, use a mix of Granny Smith, Jonathan and Pippin apples)

Streusel Topping:
⅓ c. brown sugar
¾ c. all purpose flour
6 Tbsp. butter

For crust: Put flour and salt into a bowl. Add shortening and cut into the flour mixture using a masher. The flour mixture should be

Andy's Incredible Apple Pie (Cont.)

in pea size granules before you add the water. Add water and mix well to form a ball of dough. Knead the dough gently using excess flour to keep it from getting sticky. Roll out with a rolling pin. Place in a 9½" pie plate and crimp edges by pushing the index finger of one hand together with the index finger and thumb of the other hand (the dough goes in between). Set aside.

Apple Mixture: Mix together all ingredients and place in the crust.

For Streusel Topping: Mix brown sugar and flour together until soft. Add partially melted butter and mix with your fingers. When you get nice size bits of streusel topping, put it on the pie. Add a little extra butter in little chunks on top and bake in the oven at 300° for 30-40 minutes or until golden brown. Don't forget to share!! Enjoy!!

Serves 6-8

HOMEMADE

DESSERTS

China Wok

120 Country Club Drive #62
P.O. Box 6326
Incline Village, Nevada 89450
(775) 833-3663
Reservations: Accepted

Just across the street from the Hyatt Regency is the China Wok, a small restaurant with a very big repertoire. The Family style dinners available from 11 AM to 10 PM show the range of the kitchen with "Beijing Dinner, Hong Kong Dinner, and Szechwan Dinner", each with a showcase menu from its designated region. More than two dozen-lunch specials provide dishes from all regions, too, and include soup, rice, egg roll, tea and cookies at a bargain price.

The extensive menu has plenty of delectable choices among seafood, fowl, beef, vegetables, pork, and lamb dishes in addition to a variety of soups, appetizers, rice and noodle dishes. Everyone's Chinese favorites are here, as well as some new and exciting dishes you'll want to sample again and again.

Specialties:
Mandarin, Hunan, and Szechwan

Hours:
11:00 AM - 10:00 PM, Mon. – Sat.
12:00 PM - 10:00 PM – Sun.

Credit Cards Accepted:
All Major

Hot & Sour Soup

4 c. chicken broth
1 Tbsp. wood ears *
½ pkg. bean curd *
½ c. bamboo shoots
½ c. scallion, chopped
½ c. cooked pork, cut in bite size pieces
½ tsp. pepper
½ tsp. sugar
1 Tbsp. soy sauce
2 Tbsp. vinegar
3 Tbsp. cornstarch
1 egg, beaten

Bring broth to a boil. Add vegetables and meat in the order listed above. Stir and bring to boil again after each addition. Add pepper, sugar, soy sauce and vinegar. May be prepared ahead of time up to this point. Thicken with cornstarch mixed with some water. Add egg and stir gently. Pour soup into tureen and serve hot.

* Available in Oriental markets.

Serves 4-6

Beef Pepper Steak

⅔ lb. lean beef, sliced
1 ½ tsp. soy sauce
1 tsp. red wine
2 tsp. water
1 tsp. cornstarch
4 tsp. oil
2 tsp. garlic, finely chopped
1 tsp. ginger, sliced
½ c. bell pepper, sliced
3 tsp. green onion
1 tsp. sugar
1 tsp. cornstarch
½ tsp. soy sauce
3 tsp. water

Mix beef with the soy sauce, wine and water. Add 1 teaspoon cornstarch. Mix well. Heat oil, in wok. Add beef mixture and stir-fry until beef is almost cooked. Remove from pan. Use remaining oil from pan to stir fry garlic, ginger and bell pepper. Add green onions and cook until fragrant. Add sugar, the remaining 1 teaspoon cornstarch, ½ teaspoon soy sauce and water and cook until thickened. Add meat mixture and stir-fry to mix well.

Serves 2

239

Eggplant and Hot Garlic Sauce

4 tsp. oil
1 eggplant, cut in 1" cubes
2 tsp. garlic, finely chopped
2 tsp. ginger, finely chopped
1 whole scallion, chopped
½ tsp. salt
½ tsp. sugar
¼ tsp. wine
1 tsp. soy sauce
¼ c. water
1 tsp. cornstarch
½ tsp. Szechwan peppercorns

Heat oil. Add eggplant and turn heat to medium. Stir intermittently until soft (about 5 minutes). Push to side of wok. Add garlic, ginger, and scallions. Add seasonings and soy sauce. When mixture boils, turn heat to medium, cover and simmer for 2 minutes. Add cornstarch/water mixture and Szechwan peppercorns.

Serves 2

Excellent Food

TAHOE VISTA

Sunsets on the Lake

7320 North Lake Boulevard (P.O. Box 189)
Tahoe Vista, California 96148
(530) 546-3640
Website: www.sunsetslaketahoe.com
Reservations: Strongly suggested

Sunsets on the Lake boasts an "Island Bar" complete with tiki torches, thatched umbrellas, and a panoramic view of Lake Tahoe where the sunsets are simply spectacular. Meanwhile, patrons can sit outside in comfort protected by a glass windbreaker. There are even heat lamps in the outdoor dining area to even the odds against Tahoe's mercurial weather changes. Inside, a central stone fireplace adds yet another cozy note.

Fine Northern Italian and American cuisine is the bill of fare. The olive-wood burning oven turns out pizzas, rotisserie dishes, and grilled items. All the delicious desserts are made from scratch, too. There's a nice, solid wine list with plenty of by-the-glass options.

Sunsets on the Lake also has valet parking for your boat or your car.

Specialties:
Lamb Shanks, Fresh Fish and Seafood

Hours:
From 5:00 PM, Nightly, Winter
11:30 AM - 10:00 PM, Nightly, Summer
Drinks till midnight

Credit Cards Accepted:
All Major

Spinach & Mushroom Lasagne with Tomato/Mushroom and Béchamel Sauce

1 pkg. dried spinach lasagne pasta, cooked
6 c. picked spinach
Tomato/Mushroom Sauce (recipe follows)
Béchamel Sauce (recipe follows)
3 c. Asiago cheese
marinara sauce
grated Parmesan cheese

In a 4" deep, 9 x 11" pan, assemble the lasagna in the following manner: one layer of Tomato/Mushroom Sauce, one layer of cooked noodles, one layer Tomato/Mushroom Sauce, one layer spinach leaves, drizzled Béchamel Sauce, one layer of sprinkled Asiago cheese, one layer of cooked noodles. Continue assembly, repeating this four more times so you have a total of five layers. On the top, finish with Béchamel Sauce and Asiago cheese only. Cover with foil and bake in a 350° oven for 45 minutes. Remove foil and bake an additional 15 minutes or until golden on top. Serve on top of a little marinara sauce with freshly grated Parmesan cheese.

Tomato/Mushroom Sauce

½ c. olive oil
¼ c. chopped garlic
1 onion, diced fine
2 stalks celery, diced fine
1 carrot, diced fine
1½ c. sliced mushrooms (shiitakes & white)
1 c. white wine
2 tsp. chopped fresh oregano – Salt and pepper to taste
1 (12 oz. can) Roma tomatoes, crushed by hand
1 c. sun dried tomatoes, sliced

Tomato/Mushroom Sauce (Cont.)

Warm olive oil in fairly large pot. Add garlic, onion, celery and carrot and sauté until soft, approximately 5 minutes. Add mushrooms and continue to cook until mushrooms begin to soften. Deglaze with white wine and add oregano. Once wine has mostly cooked out, add Roma tomatoes and turn heat down to a simmer. Sauce should be quite firm when ready (not watery). Add sun dried tomatoes and season with salt and pepper.

Béchamel Sauce

1 ½ c. heavy cream
1 ½ c. milk
¼ c. butter
½ c. flour
½ tsp. ground nutmeg
salt & pepper to taste

Bring cream and milk to a boil in one pot. In a separate pot, melt butter and whisk in flour so it is smooth and without lumps. Make sure heat is on low and add cream mixture to the roux, whipping continuously to avoid any lumps. Allow to simmer for 10 minutes while stirring occasionally. Make sure sauce does not stick to bottom of pot, otherwise you will have a scorched flavor. Add nutmeg, salt and pepper to taste.

Serves 8

Woodfired Pork Tenderloin with Minted Couscous , Cinnamon Burgundy Sauce & Vanilla Glazed Vegetables

1 Pork tenderloin (approximately 8 oz. per person)
1 tsp. chopped garlic
1 tsp. chopped fresh herbs (rosemary, sage, thyme)
½ c. olive oil
¼ c. balsamic vinegar
Salt & coarsely ground black pepper
Minted couscous (recipe follows)
Cinnamon burgundy sauce (recipe follows)
Vanilla glazed vegetables (recipe follows)

Trim sinew and excess fat from pork, rub with garlic, herbs, olive oil, vinegar and salt and pepper. Let pork marinade overnight. Place pork on BBQ and cook to medium rare-medium. Spoon Minted Couscous on top of plate. Slice pork into thin slices and fan out around the couscous. Pour Cinnamon Burgundy Sauce around pork and arrange Vanilla Glazed Vegetables on plate.

Minted Couscous

1 tsp. butter
2 Tbsp. olive oil
½ tsp. garlic
½ c. celery, onion and carrot, finely diced
1 c. couscous
1 c. chicken stock
2 tsp. chopped fresh mint
salt & pepper to taste

Combine first four ingredients in saucepan and cook until vegetables are tender. Add couscous and chicken stock while stirring. Turn heat down to low and cover. Let couscous steam for approximately 5 minutes, stirring occasionally until tender and all liquid is absorbed. Turn off heat. Add mint and season with salt and pepper. Use a fork to fluff up the couscous.

Cinnamon Burgundy Sauce

2 c. red wine
¼ c. soy sauce
¼ c. brown sugar
2 cinnamon sticks
10 juniper berries, crushed
3 cloves garlic
5 slices fresh ginger
juice and zest of 1 orange
3 c. veal stock

Combine all ingredients except veal stock and bring to a boil. Turn heat down to a simmer and reduce by half. Add veal stock and reduce by half again and strain.

Vanilla Glazed Vegetables

1 yam
1 bunch baby carrots
1 c. water
½ c. sugar
1 vanilla bean, split

Bake yam in 350° oven until just soft. Peel baby carrots and boil until tender. Combine water, sugar and vanilla bean in saucepan and reduce until a thickish glaze is achieved. Place sliced yam and baby carrots into glaze over low heat, turning vegetables until well coated and liquid is absorbed.

Serves 6

Spit Roasted Garlic Chicken with Grilled Polenta and Vegetables

1 whole chicken
1 c. olive oil
3 Tbsp. garlic, chopped
2 tsp. fresh chopped herbs (rosemary and thyme)
1 tsp. coarsely ground black pepper
1 tsp. garlic powder
1 tsp. paprika
1 tsp. fennel seed
1 tsp. onion powder
1 tsp. sage
chicken stock
Polenta (recipe follows)

Spit Roasted Garlic Chicken with Grilled Polenta and Vegetables (Cont.)

Rub chicken inside and out with olive oil, garlic, fresh herbs and ground black pepper. Marinade overnight. Sprinkle next 5 ingredients over chicken just before cooking. Either spit roast or oven roast the chicken in a 350° oven for 1½ hours. Remove from oven and let cool to touch. Running a sharp knife along the center, debone the chicken so you have two half chickens. Leg bone can be left intact. Place the two half chickens into roasting pan with ½" of stock in the bottom and roast in 550° oven until skin is crisp. Use reduced chicken stock in pan as sauce. Serve with Polenta and vegetables of choice.

Polenta

2 c. milk
1 c. chicken stock
1 c. polenta
½ c. Parmesan cheese
salt and pepper to taste
butter

Bring milk and chicken stock to a boil. Turn down heat to a simmer and add polenta while stirring with a whisk. Cook for approximately 5 minutes until polenta thickens. Add cheese and salt and pepper. Pour into a buttered dish so polenta is approximately 1" thick and let set for 6 hours in refrigerator. At the restaurant, this is cut into squares and grilled, but it can also be reheated in a microwave at home.

Serves 4

Crispy Saffron Risotto Cakes

8 c. chicken stock
1 Tbsp. butter
½ c. finely chopped onion
⅛ tsp. saffron threads
2 c. arborio/risotto rice
½ c. dry white wine
½ c. freshly grated Parmesan cheese
flour
Mushroom Sauce (recipe follows)
freshly chopped parsley for garnish

In a pot, bring chicken stock to a boil and turn off heat. In a separate pot, melt butter. Sauté onions and saffron over low heat until onions are soft. Add rice and wine, stirring continuously. When wine has been absorbed, begin adding the chicken stock in stages, 2 cups at a time. Wait until stock has cooked down before adding more. When the rice is just tender and all the liquid has been absorbed, stir in the Parmesan cheese. Pour risotto into flat dish or sheet pan so that risotto is approximately 1" deep in pan. Refrigerate for at least 5 hours. With biscuit cutter, cut risotto into cakes and dredge in flour. Submerge cakes in 350 ° oil and deep fry until golden brown and crisp, approximately 2 minutes. To serve, pour Mushroom Sauce into bowl. Place two risotto cakes on top of sauce and garnish with freshly chopped parsley.
Serve as an appetizer.

Mushroom Sauce

1 Tbsp. butter
1 tsp. finely chopped shallots
1 tsp. chopped garlic
2 c. sliced mushrooms
½ tsp. chopped fresh oregano
1 ½ c. veal stock
2 Tbsp. balsamic vinegar
salt & pepper to taste
freshly chopped parsley for garnish

In saucepan, melt 2 tsp. butter, add shallots and garlic and cook for 2 minutes on medium heat. Add mushrooms and oregano. Sauté until mushrooms are soft. Add veal stock and balsamic vinegar and cook down by about one half. Finish with the last teaspoon of butter and season with salt and pepper if needed. To serve, pour sauce into bowl. Place two risotto cakes on top of sauce and garnish with freshly chopped parsley.

Serves 6-8

Gorgonzola and Pear Salad

1 pear (firm but ripe)
4 c. mixed greens, lettuce/spring mix
½ c. Gorgonzola cheese,crumbled
½ c. pecans, roughly chopped
½ c. Basic Vinaigrette (recipe follows)

Cut pear in half lengthwise and remove seeds. Reserve half and dice the other half into fairly thin ½" pieces. In a salad bowl, combine the mixed greens, diced pear, half of the Gorgonzola cheese, half of the pecans and the salad dressing. Toss until greens are well coated with dressing and pile onto serving plates. Take the remaining half of the pear, cut into long thin strips and fan out on top of the salad. Crumble remaining Gorgonzola cheese and pecans on top.

Basic Vinaigrette

2 Tbsp. red wine vinegar
½ tsp. Dijon mustard
1 tsp. finely chopped shallots
1 Tbsp. freshly squeezed lemon juice
½ tsp. salt
¼ tsp. fresh ground black pepper
½ c. extra virgin olive oil

Combine first 6 ingredients in a small mixing bowl and slowly whisk in olive oil.

Serves 4

Chocolate, Bourbon, Pecan Tart with Homemade Cinnamon Ice Cream

Pie crust:
1 c. flour
¼ c. sugar
pinch salt
2 tsp. lemon zest
5 oz. butter
2 egg yolks
2 tsp. vanilla extract
2 tsp. cold water (add more if needed)

Pulse flour, sugar, salt, lemon zest and butter in food processor. Add egg yolks, vanilla and water and continue to process until dough comes together. Wrap in plastic and chill for 1 hour. Roll dough into 2 (8") tart shells and chill while making filling.

Filling:
6 large eggs (room temperature)
1 c. sugar
¾ c. corn syrup
1½ c. butter, melted and cooled
3 tsp. vanilla extract
6 oz. semisweet chocolate, cut into ¼" pieces
3 c. pecans
½ c. bourbon
cinnamon ice cream (recipe follows)

Whisk together eggs, sugar, corn syrup, butter and vanilla and stir in chocolate. Pour filling into shells and top with pecans. Bake in 325° oven for 50 minutes or until filling is set. Pour bourbon over tarts while still hot and let tarts cool.
Top with Cinnamon Ice Cream.

Cinnamon Ice Cream

2 c. heavy cream
2 c. milk
6 cinnamon sticks
½ c. sugar
8 egg yolks
2 tsp. vanilla extract
½ tsp. ground cinnamon

Heat cream, milk and cinnamon sticks over medium-high heat until small bubbles start to form around edges of pan. Remove from heat. Cover and let stand for 30 minutes. Whisk together sugar and egg yolks until well blended. Whisk 1 cup hot cream mixture into egg yolks and then return to pan with rest of the hot cream mixture. Cook over medium-low heat, stirring constantly for 2-4 minutes or until slightly thickened. DO NOT BOIL. Remove pan from heat and strain into bowl. Place bowl into ice bath and stir until cool, approximately 5-10 minutes. Stir in vanilla, ground cinnamon and cover mixture with plastic and refrigerate at least 6 hours. Place mixture in ice cream maker and follow standard directions.

Makes 2 tarts

DESSERT MENU

Boulevard Café

6731 North Lake Boulevard
P.O. Box 406
Tahoe Vista, California 96148
(530) 546-7213
Reservations: Required

Boulevard Café's intimate dining room and romantic setting make it a favorite with locals and visitors who've made it an "I'll be back" kind of place. Imaginative starters and salads include dishes like butternut squash gnocchi, potato ravioli, sweetbread salad, and pear and goat cheese salad. Pasta dishes exhibit the same flair, among them; linguine with shrimp putanesca, pappardelle with braised rabbit, and a risotto of the day.

There is always a fresh fish of the day, too, as well as ossobuco, roast duck, rack of lamb, filet mignon, loin of pork, baked scampi, and stuffed chicken breast. Boulevard Café's wine selection is equally superb.

Specialties:
Northern Italian with a California Flair

Hours:
6:00 PM - 9:30 PM, Mon. - Sun.
Closed Mondays in October & November

Credit Cards Accepted:
MasterCard, Visa

Grilled Sweetbread Salad with Wild Mushrooms

1 (8 oz.) veal sweetbread
flour for dredging
salt & pepper
canola oil
½ c. carrot, diced
½ c. onion, diced
½ c. celery, diced
1 bay leaf
10 green cardamom pods
2 c. dry white wine
2 c. veal stock
½ c. spring mix salad greens
¼ c. sesame oil (plus more for grilling)
2 Tbsp. sherry vinegar
1 Tbsp. shallots, chopped
12 shiitaki or chanterelle mushrooms

Trim off all membranes and fat from sweetbread. Pat dry. Dredge in flour seasoned with salt & pepper. Shake off excess. Sauté in canola oil until very brown, turning as needed. When well browned, add diced vegetables and spices. Stir until vegetables just begin to soften, add wine and reduce by two-thirds. Add veal stock and cover. Simmer until sweetbread is cooked through, about 15 minutes. Remove meat and cool. Reduce sauce to one-half cup, strain and reserve. Toss salad mix with oil, vinegar, shallots, salt & pepper. Arrange on plates. Brush sweetbread and mushrooms with sesame oil and grill until mushrooms are warmed through and the meat is crisp. Slice meat, divide among plates and put mushrooms on top. Serve with sauce.

Serves 4

Potato Raviolis with Porcini, Reggiano and White Truffle Oil

1 c. mashed potatoes
1 Tbsp. chopped chives
½ tsp. white truffle oil
1 Tbsp. grated reggiano
20 (3") fresh pasta squares*
1 egg, beaten
½ c. dry porcini mushrooms
1 Tbsp. Shallots, minced
½ tsp. fresh sage, chopped (plus leaves for garnish)
½ c. Madeira
salt & pepper
1 c. heavy cream
shaved Parmesan & reggiano

Mix first four ingredients and place a small amount on each pasta square (which have been brushed with beaten egg). Fold into triangles, crimp edges. Re-hydrate mushrooms by boiling in water for 10 minutes. Roughly chop the mushrooms, place in pan with shallots, sage, Madeira, salt & pepper and reduce until liquid is almost gone. Add cream and reduce until thickened. Boil ravioli and toss in sauce. Top each serving with shaved cheeses, truffle oil and sage leaves.

*wonton wrappers work well

Serves 5

Fritelle with Crab and Shrimp
(Italian-style crabcake)

2 c. crabmeat, drained (any type will work)
2 c. rock shrimp, cooked and chopped
1 large potato, boiled and chilled
½ c. onion, grated
¼ c. Parmesan cheese
chopped chives
salt & pepper to taste
2 eggs
1 tsp. chopped fresh tarragon (optional)
flour, beaten eggs & bread crumbs
olive oil

Combine first nine ingredients. Mix with your hands until the potato is well broken up and the mixture holds together. Form into cakes, dredge in flour, then egg wash, then fresh bread crumbs. Fry in olive oil until golden brown. Serve with your favorite sauce.

Yields approx. 20 large cakes

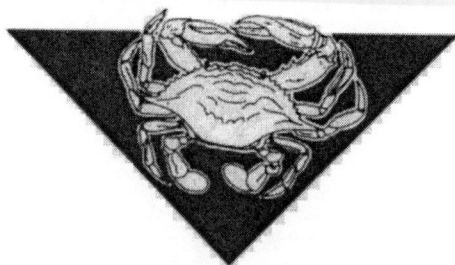

Almond Panna Cotta

5 c. heavy whipping cream
¾ c. sugar
¼ c. honey
½ tsp. vanilla extract
¼ tsp. almond extract
4 gelatin sheets
berries (any favorite)
toasted almonds

Combine cream, sugar, honey, vanilla and almond extract in sauce pan. Bring to a low boil. Soften gelatin sheets in cold water and add to cream, stirring until melted. Ladle into cups and refrigerate overnight. To serve, unmold onto plate and garnish with berries and toasted almonds.

Serves 8

Nut Meringue Cookies

2½ c. ground almonds
1½ c. sugar
2 Tbsp. cornstarch
1 Tbsp. anise seeds
12 egg whites
pinch cream of tarter

Mix nuts, sugar, cornstarch and anise seeds. Beat egg whites with cream of tartar to stiff peaks. Fold in nut/sugar mixture. Place in pastry bag and pipe onto buttered and floured sheet pan. Any shape or size will work - have fun! Work quickly, don't let the mixture deflate. Bake at 250° until dry and golden, about 90 minutes.

Captain Jon's Seafood

7220 North Lake Boulevard (P.O. Box 157)
Tahoe Vista, California 96148
(530) 546-4819
email: AJ@LTIS.com
Reservations: Strongly Suggested

Inviting fireplaces and a view of Tahoe are just a few of the attractions at Captain Jon's. There's outdoor dining (and boat parking) in fine weather, and a menu that delights diners all year Round. While you select your comestibles, you are invited to dip fresh French bread in a mixture of olive oil and balsamic vinegar flavored with garlic and Parmesan. House specialty Oysters Rockefeller have a Captain Jon twist. They are baked in a light lemon-butter sauce and topped with Brie. Imaginative entrees include fresh fish and meat selections paired with thoughtfully chosen and prepared accompaniments, artfully presented.

Service includes those extra touches you expect from fine dining. A palate-refreshing sorbet is offered before your entree. All the wines on the list are available by the glass. Fine soups, crisp salads, and delectable desserts round out the bill of fare.

Specialties:
Fresh seafood prepared in a variety of ways

———————————

Hours:
Lunch on the Pier and in Boat House late June - early Sept. only
Dinner: 5:30 PM, Nightly
Happy Hour: 4:00 PM - 7:00 PM, Nightly

———————————

Credit Cards Accepted:
American Express, MasterCard, Visa

261

Oysters Rockefeller

½ c. Rocky Mix (recipe follows)
4 shucked oysters (reserve shells)
2 oz. brie cheese
1 c. heavy cream

Rocky Mix:
2 pieces bacon, rendered & crumbled (reserve fat)
¼ c. bell peppers, diced
⅛ c. fennel, diced
¼ c. red onions, diced
2 tsp. Garlic, minced
¼ c. shot Pernod
½ c. fresh spinach, chopped

Evenly divide Rocky Mix among oyster shells. Place oysters on top then place ½ oz. brie cheese on each oyster. Heat heavy cream and pour over the top. Bake for 15-18 minutes at 450°. Heat bacon fat. Sauté peppers, fennel, red onions and garlic. Add Pernod and chopped spinach.

Serves 4

262

Salmon En Croute

4 oz. puff pastry dough
2 Tbsp. fresh spinach
½ c. Fish Mousse (recipe follows)
4 oz. fresh salmon
1 egg

Roll out dough into ½ inch flat square 6" x 6". Place spinach in center of dough, add Fish Mousse on top of spinach then place a 4 oz. cut of salmon on top. Roll out another 6" x 6" piece of dough and place on top. Shape into a fish and seal the edges firmly. Make an egg wash (1 egg plus 2 Tbsp. water) and brush over the croute. Bake at 500° for 8-10 minutes. Remove from oven and let set for 5 min. Then bake again at 450° for 8-10 minutes more.

Fish Mousse

8 oz. salmon
4 oz. scallops
4 oz. rock shrimp
1 Tbsp. cold butter
2 Tbsp. heavy cream
1 tsp. chopped shallots
2 tsp. chopped garlic
3 egg whites

Blend all ingredients together in a blender or Cuisinart. Refrigerate until set.

Serves 1

Lobster Whiskey

¼ c. whiskey
½ c. pureed tomatoes
¼ c. heavy cream
½ c. clam juice
2 Tbsp. chopped green onions, chopped
¼ c. tomatoes, diced
dash cayenne
dash nutmeg
pinch rosemary, chopped
1 (2 lb.) par boiled lobster (8 minutes)

Combine all ingredients, bring to a boil. Add lobster and bake for 20 minutes. Baste every 5 minutes. Split lobster in half and place it on a dish. Pour sauce over lobster and serve.

Serves 1

Berries Romanoff

½ c. vanilla ice cream, slightly softened
½ c. whipped cream
¼ c. raspberry sherbet, slightly softened
½ c. sliced berries (strawberries, raspberries, blackberries, blueberries)
¼ c. Grand Marnier
2 Tbsp. raspberry puree
1 tsp. pure vanilla
whipped cream
powdered sugar

Fold first seven ingredients together. Top with whipped cream and powdered sugar.

Serves 1

Blue Onion Catering & Event Planning

7019 North Lake Boulevard
Tahoe Vista, California 96143
P. O. Box 711
Tahoe City, California 96145
(530) 546-3913
(800) 353-4050
Reservations: Essential

Blue Onion can make your dreams a reality. From event planning to service, theirs is a highly-skilled and caring staff. Blue Onion's cuisine is unique and imaginative, a blend of classic technique with the latest global influences and light, fresh flavors. From a cocktail party in your parlor to a mountain-top wedding, and just about anything in between (they'll find just the right place, if you don't have one), Blue Onion will fill your special time with wonderful memories.

Blue Onion can help you find just the right invitations, place cards, musicians, photographers, props, flowers, ice sculptures, and more. Each menu is custom-created. Some recent themes have included: paella party, fondue dinner, classic barbecue, sushi bar, Mexican fiesta, Mediterranean table, tapas party. One satisfied customer says: "all our guests were overwhelmed by the excellent food, the bar and the service". From an intimate anniversary dinner to the wedding of your dreams.

Specialties:
Full-service catering, award-winning cuisine

Credit Cards Accepted:
Visa, MasterCard

Caramelized Ginger Scones

2 Tbsp. fresh ginger, chopped
½ Tbsp. butter
3 c. all-purpose flour
5 Tbsp. granulated sugar
¾ Tbsp. baking powder
¾ tsp. salt
¾ c. butter
1 c. buttermilk
1 egg, beaten
cinnamon sugar (1 Tbsp. sugar & 1 Tbsp. cinnamon)

Preheat oven to 400°. Over medium heat sauté fresh chopped ginger in ½ tablespoon butter until golden brown and caramelized, set aside. In large mixing bowl combine flour, sugar, baking powder and salt. Using your fingers, crumble the butter into the dry mix until the butter forms pebble shapes. Add caramelized ginger. Stir in buttermilk – do not over mix, the key to a good scone is a semi-dry under mixed batter. Using an ice cream scoop, scoop out batter onto parchment lined baking sheet and flatten with palm of hand. If desired, brush with egg wash and sprinkle with cinnamon sugar. Bake about 15 minutes or until golden brown.

Makes 2 dozen scones

Orange Pistachio Biscotti

1 ½ c. all purpose flour
½ tsp. baking soda
¼ tsp. salt
¾ c. granulated sugar
2 large eggs
1 tsp. vanilla extract
2 Tbsp. orange zest, grated
⅔ c. pistachios, chopped

Preheat oven to 350°. Line a baking sheet with parchment and set aside. In large mixing bowl combine flour, baking soda, salt and sugar. Using a wooden spoon or rubber spatula, blend the eggs, vanilla, orange zest and pistachios into the dry ingredients forming a thick sticky dough. Turn the dough over onto a lightly floured work surface. Cut the dough into 4 equal pieces and shape each piece into a 12-inch long log. Place logs onto baking sheet and press down on the logs to flatten them slightly. Bake for about 12 minutes, until firm to the touch but not golden brown (¾ baked). Let cool completely. Using a sharp serrated knife, cut the logs into ⅓ " thick slices. Lay the biscotti on parchment lined baking sheet and bake for 10 to 15 minutes, or until lightly toasted. As the biscotti cools they will become crisp.

Makes 3 dozen biscotti

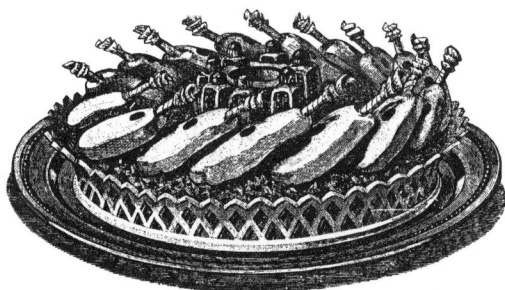

Rosemary Brioche Dinner Rolls

1 lb. unbleached all purpose flour or organic bread flour
½ c. unsalted butter, melted
2 large eggs
1 tsp. kosher salt
1 ½ tsp. sugar
2 tsp. active yeast
⅓ c. warm water (100°)
2 Tbsp. fresh rosemary, chopped

Place all of the above ingredients in a mixer. Using the dough hook attachment, mix for 20 minutes. If the dough is not coming together or is too wet, add a few extra pinches of flour. If the dough is too dry and not forming a smooth ball, add up to a tablespoon of warm water. Transfer dough to a large buttered bowl and cover tightly with plastic wrap. Let rise at room temperature until doubled in size, 2 to 3 hours. Deflate the dough by "punching" it with your fist. Cover bowl with plastic wrap and refrigerate overnight or let rise at room temperature 4 to 6 hours until double in size for the second time. Scale the dough into 2 oz. balls and roll freehand or place in brioche molds. Let rise at room temperature for 2 to 3 hours. Bake in preheated oven at 400° for 20 to 30 minutes or until golden brown.

Makes 2 to 3 dozen dinner rolls

Bakery

Thai Cole Slaw

Dressing:
½ c. sesame seed oil
½ c. olive oil
1 Tbsp. garlic, chopped
1 Tbsp. toasted sesame seeds
½ c. rice wine vinegar
¼ c. pickled ginger, chopped

Salad:
1 small head of Napa cabbage, shredded
½ head of red cabbage, shredded
¼ lb. of snow peas, blanched

Mix dressing ingredients together. Toss dressing and salad together. Let marinate 1 hour and serve chilled.

Makes 6-8 servings

Tahoe City

Jake's on the Lake

780 North Lake Boulevard (In the Boatworks Mall)
P.O. Box 6925
Tahoe City, California 96145
(530) 583-0188
Reservations: Suggested

Sail on in to Jake's on the Lake, and you can have a valet park your boat. No surprise, then, that Jake's specializes in fresh seafood, with several fresh catch items available every night. There's outdoor deck dining, with a view toward Tahoe's South Shore, 22 miles distant. The lower deck is for drinks and appetizers. Jake's boasts the finest liquors on the lake. They also take pride in their "innovative appetizers." Here, too, seafood is the star of the show. During happy hour - Sunday through Thursday from 4:30 to 6:30 p.m. there are half-price specials in the bar.

The upstairs deck is the venue for dining. In addition to the fresh fish, Jake's offers a good variety of beef, chicken, and pasta dishes as well as a marinated rack of lamb. There is also a nicely varied wine list

Specialties:
Fresh Fish, Innovative Appetizers

Hours:
(June 15 to September 15)
11:30 AM - 2:30 PM, daily
2:30 PM - 5:00 PM, Bar menu
5:00 PM - 10:30 PM, nightly
(September 16 to June 14) weekends only
11:30 AM - 2:30 PM,
5:30 PM - 10:00 PM

Credit Cards Accepted:
American Express, MasterCard, Visa, Discover

Seafood Gumbo

⅛ tsp. each, cayenne pepper, paprika and salt
⅛ tsp. each, white pepper, black pepper, thyme, oregano and ground bay leaf
¼ c. margarine
¼ c. onion, chopped
¼ c. green pepper, chopped
¼ c. celery, chopped
1½ tsp. garlic, chopped
1½ tsp. gumbo filé
6 c. clam broth or fish stock
1 c. shucked oysters
¼ lb. rock shrimp
¾ lb. crab meat
2 c. cooked rice

In a small bowl, combine the cayenne pepper, paprika, salt, white pepper, black pepper, thyme, oregano and bay leaf. Set aside. In a large heavy stock pot, melt the margarine over medium heat. Cook the onions, green peppers and celery for 5 minutes. Add the garlic, filé gumbo and spice mixture. Cook for about 8 minutes or until vegetables are soft and spices are aromatic. Mix may stick to the pan so watch it carefully and stir often. Add clam broth, bring to a boil, reduce to a simmer and cook for 45 minutes. While the soup is cooking, poach the oysters in ½ gallon lightly salted water for 5 minutes. Drain, cool and chop. Add shrimp and crab to soup. Bring to a boil and turn off instantly. Add oysters, add rice and serve.

Serves 8-10

Rack of Lamb

1 Tbsp. coarse ground black pepper
1 Tbsp. kosher salt
1 Tbsp. virgin olive oil
1 Tbsp. garlic, minced
1 Tbsp. rosemary, crushed
4 each lamb racks (Frenched) about 3½ to 4 lbs.
Dijon Herb Paste (recipe follows)
Chutney Butter (recipe follows)
Mint sprigs for garnish

Mix pepper, salt, oil, garlic and rosemary in small bowl. Rub on to lamb. Bake lamb in a hot oven for about fifteen minutes or until just rare. (If using a meat thermometer it should be about 105°). Cool and spread with Dijon paste. At this point lamb can be refrigerated until needed. Heat oven to 450°. Place lamb on oven rack and cook to desired doneness. Remove from oven, let sit for five minutes in a warm spot and carve into chops. Serve garnished with mint sprigs and a side of softened chutney butter.

Dijon Herb Paste

1 Tbsp. rosemary
2 garlic cloves
1 bay leaf
1 Tbsp. olive oil
1 Tbsp. red wine vinegar
¾ c. Dijon mustard
2 tsp. Chervil (or fresh parsley)
2 tsp. black pepper
2 tsp. thyme
2 tsp. basil

Puree first five ingredients in blender.   Puree to a paste.   Add remaining five ingredients and mix well.

Chutney Butter

2 Tbsp. cream
¾ c. butter
1 tsp. lemon juice
¼ c. ketchup
½ Tbsp. Worcestershire sauce
½ c. Mayor Grey's mango chutney (pureed)
¼ c. mint jelly

Whip cream and butter until soft.   Combine all other ingredients and blend well. Chill. Will keep for about six weeks.

Serves 4

Mediterranean Chicken Sandwich

1 sour dough roll (or bread)
3 Tbsp. olive Tapanade (recipe follows)
2 tsp. Herb Mayonnaise (recipe follows)
2 tomato slices
salad greens
4 red pepper, julienne strips
2 red onion slices
1 marinated chicken breast (grilled and chilled)

Toast roll lightly. Spread olive mixture on one side and herb mayo on the other. Arrange tomato, greens, pepper, onion and chicken on roll.

Serves 1

Olive Tapanade

½ c. Kalamata olives (pitted)
½ c. olive oil
½ Tbsp. garlic, chopped
½ Tbsp. shallot, chopped
1 ½ Tbsp. red onion, chopped
2 Tbsp. red pepper, chopped
2 Tbsp. green pepper, chopped

Combine all ingredients in food processor and process until semi-smooth. Mixture should be a little rough, not totally pureed.

Yields 1 cup

Herb Mayonnaise

1 c. Best Foods mayonnaise
2 Tbsp. Dijon mustard
1 Tbsp. dried chervil
1 Tbsp. fresh basil, chopped
2 Tbsp. fresh parsley, chopped
4 green onions, chopped

Combine all ingredients in mixing bowl and mix thoroughly.

Yields 1 cup

Tortilla Grilled Fresh Fish

1 batch Tortilla Breading Crust (recipe follows)
8 firm white fish filets, cut fairly thin (Halibut or Sea Bass work well)
½ c. canola oil
1 batch Avocado Aioli (recipe follows)
cilantro sprigs for garnish
lime wedges for garnish

Place the tortilla crust on a flat baking sheet. Press the serving side of the fish into the Tortilla Breading Crust. You need only a light layer on the fish. In a 12" non-stick skillet, heat half the oil to medium heat. Sauté four of the fish filets crust side down until crisp. Remove to a baking pan crust side up. Repeat process with other four filets. Handle the fish with care. Place pan of fish in 400° oven and cook until just done, about five minutes, depending on the thickness of the fish. Remove to warmed serving plates, top with a dollop of the avocado aioli and garnish with a sprig of cilantro and a lime slice or wedge.

Serves 8

Tortilla Breading Crust

8 corn tortillas
1 Tbsp. cumin
1 Tbsp. chili powder
½ Tbsp. kosher salt

Slice tortillas. Deep fry until crisp. Cool. Puree in food processor until very fine. Add seasonings and mix well.

Avocado Aioli

1 ripe Haas avocado
¼ c. chopped cilantro
1 c. mayonnaise
3 Tbsp. fresh lime juice
½ tsp. cayenne pepper (or to taste)
½ Tbsp. kosher salt (or to taste)

Peel and roughly chop avocado. Chop cilantro. Combine all ingredients in food processor. Blend until smooth.

Serves 8

Ahi Poke

1 lb. diced fresh ahi
⅓ c. diced green onions
1 tsp. chili flakes
3 Tbsp. toasted sesame seeds
1½ Tbsp. sesame oil
¼ c. soy sauce
¼ c. pickled ginger, chopped
1 tsp. kosher salt
8 egg roll wrappers
1 egg white
cornstarch
vegetable oil

Combine first 8 ingredients in a bowl and mix well. Let sit for about 15 minutes. Drain off excess juice in strainer. Place about 2 ounces in a 7"x 7" egg roll wrapper and roll in a traditional egg roll style. Seal end with egg wash* and dust with cornstarch so they don't stick. Heat oil to 360°. Deep fry roll for about 1 minute. They should still be rare in the middle. Cut on bias and serve.

*egg wash - beat white of egg

Serves 8

Sunnyside Resort Chris Craft Dining Room

1850 West Lake Boulevard (P.O. Box 5969)
Tahoe City, California 96145
(530) 583-7200
(800) 822-2SKI
Website: www.hulapie.com
Reservations: Suggested

Hospitality at Sunnyside goes back to 1908 when its wealthy private owner played host to such luminaries as Winston Churchill. It has been a resort since 1946 and was completely refurbished in 1987. Accessible by boat to the Sunnyside Marina, or by road along SR 89, Sunnyside's Chris Craft Dining Room provides an unobstructed view of Lake Tahoe and the Sierra Nevada, with al fresco dining available on the spacious patio in season. The dining room takes its name from the mahogany paneling and pictures of Chris Craft boats.

Friendly service is a memorable feature of the restaurant that serves up a tempting selection of fresh fish, pastas, chicken, and grilled meats. There is also a chef's special every night of the week, plus a homemade soup of the day. Be sure to save room for dessert. They are made fresh daily in Sunnyside's kitchens. For relaxing, there's a giant stone fireplace in the lounge, and on Friday evenings, you'll find live music for dancing from 7 until 10 PM.

Specialties:
Fresh fish, Prime Rib & Pasta

Hours:
4:00 PM - 9:30 PM (to 10 PM on weekends), Winter
10:00 AM - 10:00 PM, Summer

Credit Cards Accepted:
American Express, MasterCard, Visa, Discover

Sunnyside Ahi Fish Taco

1 Tbsp. oil
1 (3oz. piece) fresh Ahi (about ½" round, 3" long)
1 flour or corn tortilla
2 Tbsp. ranch dressing
¼ c. shredded cabbage
2 Tbsp. diced tomato

Heat sauté pan with a little oil. Add fish. Cook to desired doneness. At the same time, warm tortilla. In tortilla put the ranch dressing, cabbage, tomato and fresh sautéed fish. Top with your favorite salsa.

Serves 1

Corn Husk Salmon

Atlantic salmon oven baked with fresh roasted corn, grilled tomato, cilantro and garlic butter

1 corn husk
3 Tbsp. white wine
1 (8 oz.) salmon filet - score top (cut crisscross ½ way in depth)
2 slices fresh grilled tomato (marinate in olive oil, garlic, cilantro, then grill on bbq. just a bit for flavor)
¼ c. fresh corn off the cob
1 tsp. fresh cilantro, chopped
¼ c. garlic butter, melted
salt & pepper

Corn Husk Salmon (Cont.)

Soak corn husk in water for 5 minutes. Put white wine in bottom of baking dish. Place corn husk in wine in baking dish. Place salmon on corn husk. Place grilled tomato slices on top of salmon. Sprinkle corn on top of tomatoes. Sprinkle cilantro on top of tomatoes. Pour melted garlic butter over top. Sprinkle pinch of salt & pepper over top. Bake at 350° for 12-15 minutes.

Serves 1

Chicken Chili Relleno with Roasted Tomato Salsa

Use Anaheim chilies for this dish. To roast chilies, rub them with a light amount of olive oil. Place on a sheet pan and bake at 400° for about 12 minutes or cook over an open flame to char outside skin of chili. When done, place in a container and cover tightly with plastic wrap. When cool, peel chilies and cut a small slit in the side and remove seeds.

Filling for 4 Anaheim chilies:
1 (8 oz.) boneless, skinless chicken breast, grilled and diced
½ c. pepper Jack cheese, diced
½ c. roasted red bell peppers, diced
½ c. roasted fresh corn off the cob
salt & pepper

Chicken Chili Relleno with Roasted Tomato Salsa (Cont.)

Combine stuffing and fill each chili.

Breading:
flour
2 eggs and 1 c. milk (mixed)
1 c. panko bread crumbs*

Roll chilies in flour, then egg and milk mixture, then bread crumb mix. Sauté chilies in a hot pan with a little butter.

Serves 2

Salsa

4 Roma tomatoes
½ yellow onion
1 jalapeno
3 garlic cloves
1 tsp. cilantro (chopped)
salt and pepper
cumin
sour cream

Boil tomatoes, onions, jalapeno and garlic cloves in a little water until tender. Puree ingredients in food processor then add cilantro, salt, pepper and cumin to taste. To serve, place salsa on plate, then chili and garnish with sour cream.

Yields approx. 1 ½ cups

*Panco bread crumbs can be found at an oriental market.

Black Bean Chili

⅓ c. olive oil
1 red bell pepper, diced
1 yellow bell pepper, diced
1 green bell pepper, diced
1⅓ c. diced onion
1 jalapeno, diced
1⅓ Tbsp. garlic, chopped
2 Tbsp. chili powder
2 Tbsp. cumin
⅔ tsp. cayenne pepper
⅔ Tbsp. black pepper
1 (15 oz. can) cooked black beans
1 (15 oz. can) diced tomato
1 (8 oz. can) tomato sauce

In hot olive oil, sauté peppers, onions, jalapenos and garlic until translucent, about 10 minutes. Add spices and stir. Drain black beans and add with remaining ingredients. Simmer for ½ hour.

Yields 8 cups

Sunnyside's Seared Ahi

4 (7 oz.) Ahi steaks (preferably Hawaiian yellow fin tuna)
kosher salt & pepper
2 c. Garlic Roasted Smashed Potatoes (recipe follows)
1½ c. roasted vegetables (red, green & yellow bell peppers, zucchini, mushrooms, red onions) all cut into 1" pieces
1 c. roasted Red Bell Pepper Cream Sauce (recipe follows)

Start your barbecue and bring to a medium to hot heat. You may also use a sauté pan on the range. Lightly season one side of your Ahi with kosher salt and fresh ground pepper. Place Ahi on the grill and cook for about 3-4 minutes per side for medium rare or cook longer for desired doneness. Place ½ cup garlic smashed potatoes in the center of your 4 plates. Surround the potatoes with the roasted vegetables. Place Ahi on top of potatoes and finish with ¼ cup of red bell pepper cream sauce. Garnish with fresh chopped parsley and lemon wedge.

Garlic Roasted Smashed Potatoes

1 lb. potatoes, peeled and cut into 3" pieces
2 Tbsp. butter
4 Tbsp. sour cream
8 garlic cloves, lightly oiled and baked in 350° oven until golden brown
cream
salt and pepper to taste

Boil potatoes in water with a pinch of salt until done. Strain off water and add butter, sour cream and chopped roasted garlic cloves. Mix with hand masher or electric blender and thin with cream and salt and pepper to taste.

Roasted Red Bell Pepper Cream

2 small red bell peppers, seeded and cut into 1" pieces
¼ c. diced red onion
1 sprig fresh thyme
1 Tbsp. olive oil
6 Tbsp. heavy cream
2 Tbsp. butter
juice from ½ of a lemon

Sauté red bell peppers, red onion and thyme in olive oil until tender. Add cream and bring to a boil. Place in blender and puree. Add butter and lemon juice.

Serves 4

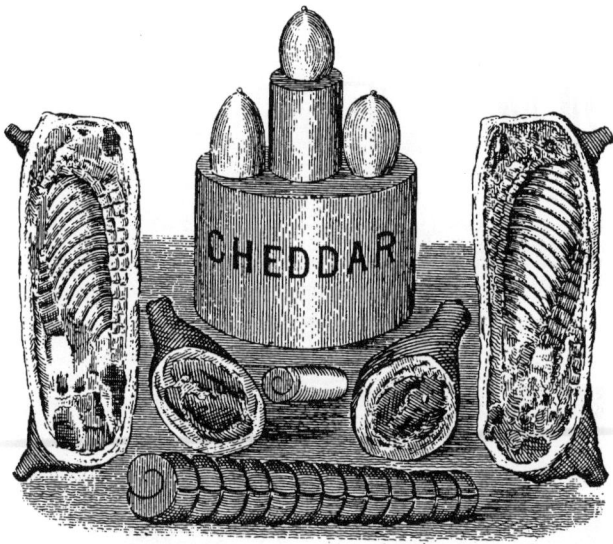

TRUCKEE AREA

Breakfast
NOW BEING SERVED

Squeeze In

Commercial Row
P.O. Box 1001
Truckee, California 96160
(530) 587-9814
Reservations: Not accepted

As the name tells you, Squeeze In is small. The building is from the 1800's. The eclectic collection of bric-a-brac on one wall are gifts from patrons, who are also encouraged to add to the "graffiti wall". Kids are welcomed with crayons and gift baskets. Singles are invited to sit together at a community table on weekdays. Squeeze In provides a variety of newspapers for browsing, and checkers for the two checker-board-topped tables.

There are 57 different omelets, all whimsically named to honor local folk. The ingredients are sautéed in a butter-wine sauce, and they are topped with either cheese, mushroom or tomato sauce. You can split an omelet, or add meat, cheese, veggies, or avocado to the recipe if you choose. Other breakfast items are available, too. There are triple-decker sandwiches; too - 23 listed - also bearing unusual monikers. Soups, salads and specials (with a Mexican accent), plus beverages including beer, wine and champagne round out the menu.

Specialties:
Creative Omelets named for local "characters"

―――――――――――――

Hours:
7:00 AM - 2:00 PM, daily

―――――――――――――

Credit Cards Accepted:
None

Grilled Lola

3 slices sour dough bread
mayonnaise
Jack cheese
1 slice avocado
fresh baby spinach
4-5 slices cooked bacon

Grill 3 slices sour dough bread with mayonnaise and Jack cheese on top. Place a slice of avocado on one piece and a handful of fresh baby spinach on another. Add 4-5 slices cooked bacon. Assemble and serve with pasta salad.

Serves 1

Casa Dia

1 corn tortilla
refried beans
Jack cheese
eggs (over easy or cooked to order)
salsa
avocado
sliced olives
sprouts
sour cream

Grill tortilla with refried beans and Jack cheese on top. Place eggs on top of beans and cheese. Cover with salsa, avocado and sliced olives. Serve with sprouts and sour cream on the side with a choice of corn or flour tortilla for dipping.

Serves 1

Eric Sandwich

1 large flour tortilla
Jack cheese
avocado
scrambled eggs
cooked bacon
salsa
sour cream
alfalfa sprouts

Grill flour tortilla with jack cheese and avocado on top. Place scrambled eggs on top. Add bacon and salsa and wrap. Serve with sour cream and alfalfa sprouts on the side.

Serves 1

Black Bean Soup

½ lb. black turtle beans
4 c. water
¾ c. onions, chopped
½ c. green pepper, chopped
½ c. carrots, chopped
½ c. celery, chopped
1 smoked pork hock
4 c. chicken stock
1 tsp. salt
1 tsp. dried thyme
1 tsp. dry mustard
2 cloves garlic, minced
½ tsp. pepper

In a large stockpot soak beans in water 24 hours. To the beans and water, add onions, green pepper, carrots, celery and pork hock. Heat to a boil. Skim, reduce heat to simmer and add chicken stock, salt, thyme, mustard, garlic and pepper. Cover and cook until the beans are tender, about 4 hours.

Serves 8

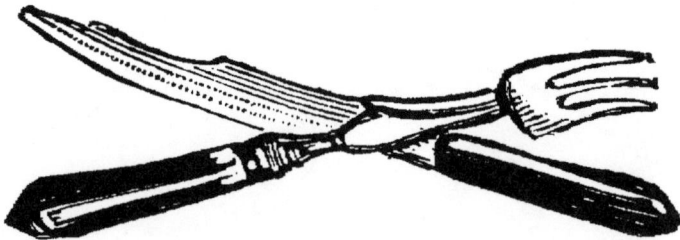

Graham's

1650 Squaw Valley Road (Olympic Valley)
P.O. Box 7563
Tahoe City, California 96145
(530) 581-2199
e-mail: graham@dinewine.com
Reservations: Suggested

Situated at the foot of Squaw Peak in breathtakingly beautiful Squaw Valley, Graham's is an oasis of fine dining in a spacious setting with vaulted ceilings, a stone fireplace, and tables dressed with crisp white linens. The seasonal menu presents an engaging assortment of choices. Among them you may find lamb, duck, beef, fish, shellfish, chicken, and pork. There are also imaginative vegetarian items such as Eggplant Marrakesh with tomatoes, brown rice, garbanzo beans, and feta cheese.

Starters may include strudel filled with wild mushrooms and Camembert with sun-dried tomato tapenade, or perhaps corn risotto topped with grilled prawns. Pastas, salads, and homemade soups are on the menu, and the wine list includes 450 choices.

Specialties:
Southern European Country Cuisine

Hours:
6:00 PM - 10:00 PM, Wed. - Sun.

Credit Cards Accepted:
American Express, MasterCard, Visa

Grilled Salmon with Orange Saffron Glaze

Glaze:
4 c. orange juice
¾ c. honey
pinch of saffron (be generous)

4 (8 oz.) salmon filets
salt & pepper to taste

Combine glaze ingredients in small saucepan and reduce by two-thirds. Grill salmon filet, seasoned with salt and pepper, for approximately 3 minutes per side. Brush each side with glaze just before finished cooking.

Serves 4

Summer Vegetable Medley

1 red bell pepper, small diced
1 red onion, small diced
1 corn cob (fresh, off cob, uncooked)
4 Tbsp. butter
¼ lb. snap peas
salt & pepper to taste
2 Tbsp. Parsley, chopped
½ tsp. marjoram
½ tsp. chives (or your favorite herb)
2 Tbsp. white wine

Sauté peppers, onions and corn in butter approximately 2 minutes over medium heat. Add snap peas and cook two minutes. Season with salt and pepper. Add fresh herbs. Splash with white wine (be sure to cook out alcohol).

Serves 2

Blueberry Crisp

Brisee:
1⅛ c. all purpose flour
½ c. cold butter
1 pinch of salt
½ tsp. sugar
⅛ c. cold water

Using paddle attachment of an electric mixer, mix flour, butter, salt and sugar to a course meal consistency. Add water. Mix until dough comes together. Set aside.

Filling:
1 ½ quarts blueberries
2 Tbsp. cornstarch
½ c. sugar
zest of 1 lemon
pinch of salt

Mix all filling ingredients together. Set aside.

Topping:
2 c. flour
1 c. brown sugar
1 c. nuts or oatmeal
½ tsp. cinnamon or ginger
pinch of salt
½ lb. soft butter

Blueberry Crisp (Cont.)

Mix all dry ingredients together. Cut in butter until crumbly.

Assemble:
Line an 11x 15½" baking dish with brisee. Sprinkle berry mixture over brisee. Top with topping. Bake at 400° for 30 minutes. Lower heat to 350° and bake until golden brown and set, about 20-30 minutes longer.

Serves 12

MARTIS VALLEY Grille

Martis Valley Grille

P.O. Box 129 (Northstar)
Truckee, California 96160
(530) 562-2460
E-mail: cbanovich.ns@boothcreek.com
Reservations: Accepted

Recently voted "Best of Show" from the "Food and Wine Jubilee", Martis Valley Grille is that kind of place that makes you feel welcome, because there really is "something for everyone". Breakfast includes homemade omelets, Grand Marnier French toast, and huevos rancheros. An extensive lunch menu features fresh salads, and grilled specialties. The dinner menu accommodates all from the heartiest appetite with a one-pound Porterhouse steak to a special selection for kids under 12. In between you'll find hickory smoked baby back ribs, marinated and grilled giant tiger prawns, veal, steak, chicken, salmon, and pasta of the day with an all-you-can-eat-option.

Family style dinners include soup and salad, entrée with all the trimmings, AND desert! If your group is really big, no problem, Martis Valley Grille can handle large parties. Don't forget to check out the Cafe for a fine selection of sandwiches, potpies, salads and soups. There are appetizers in the bar. In winter, enjoy sleigh rides.

Specialties:
Family style dining with upscale steak & seafood menu

Hours:
5:00 PM - 9:30 PM, (dinner only during winter)
7:30 AM - 2:30 PM, Summer

Credit Cards Accepted:
American Express, MasterCard, Visa

299

Grilled Jumbo Shrimp Drizzled with Lemon Chipotle Butter

20 very large shrimp, deveined, shell on
½ c. Cajun seasoning
1 c. olive oil
1 lemon, sliced
2 Tbsp. cilantro, chopped
½ lb. butter, melted
3 Tbsp. canned chipotle chile paste
1 Tbsp. garlic, chopped
2 lemons, zested and juiced
salt and pepper to taste

Marinate shrimp in the Cajun seasoning, olive oil, lemon and cilantro for 3-4 hours. Heat grill or broiler to medium-high heat. Grill the shrimp with the shells on. The shells keep the meat moist and add a whole new realm of flavor to the shrimp. This should take about 8-10 minutes. Baste with marinade repeatedly while cooking. Mix the melted butter, chipotle chile, garlic, lemon juice and zest and season with salt and pepper as needed. Use this mixture to drizzle atop the shrimp. Roasted garlic mashed potatoes or a nice nutty wild rice blend would accompany this dish well.

Serves 4

Broiled Mahi Mahi with Grilled Pineapple Salsa and Lemon

4 (8 oz. portions) mahi mahi, skinned & boned
salt and pepper to taste
½ pineapple, grilled and diced
1 red bell pepper, diced ¼ inch
½ red onion, diced ¼ inch
½ bunch cilantro, chopped
1 serrano pepper, seeded & chopped
salt & pepper
1 tsp. cumin
1 c. rice wine vinegar
¼ c. olive oil
1 c. butter
¼ c. lemon juice
1 tsp. garlic, minced

After skinning and boning the mahi mahi, heat your grill to medium-high and season the fish with salt and pepper. Peel and slice the pineapple in ¼ inch thickness. Season lightly and grill until tender, should not be falling apart or mushy. Let cool, dice and mix with the remainder of the veggies and the seasonings, vinegar and olive oil. Let marinate for 3-5 hours. Melt butter and mix with lemon juice and garlic. Once the fish is grilled, top with the salsa and drizzle with the lemon butter.

Serves 4

TIMBERCREEK
restaurant

Timbercreek @ Northstar

P.O. Box 129
Truckee, California 96160
(530) 562-2284
e-mail: cbanovichns@boothcreek.com
Reservations: Suggested

Timbercreek was voted one of Tahoe's best restaurants, recently receiving the 2nd best of show in the "Food and Wine Jubilee"! Timbercreek has indoor and outdoor dining, a full bar and lounge, and two menus - one for cafe casual dining and appetizers, the other for the cuisine for which Timbercreek is known. Dishes may include California Cabernet filet smothered in caramelized shallots, honey-barbecued salmon on a bed of grilled fennel, or rack of Sonoma lamb in a garlic demi sauce. Pastas and vegetarian dishes are offered, too. The menu even has suggestions for wine and food pairings.

Their wine list is a well-chosen selection of moderately priced wines. Among the luncheon dishes are burgers and sandwiches as well as Mediterranean cioppino, house-cured gravlax, pasta of the day, and old-fashioned pot pies. Breakfast runs the gamut from Belgian waffles to huevos rancheros, variations on eggs Benedict, and "hearty mountain breakfasts". A place for all reasons, Timbercreek can accommodate large groups, and has a special children's menu, too.

Specialties:
American Mediterranean with a hint of Pacific Rim

Hours:
7:00 AM - 9:00 PM, Winter, daily
5:00 PM - 9:00 PM Summer, daily

Credit Cards Accepted:
American Express, MasterCard, Visa

Black and Blue Caesar Salad

1½ heads romaine lettuce
4 (4 oz.) Filet mignon tournedos, seasoned and grilled
⅔ c. Caesar salad dressing
20 beefsteak tomato wedges
24 pieces artichoke hearts
¾ c. crumbled blue cheese
¾ c. crumbled bacon
¾ c. croutons
¾ c. carrots, julienne
6 Tbsp. grated Parmesan
28 pitted kalmata olives

Clean and chop the romaine lettuce. Dry thoroughly. Grill the filets to desired doneness and set aside. Toss the romaine with the dressing liberally and coat well. Place in a serving plate or bowl and top with the remaining salad ingredients. To finish, slice the filet thinly and fan on top.

Serves 4

Mediterranean Seafood Paella with Herb Aioli

olive oil for sautéing
8 oz. chorizo sausage, cooked and diced
2 (8 oz.) chicken breasts, grilled and diced
24 Manilla clams
8 jumbo shrimp with heads on
1 lb. Chilean sea bass
8 Dungeness crab legs
5 c. Broth Base (recipe follows)
salt & pepper
6 c. Saffron couscous (recipe follows)
1 c. Herb Aioli (recipe follows)

Place olive oil in a hot pan . Sauté all of the meat and seafood until the sea bass is golden. Ladle in the Broth Base and simmer, covered, until clams are opened. Season with salt and pepper to taste. Place warm saffron couscous mixture in center of your large flat soup bowl. Spoon cooked seafood and meat over the couscous and ladle broth over the top of that. Place Herb Aioli in a squirt bottle and squeeze a few streams atop the fish.

Broth Base

1 carrot, diced
1 small onion, diced
3 Roma tomatoes, diced
¼ c. olive oil
½ c. white wine
5 c. fish broth
¼ tsp. saffron
1 tsp. garlic
1 Tbsp. chopped basil
1 bay leaf
salt & pepper to taste

Sauté vegetables lightly in olive oil for 5 minutes. Add white wine, fish broth, saffron and remainder of seasonings. Bring to a simmer for 30 minutes.

Saffron CousCous

6 c. warm water
1 Tbsp. butter
salt & pepper to taste
6-8 fibers saffron
3 c. dry couscous

Bring water, butter and seasonings to a boil and remove from heat. Add saffron and let steep for 20 minutes, covered. Reheat before adding the couscous. The couscous does not need to be cooked, but just allowed to sit and absorb the moisture from the hot infusion. It will usually double in volume. Fluff before serving and serve warm.

Herbed Aioli

5 egg yolks
½ c. white wine vinegar
1 Tbsp. garlic
1¼ Tbsp. olive oil
1 Tbsp. cilantro, chopped
1 Tbsp. basil, chopped
salt & pepper
½ tsp. Tabasco sauce
½ tsp. sugar

In a food processor, combine the yolks, vinegar and garlic and process at high speed. Add the oil into the mix at a slow drizzle to ensure a proper emulsification. If the mixture starts to get too thick, add a little warm water in between oil intervals. When all oil is blended, turn off and move mixture to a mixing bowl and add remaining ingredients. Refrigerate and reserve for up to 5-6 days.

Serves 4

Peppered Ahi Sashimi with Blackberry Hoisin Sauce

12 oz. #1 grade ahi tuna
½ c. black peppercorns, toasted, medium ground
sesame oil & olive oil
1½ c. hoisin sauce
1 c. blackberries
½ c. chambord liqueur
2 c. red cabbage, very thinly sliced
1 c. bean sprouts
2 Tbsp. green onions, sliced
½ c. carrots, julienne
rice wine vinegar
2 Tbsp. wasabi, mixed with water to form a paste

Peppered Ahi Sashimi with Blackberry Hoisin Sauce (Cont.)

Clean tuna and cut into loins 3 inches in diameter. Coat with peppercorns and pack firmly. In a sauté pan, heat a mix of sesame oil and olive oil to medium-high heat and sear ahi until golden brown on all sides. Be careful not to burn! Do not over cook. It will only take a couple of minutes on each side at the most. Remove from the pan and cool. Wrap in plastic and freeze. This ensures that all parasites are killed and the tuna keeps a nice round shape. Mix the hoisin, blackberries and Chambord and simmer lightly for 20 minutes. Let cool. Mix the vegetables together and sprinkle with rice wine vinegar and sesame oil. Place some of the mix in the center of the plate. Remove the ahi from the freezer and let defrost 30 minutes before slicing, then slice 6-7 thin slices on the bias and fan them on the plate around the slaw mixture. Drizzle the plate with the sauce and put three small balls of wasabi around the plate. Enjoy!

Serves 4

Double Pork Chop with Sun-dried Apricot and Chile Chutney

1 ½ c. dried apricots
2 Anaheim chiles, roasted, peeled, seeded, and diced
¼ c. red onion, diced
2 Tbsp. Cilantro, chopped
2 c. orange juice
1 Tbsp. chili powder
½ Tbsp. cayenne
1 Tbsp. cumin
1 Tbsp. garlic
4 (10 oz.) bone in pork chops
salt & pepper
4 c. roasted garlic mashed potatoes

Combine all ingredients except pork chops and potatoes in a pot for the chutney and bring to a medium simmer for about 45 minutes. Season accordingly and reserve. Season pork chops with salt and pepper and grill on a BBQ until desired doneness, about 10-15 minutes for medium-well. When pork chops are done, place one cup of roasted garlic mashed potatoes in the center of the plate, pork chop atop and spoon some of the chutney on top of that.

Serves 4

STEAKS & CHOPS

Pan Roasted Muscovy Duck Atop Thai Red Curry Sauce

olive oil
4 (8 oz.) Muscovy duck breast, trimmed
salt and pepper
4 c. Saffron CousCous, warmed (see recipe page 306)
12 pieces baby bok choy, halved and blanched
2½ c. Thai Red Curry Sauce (recipe follows)

Preheat oven to 325°. Heat a large sauté pan to medium-high heat. Add a dash of olive oil and let heat until almost smoking. Season duck breasts with salt and pepper and sear on both sides, searing skin side until almost crisp. Retain in pan, skin side up, and roast for 5-7 minutes or until desired doneness. Remove duck breasts from pan when done and reserve the pan. The juices will be used for the sauce. Let breasts sit for 5-6 minutes before slicing to retain all of the juices. Slice into 6 pieces. Place Saffron CousCous in center of the plate and surround that with the blanched bok choy. Fan the duck breasts atop the couscous and drizzle with Thai Red Curry Sauce.

Thai Red Curry Sauce

1 ½ Tbsp. red curry paste
2 ½ c. beef demi-glaze (available in specialty markets)
1 Tbsp. soy sauce
1 Tbsp. rice wine vinegar
¼ c. honey
1 tsp. ginger
½ tsp. Sambal chile paste (available in grocery stores)
1 tsp. fresh garlic
1 Tbsp. cilantro
1 Tbsp. scallions

Combine all ingredients except for cilantro and scallions in the sauce pan that was used for the duck. Bring to a boil and reduce to simmer for 10 minutes. Add cilantro and scallions right before serving.

Serves 4

SOUTH
LAKE TAHOE

PRIMAVERA

Primavera

Caesar's Tahoe
55 Highway 50
Lake Tahoe, Nevada 89449
(775) 588-3515
Reservations: Suggested

Primavera offers Northern Italian cuisine, which includes a plenitude of pastas, veal, seafood and more. Appetizers such as the hearty antipasti plate are great for a pair to share. Among the things that make Primavera special are house-made sausage, hand cut noodles, and daily pasta, soup and fish specials. Specialties include traditional lasagna and lobster cannelloni.

The manager is a wine expert whose well-tended wine list includes both domestic and Italian wines with a number of "wine flights" so that you can create your own wine tasting experience. Complete your meal with a cappuccino and homemade dessert.

Specialties:
Fresh seafood, veal and pasta dishes with an Italian flair

Hours:
6:00 PM, nightly

Credit Cards Accepted:
All major

Fennel Sausage and Wild Mushroom Lasagna

Meat Sauce:
1 lb. fennel sausage, crumbled
1 ¼ lb. mushrooms, assorted wild, sliced
¾ oz. dried porcini mushrooms
3 oz. prosciutto, chopped
½ bunch parsley, chopped
½ onion, minced
3 Tbsp. garlic, slivered
1 ½ tsp. rosemary, chopped
6 fresh sage leaves
1 (28 ½ oz. can) whole pear tomatoes in juice
salt & pepper to taste

Béchamel Sauce:
1 stick butter
1 ½ qts. milk
1 c. flour
Spinach lasagna noodles, cooked

Toppings:
1 ½ lb. mozzarella, sliced
2 c. fresh grated Parmesan cheese

In a 5 qt. Dutch oven, over medium heat, sauté sausage, mushrooms, prosciutto, parsley, onion and garlic until well browned. Add rosemary, sage, tomatoes and salt and pepper to taste. Simmer until heated through, stirring occasionally. For Béchamel Sauce: Melt butter, stir in flour. Add milk slowly and simmer to make a medium white sauce. In 9 x 13" casserole dish layer noodles, meat sauce, then top with Béchamel Sauce, mozzarella and Parmesan cheese. Bake uncovered at 350° for 45 minutes or until cheese is golden.

Serves 6

Sautéed Prawns with Garlic, Sage and Lemon

¼ c. olive oil
20 large prawns (peeled and de-veined) (12 to a pound size)
kosher salt & black pepper to taste
1 Tbsp. garlic, slivered
15 leaves fresh sage, chopped
¾ c. dry vermouth
juice of ½ lemon
¾ c. chicken stock
1 c. butter, softened
8 oz. cooked linguini

Pour olive oil into a hot sauté pan. Season shrimp with salt and pepper. Add seasoned shrimp to hot oil, sauté briefly. Add garlic and sage. Deglaze pan with vermouth, juice from half a lemon and chicken stock. Reduce liquid by half. Add softened butter, swirl pan to emulsify the butter. Adjust seasoning and serve over linguini pasta.

Serves 4

ITALIAN

Artichoke Bruschetta

10 artichokes
2 tsp. fresh lemon juice
1 anchovy filet, finely chopped
3 cloves garlic
2 Tbsp. Nicoise olives, pitted and finely chopped
2 Tbsp. extra virgin olive oil
1 Tbsp. Italian parsley, chopped
8 slices peasant bread
kosher salt & black pepper to taste

Peel off outer leaves of artichokes and trim off the tops of remaining leaves, remove stem. Cook artichokes in boiling salted water with lemon juice until just done (approximately 45 minutes or pass a knife through center of artichoke to determine doneness). Partially cool and then chop coarsely. Add anchovy, two cloves of garlic, minced, olives, 1 tablespoon of olive oil and parsley to artichokes. Adjust seasoning. Toast the peasant bread slices and then rub with remaining garlic clove and brush with 1 tablespoon olive oil. Serve bruschetta topped with artichoke mixture.

Serves 4

Roasted Striped Bass with Fennel and Artichokes

4 (7 oz.) striped bass fillets
kosher salt & black pepper to taste
¼ c. extra virgin olive oil
8 slices lemon
1 Tbsp. garlic, slivered
1 c. fennel, finely julienned
12 baby artichokes
1 Tbsp. Italian flatleaf parsley, chopped
8 oz. cooked, buttered pasta (spaghetti or spaghettinni)

Rinse fish fillets, dry with paper towel. Season with salt & pepper. Rub fish with oil and 2 of the lemon slices. Place in an oiled baking dish with garlic, fennel and artichokes. Top fish with the remaining lemon slices, sprinkle with salt, pepper and parsley. Bake in 450° oven for approximately 20 minutes. Serve over buttered pasta.

Serves 4

Two Colored Linguini with Four Cheeses

2 Tbsp. olive oil
1 tsp. garlic, slivered
½ c. chicken stock
½ c. heavy cream
2 Tbsp. goat cheese
2 Tbsp. Gorgonzola cheese
2 Tbsp. provolone cheese, grated
2 Tbsp. Parmesan cheese
2 oz. egg linguini, cooked
2 oz. spinach linguini, cooked
kosher salt & black pepper to taste
1 Tbsp. toasted pinenuts

Two Colored Linguini with Four Cheeses (Cont.)

In a hot sauté pan add olive oil and garlic. Simmer briefly. Add stock and cream, reduce. When reduced by approximately half, add cheeses and cooked pasta and toss. Check seasonings and adjust. Place on serving plate. Top with pinenuts, freshly grated Parmesan cheese and freshly ground black pepper.

Serves 2

Strawberries in Amaretto Sabayon

8 egg yolks
½ cup sugar
pinch salt
¾ c. Amaretto
¼ c. orange juice
1 c. heavy cream
2 pts. fresh strawberries
½ c. granulated sugar

Whip yolks, sugar and salt in a bowl with a hand whip. Mix in Amaretto and orange juice. Place in double boiler over simmering water and whip continuously until thick and tripled in volume (about 20 minutes). Put bowl in an ice bath and whisk until cold. Pour heavy cream into separate bowl and use an electric mixer to whip to soft peak. Fold whipped cream into Sabayon with a rubber spatula ⅓ at a time. Refrigerate until ready to use. To serve: Clean and quarter fresh strawberries. Toss berries in granulated sugar, enough to coat the berries. Let sit 5-10 minutes, re-toss berries. Place berries on plate or in a bowl and spoon Sabayon over. Enjoy!

The Cork & More

Wines • Gifts • Gourmet Groceries

The Cork & More

1032 Al Tahoe Boulevard
South Lake Tahoe, California 96150
(530) 544-5253

Everybody goes to the Cork & More because there is always something new and delicious to discover. Now in its 24th year, the Cork & More has expanded to include a full service deli, and catering for anything from an intimate dinner for two to a bash for 800. Cork & More's delightful assortment of fine foods allows you to pick up a delectable dinner or pack up everything you need for a picnic. There are even picnic tables so you can eat outside. Choose from freshly made salads and entrees to appetizers and gourmet cheeses. There is a great collection of wines both California and imported, and beers. Contemporary gift items include kitchen accessories and tabletop decor. The selection is unique with items you just won't find anyplace else. It's just plain fun!

Specialties:
Full service deli with unique gift items, wine and catering

Hours:
10:00 AM - 7:00 PM, Daily

Credit Cards Accepted:
American Express, MasterCard, Visa, Discover

House Torte Stuffed Mushrooms

¼ c. pesto
¼ c. sun dried tomatoes
¼ c. herb cream cheese
25 mushroom caps
Provolone cheese, thinly sliced

In a food processor, cream together pesto, sun dried tomatoes and herbed cream cheese. Fill mushroom caps with a generous amount of creamed mixture. Top with provolone cheese. When ready to serve, place under broiler for 2-3 minutes until cheese is bubbly and browned.

Serves 10-12

Basil Gorgonzola Torte

1 c. pine nuts
1 c. pesto
½ c. capers
1½ lb. cream cheese
1 lb. unsalted butter
⅓ lb. Gorgonzola cheese

Line a loaf pan with plastic wrap. Toast pine nuts and grind in food processor. Press pine nuts firmly in the bottom of the loaf pan. Drain capers and pesto (overnight would be great). Cream the cream cheese and butter together in a food processor. Set aside ⅔ of the cream cheese/butter mixture. Cream remaining ⅓ of cream cheese/butter mixture with Gorgonzola cheese. Layer in loaf pan on top of pine nuts: ½ of the cream cheese/butter mixture, ½ of the pesto, ½ of the Gorgonzola mixture, capers, remaining Gorgonzola mixture, remaining pesto and remaining cream cheese/butter mixture. Refrigerate overnight. Serve with mild crackers or French baguette slices.

Serves 6-8

German Potato Salad

3 lbs. red potatoes
¼ c. chicken broth
½ c. olive oil
2 Tbsp. red wine vinegar
1 Tbsp. Dijon mustard
1 clove garlic, chopped
½ tsp. black pepper
½ tsp. Maggi seasoning *
½ tsp. oregano
¼ small red onion, diced
4 slices crisp bacon, crumbled

Boil potatoes until soft in center and drain. Slice potatoes while still warm. Heat chicken broth and pour over potatoes. Make dressing by mixing oil, vinegar, mustard, garlic, black pepper, Maggi and oregano. Pour over potatoes and add all remaining ingredients to salad and toss.

* Available in supermarkets

Serves approximately 12

324

The
Christiania Inn

The Christiania Inn

3819 Saddle Road
P.O. Box 18298
South Lake Tahoe, California 96151
(530) 544-7337
Website: www.christianiainn.com
Reservations: Suggested

The Christiania is nestled just below the ski slopes of Heavenly. Accommodations include unique rooms and suites, all with continental breakfast brought to your door each morning. The charming Alpine-style dining room, with its cozy stone fireplace, has glass doors to show off the extensive wine collection that complements a dazzling gourmet menu, augmented by daily fish and pasta specials, and prepared by a staff of superb chefs. Among the dessert selections are spectacular Bananas Flambé, Cherries Jubilee, and Flaming Baked Alaska.

Holidays are special at The Christiania Inn, from the Winter wonderland toy land for Christmas, to a sophisticated New Years Eve Dinner. Live music is featured on Weekends during the Winter season and every night between Christmas and New Years day. "Romantic Packages" include room and dinner, and catering is available for any special event, wedding, or party.

Specialties:
American Continental cuisine. Ski to their doorstep!

Hours:
5:30 PM - 10:00 PM, Daily, Winter & Summer
Spring & Fall: Closed Mondays

Credit Cards Accepted:
MasterCard, Visa

Tomato Bruschetta

1 sourdough baguette
⅓ c. extra virgin olive oil
1 Tbsp. Garlic, minced
1 c. tomatoes, diced
½ c. sun dried tomatoes, diced
¼ c. fresh basil, julienned
3 Tbsp. capers
3 Tbsp. vinegar
goat cheese, crumbled
baby greens
kalamata olives

Cut sourdough baguette on the bias, about ½" thick (16 slices). Mix together tomatoes, sun dried tomatoes, basil, capers and vinegar. Brush baguette slices with olive oil and garlic. Lightly grill, then top with a spoonful of the tomato mixture and the crumbled goat cheese. Bake 10 to 15 minutes at 350°. Serve with a small handful of baby greens and kalamata olives.

Makes 16 slices

Christiania Caesar Salad

3 anchovies
3 Tbsp. Dijon mustard (do not substitute)
2 Tbsp. fresh garlic, chopped (do not use bottled garlic)
1 egg yolk
½ c. olive oil
¼ c. red wine vinegar
dash of Tabasco
dash of Worcestershire
medium size head of romaine
juice of ½ lemon
¼ c. Parmesan cheese
½ c. seasoned croutons

In a wooden bowl, using two forks, mash the anchovies until a paste has formed. Add mustard, garlic, egg yolk, olive oil, vinegar, Tabasco and Worcestershire, whisking constantly until smooth. Slice romaine. Put in bowl with dressing. Squeeze lemon juice over and sprinkle with the Parmesan cheese. Add croutons and toss.

Serves 2-4

Grilled Salmon on a Bed of Black Beans with Green Chile Apricot Chutney

½ lb. black beans
¼ lb. bacon
4 cloves garlic, chopped
2 stalks celery, chopped
1 carrot, chopped
1 jalapeño pepper, chopped
1 bay leaf
1½ tsp. chili powder
1 tsp. cumin
salt & pepper to taste
4 c. chicken stock (more if needed)
3 lb. salmon fillet, grilled

Green Chile Apricot Chutney:
1 lb. chilies (Anaheim & Jalapeños)
½ lb. dried apricots
1 c. sugar
1 tsp. oregano
1 tsp. coriander
½ c. cider vinegar
½ tsp. salt

Soak beans overnight. Drain. Sauté next 9 ingredients. Add to the beans with the chicken stock. Stir well. Simmer until beans are tender. About 30–45 minutes. Add more stock if it dries out too quickly. Grill salmon.

Green Chile Apricot Chutney: Dice chilies and apricots and simmer with remaining ingredients until the consistency of a relish, approximately 20 minutes. Place beans on the bottom of the plate, put grilled salmon filet on top and finish with the apricot chutney.

Serves 6

Rosemary Cabernet New York Steaks

4 (10 oz.) New York steaks
1 c. extra virgin olive oil
1 c. Cabernet wine
3 rosemary sprigs, picked off the stem
12 garlic cloves, lightly smashed
fresh ground pepper to taste
kosher salt to taste
Roasted Garlic Green Peppercorn Butter (recipe follows)

Combine the olive oil, wine, rosemary, garlic and pepper. Marinate the steaks in the oil mixture for 4 hours, turning every hour. Season with kosher salt, then grill to desired temperature. Serve with Roasted Garlic Green Peppercorn Butter.

Roasted Garlic Green Peppercorn Butter

1 c. sweet butter
½ c. roasted garlic
2 Tbsp. green peppercorns
2 Tbsp. fresh chopped chives
kosher salt and pepper to taste

Mix the above ingredients together in a food processor or with a hand blender.

Serves 4

Salmon Gravlax

salmon
coarse sea salt
ground black pepper to taste
chopped dill
brandy
powdered English mustard
salt & pepper to taste
Dill Sauce (recipe follows)

Select good quality salmon, dust with coarse sea salt, cover and leave for 24 hrs. Remove any excess salt by gently brushing off. Season well with ground black pepper and chopped dill. Drench well with brandy and dust with powdered English mustard and salt and pepper. Cover with Dill Sauce Leave again for 24 hours, slice as thinly as possible and serve well chilled.

Dill Sauce

½ c. mayonnaise
½ c. heavy cream
2 Tbsp. chopped fresh dill
1 Tbsp. Dijon mustard
2 Tbsp. brandy
salt & pepper to taste

Mix all ingredients together and serve with Salmon Gravlox.

Serves 6-12 (Depending on size of salmon).

Spiced Tomato Soup

¼ c. onions, chopped
1 clove garlic, chopped
¼ c. celery, chopped
2 Tbsp. Carrots, chopped
olive oil
½ lb. very ripe tomatoes, roughly chopped
2 c. Strong chicken stock
2 tsp. mace
3 tsp. allspice
2 Tbsp. butter
salt & pepper to taste

Heat olive oil in a sauté pan. Over very low heat, cook the onions, garlic, celery and carrots. Add the tomatoes and cook for a few more minutes. Add the chicken stock and cook for 10 minutes. Add the spices and cook for another 10 minutes. Puree in a blender while adding the butter, salt and pepper.

Serves 4

Cranberry Orange Muffins

2 c. fresh cranberries, chopped
⅓ c. sugar
¼ c. orange juice
1 Tbsp. orange rind, grated
½ c. butter, softened
1 c. sugar
1 egg, beaten
2 c. unbleached flour
1 tsp. baking powder
½ tsp. baking soda
½ tsp. salt

Mix the cranberries with ⅓ cup sugar, orange juice and rind. Set aside. Cream the butter, adding 1 cup sugar and beaten egg. Add dry ingredients to creamed mixture. Gently mix in cranberries. Fill greased muffin cups three-fourths full. Bake at 375° for 20 minutes.

Yields 12 muffins

Pumpkin Brulé

2 c. heavy cream
1 c. sugar
9 egg yolks
1 c. pumpkin puree
1 tsp. cinnamon
1 Tbsp. nutmeg
2 tsp. vanilla
4 Tbsp. brandy

Heat cream and sugar to boiling. Let cool for 10 minutes. Add cream mixture to lightly beaten egg yolks. Add remaining ingredients and mix well. Pour mix into 6 ramekins. Place in a water bath (baking pan with water half way up the sides of the ramekins). Cover with foil and bake at 300°. Check after 30 minutes and continue baking until custard is smooth and set.

Good **FOOD**

Sonnie's & Lori's FAVORITE RECIPES

Sonnie Imes

Sonnie's Favorites

Salmon Spread

1 large can salmon
1 (8 oz. pkg.) cream cheese, softened
1 Tbsp. onion, grated
1 Tbsp. lemon juice
1 Tbsp. horseradish
½ c. walnuts
½ c. parsley, chopped

Clean all skin, bones and dark meat from salmon. Blend salmon with cream cheese and add onion, lemon juice and horseradish. Chill several hours or overnight. Form salmon into a log and roll into the nuts and parsley. Serve with crackers.

Serves 4-6

HOME COOKING
That will Please you

Tomato Bisque

¼ lb. bacon
4 large garlic cloves, minced
1 onion, finely chopped
6 celery stalks, finely chopped
1 bay leaf
1 tsp. thyme
1 (28 oz. can) tomatoes, diced (reserve juice)
1 (6 oz. can) tomato paste
2 Tbsp. butter
3 Tbsp. flour
1 qt. milk
½ onion, finely chopped
1 small bay leaf
2 whole cloves
salt & freshly ground pepper

Cook bacon in large skillet. Remove bacon (use as desired). Add garlic to fat and sauté until lightly browned. Add onion, celery, bay leaf and thyme and sauté until onion is transparent. Add tomatoes and tomato paste and bring to a boil, stirring occasionally. Reduce heat, cover and simmer 30 minutes. Heat butter in large saucepan. Stir in flour and bring to boil, stirring constantly. Remove from heat and slowly add milk, then next 3 ingredients. Place over medium heat and cook uncovered 45 minutes, stirring occasionally. Add tomato mixture. Add salt and pepper to taste. Cover and simmer, stirring occasionally, about 15 minutes.

Serves 8–10

Chinese Cole Slaw

1 large green cabbage, shredded
1 bunch green onions, chopped (including tops)
1–2 oz. pkg. slivered almonds
¼ c. sesame seeds
1½ Tbsp. butter
2 pkgs. chicken flavored Ramen noodles

Dressing:
¾ c. oil
6 Tbsp. rice vinegar
4 Tbsp. sugar
1 Tbsp. Accent
1 tsp. salt
1 tsp. pepper
sauce pkg. from Ramen noodles (use both packages)

Mix all ingredients and shake in jar. Refrigerate.

Place cabbage and green onions in a large bowl. Brown almonds and sesame seeds in butter. Crush uncooked noodles, saving the sauce package from Ramen to use in dressing. Set aside. Don't add crumbled noodles, onion, and sesame seed mixture until ready to serve.

Serves 15

Calico Salad

2 (10 oz. cans) shoe peg corn, drained
1 (15 oz. can) French cut green beans, drained
1 (15 oz. can) LeSeur peas, drained
1 c. celery, diced
1 c. carrots, grated
1 c. green pepper, chopped
½ c. pimento
½ c. onion, diced
1 (24 oz. bottle) Kraft-Free Italian salad dressing
⅔ – ¾ c. brown sugar

Combine vegetables. Mix together Kraft-Free Italian salad dressing and brown sugar to taste. Pour over vegetables and refrigerate overnight. Keeps 3 weeks in covered dish.   Serves a bunch

Pea Salad

1 head lettuce, finely chopped
1 (10 oz. pkg.) frozen peas, thawed
1 bunch green onions, sliced
2–3 stalks celery, diced
1 can water chestnuts, sliced

Dressing:
1 c. mayonnaise
1 Tbsp. sugar (heaping)
1 Tbsp. cider vinegar
¾ tsp. salt
¼ tsp. garlic powder

Cheddar cheese, shredded or Parmesan cheese, grated
bacon bits hard cooked eggs, chopped

Pea Salad (Cont.)

Layer lettuce, peas, green onions, celery and water chestnuts. Combine dressing ingredients and add to top over water chestnuts. Top with cheddar cheese or Parmesan cheese, bacon bits and hard cooked eggs.

Serves 6-8

Harvard Beets

5 medium beets
1 Tbsp. cornstarch
1 Tbsp. sugar
½ tsp. salt
dash of pepper
⅔ c. water
¼ c. vinegar

Prepare and cook beets. Cut into slices. Mix cornstarch, sugar, salt and pepper in 2-qt. saucepan. Gradually stir in water and vinegar. Cook, stirring constantly, until mixture thickens and boils. Boil and stir 1 minute. Stir in beets. Heat.

Serves 4

Cheesy Potatoes

⅓ c. onion, chopped
½ c. + 2 tsp. butter
1 can cream of chicken soup
1 pt. sour cream
1½ c. cheddar cheese, shredded
6–9 medium potatoes, boiled, cooled & grated
1 ½ c. corn flake cereal

Sauté onions in ½ cup of butter until onions are clear. Blend in soup, sour cream and cheese. Slowly fold in grated potatoes. Fold until potatoes are completely mixed with sauce. Pour into a 2-½ qt. buttered casserole dish. In a skillet, mix corn flakes with 2 teaspoons butter and top casserole with these ingredients. Bake in preheated oven at 350° for 20–25 minutes.

Serves 8

Sweet & Sour Sauce

¼ tsp. ginger, grated
2 (8 ¼ oz. cans) pineapple tidbits
2 (8 oz. cans) tomato sauce
⅓ c. vinegar
⅓ c. brown sugar, packed
3 Tbsp. soy sauce
1 clove garlic, minced

Combine all ingredients. Simmer covered for 1 hour and 30 minutes. Serve over cooked pork, chicken or meat.

Yields 1 qt.

Sonnie's Almond Roco

1 lb. butter
2 c. sugar
2 c. whole almonds
7 regular size Hershey bars
¼ c. ground almonds

Combine butter, sugar and whole almonds in a saucepan. Cook until temperature reaches 300° (about 40 minutes). Pour into a cookie sheet or oblong pan with a 1" lip around it. Place the 7 Hershey bars on top and add the ground almonds. (The Hershey bars will melt.) Cool and then crack into chunks.

Barb's Lemon Cake

Cake:
1 pkg. super moist lemon cake mix (use Betty Crocker)
1 large pkg. lemon Jell-O
¾ c. corn oil (you can use any kind of oil you want)
¾ c. water
4 eggs
Topping:
fresh lemon juice (use bottle juice if you can't get fresh)
2 c. powdered sugar

Mix all the cake ingredients in large bowl until Jell-O is well dissolved. Put in one large baking dish or two 8" x 8" aluminum baking pans. Bake at 350° for about 30–35 minutes or until cake is done. Take out immediately and take a large fork and poke holes throughout the top of the cake. For the topping, mix lemon juice and powdered sugar together until powdered sugar is completely dissolved. Liquid should be kind of thick. Put topping on the cake and spread all over the top. Serves a bunch

Ground Almond Torte

1 c. whole toasted almonds
¾ c. butter
¾ c. sugar
2 large eggs
½ tsp. vanilla
¼ tsp. almond extract
¾ c. all-purpose flour

In a blender, whirl ⅔ cup of the toasted almonds, half at a time, stirring every 15 seconds, until very finely ground. Watch carefully, if blended too many nuts will turn to butter. In large bowl of an electric mixer, beat butter and sugar until creamy. Add eggs, one at a time, beating well after each addition. Beat in vanilla and almond extract. On low speed, thoroughly mix in flour and ground almonds. Scrape into a buttered 8 or 9 inch tart or cake pan with a removable bottom. Smooth surface of batter with a spatula. Arrange remaining whole toasted almonds on top. Bake in a 350° oven until center springs back (25–30 minutes). Cool on a rack. Remove pan sides.

Serves 6-8

Lori Lacey

Crab Quiche

1 egg
4 tsp. all-purpose flour
½ c. mayonnaise
½ c. milk
1 c. Gruyere cheese, grated
1 c. flaked fresh crab meat
2 Tbsp. green onion, finely chopped
1 pre-baked 9" pie crust shell

Preheat oven to 350°. Beat egg with a wire whisk, blend in flour and beat in mayonnaise. Add milk and blend well. Fold in cheese, crab and onion. Fill pie shell and bake for 45 minutes or until toothpick inserted in center comes out clean.

Serves 6

Spinach Balls

2 (10 oz. pkgs.) frozen chopped spinach
2 c. crumbled seasoned stuffing mix
¾ c. onion, chopped
4 eggs, beaten
¾ c. (1 ½ sticks) melted butter
¾ c. grated Parmesan cheese
½ tsp. garlic powder
½ tsp. thyme
½ tsp. freshly grated pepper

Spinach Balls (Cont.)

Preheat oven to 350°. Thaw the spinach. Squeeze as dry as possible. Mix with the remaining ingredients, reserving ¼ cup of the cheese. Roll into balls the size of walnuts. Roll in the remaining Parmesan cheese. Bake for 30 minutes. Serve on a platter. Pass with toothpicks. If freezing for later use, do not roll in the remaining cheese. Place on a cookie sheet and freeze until firm. Place in plastic bags in the freezer. When ready to use, thaw for 10 minutes. Roll in the Parmesan cheese and bake.

Yields 4 dozen

Curried Stuffed Eggs

12 hard-cooked eggs, shelled
4 tsp. fresh lemon juice
1 Tbsp. curry powder
2 Tbsp. minced green onion
2 tsp. soy sauce
mayonnaise to moisten
chutney

Halve eggs lengthwise and remove yolks. Mash yolks well with fork. Add the lemon juice, curry powder, onion and soy sauce. Moisten with the mayonnaise. Fill the shells. Garnish each stuffed egg with a small piece of chutney.

Yields 24

Layered Mexican Delight

2 avocados
2 tsp. lemon juice
1 pkg. taco seasoning mix
1 c. sour cream
2 Tbsp. mayonnaise
4 oz. cheddar cheese, shredded
4 oz. Jack cheese, shredded
2 tomatoes, diced
2 (4 oz. cans) black olives, chopped
4 green onions, chopped
picante sauce
tortilla chips

Purée the avocados together with the lemon juice in a food processor or blender until smooth. Spread evenly onto a 10-12" flat plate. Blend the taco seasoning into the sour cream and mayonnaise. Spread over the avocado mixture. Layer the remaining ingredients over the sour cream mixture, making sure that each layer is even and ending with the green onions on top. Sprinkle with the picante sauce and place the tortilla chips around the edges of the plate.

Serves 8-10

Deluxe Potato Salad

6 lb. medium potatoes

Dressing:
3 c. mayonnaise
1 ½ c. onion, finely chopped
1 ½ c. cucumber, pared and cubed
2 hard cooked eggs, chopped
1 (4 oz. can) pimientos, drained and diced
⅔ c. dill pickle, chopped
⅓ c. pickle juice
3 Tbsp. cider vinegar
1 Tbsp. salt

cherry tomatoes
ripe olives

In boiling salted water to cover, cook unpared potatoes, covered, just until tender - about 30 minutes. Drain. Refrigerate until cold. In large bowl, combine mayonnaise, onion, cucumber, eggs, pimientos, pickles, pickle juice, vinegar and salt. Mix well. Peel potatoes and cut into 1" cubes. Add to dressing. Toss until potatoes are well coated. Refrigerate, covered, until well chilled (several hours or overnight). To serve: Garnish with cherry tomatoes and ripe olives.

Serves 12

Smoked Turkey Tetrazzini

Sauce:
¾ c. butter or margarine
¾ c. all-purpose flour
3 tsp. salt
⅛ tsp. nutmeg
dash cayenne
1 qt. milk
2 c. chicken stock
4 egg yolks
1 c. heavy cream
½ c. dry sherry

1 (1 lb. pkg.) thin spaghetti
6 c. smoked turkey or chicken
4 (4 oz. cans) whole button mushrooms
2 (8 oz. pkgs.) sharp cheddar cheese, grated (4 cups)

To make sauce: Melt butter in large saucepan. Remove from heat. Stir in flour, salt, nutmeg and cayenne until smooth. Gradually stir in milk and 2 cups stock. Bring to boiling, stirring constantly. Boil gently, stirring constantly, 2 minutes or until slightly thickened. In a small bowl, beat egg yolks with cream. Gently beat in a little of the hot mixture. Return to saucepan. Cook over low heat, stirring constantly, until sauce is hot. Do not let it boil. Remove from heat. Add sherry. Cook spaghetti as package label directs and drain. Return spaghetti to kettle. Add 2 cups sauce and toss until well blended. To remaining sauce, add cut up chicken and the mushrooms. Divide spaghetti into two 12 x 8 x 2" baking dishes, arranging it around edges. Spoon half of turkey mixture into center of each. Sprinkle 2 cups cheese over spaghetti in each dish. Cover with foil. Bake, covered, at 350° for 45 minutes or until piping hot.

Serves 12

Chicken Mozzarella

¾ c. butter
1 c. fresh mushrooms, sliced
salt & pepper
½ c. parsley, chopped
1 c. flour
red pepper
8 chicken breasts, skinned, deboned and pounded thin
4 Tbsp. Madeira wine
⅔ c. dry white wine
1 lb. sliced mozzarella cheese

Heat 4 tablespoons of the butter in a heavy skillet. When hot, add the mushrooms and cook 4 or 5 minutes, stirring occasionally, taking care not to allow them to brown. Season lightly with salt and pepper. Mix in parsley and set aside. In a paper bag, combine flour, salt and red pepper. Add the breasts one at a time and shake to coat with the mixture. Shake off any excess. Heat the remaining butter in a heavy skillet over moderate heat. When butter foams, add the breasts (only as many as the pan will accommodate without crowding). Sauté 3 minutes on one side, then turn and sauté 3 minutes on the second side. Arrange the breasts in a shallow baking pan that just holds them comfortably and can go to the table. Spoon some of the mushrooms and parsley mixture over each of the breasts. Add both wines to the same skillet that you browned the chicken in. Heat on high and allow to boil. Remove from stove and pour over breasts. Bake in 300° oven for about 20 minutes. During last 3 minutes, place 1 slice of cheese over each breast.

Serves 8

Chicken Cordon Bleu

3 whole chicken breasts, skinned and deboned
3 slices boiled ham
3 slices Swiss cheese
1 c. flour
1 tsp. salt
½ tsp. monosodium glutamate
½ tsp. pepper
½ tsp. paprika
2 eggs
4 Tbsp. milk
1½ c. fine, dry bread crumbs
3 Tbsp. butter
½ c. chicken broth or bouillon
½ c. sauterne
2 Tbsp. dried parsley flakes
1 can cream of chicken soup
½ c. sour cream

Split each chicken breast in half. Put each piece between two sheets of saran wrap. Pound thin to twice the original size, using mallet. Cut ham and cheese slices in half. Fold chicken piece in half with ham and cheese sandwiched between halves. Seal edges of chicken by pounding together. Mix flour with salt, monosodium glutamate, pepper and paprika. Coat each breast with flour mixture, shaking off excess. Dip in slightly beaten egg which has been mixed with the milk, then roll in bread crumbs. Brown slowly in butter. Add chicken broth and sauterne. Sprinkle with parsley. Cover and simmer until chicken is tender, about 1 hour. Remove chicken to warm serving plate. Blend undiluted soup into pan drippings. Gradually stir in sour cream, heating gently. Serve chicken and gravy over rice or noodles.

Serves 6

Cranberry-Stuffed Cornish Hens

⅔ c. chopped cranberries
2 Tbsp. sugar
1 tsp. shredded orange peel
¼ tsp. salt
⅛ tsp. ground cinnamon
3½ c. toasted raisin bread cubes
3 Tbsp. butter or margarine, melted
1 Tbsp. orange juice
4 (1-1½ lb.) Cornish game hens
salt
cooking oil
¼ c. orange juice
2 Tbsp. butter or margarine, melted

In bowl, combine chopped cranberries, sugar, orange peel, salt and cinnamon. Add raisin bread cubes, sprinkle with 3 tablespoons melted butter or margarine and the 1 Tbsp. of orange juice. Toss lightly to mix. Season cavities of hens with salt. Lightly stuff birds with cranberry mixture. Pull neck skin to back of each bird and fasten securely with a small skewer. Tie legs to tail, twist wing tips under back. Place Cornish game hens, breast side up, on a rack in a shallow roasting pan. Brush hens with cooking oil, cover loosely with foil. Roast at 375° for 30 minutes. Combine the ¼ cup orange juice and 2 tablespoons melted butter or margarine. Uncover birds, baste with orange juice mixture. Roast, uncovered, until done (drumstick can be twisted easily), about 1 hour longer. Baste once or twice with orange juice mixture.

Serves 4

Chicken Breast Florentine

4 chicken breasts, boneless & skinless
2 tsp. olive oil
1 tsp. shallots, minced
1 tsp. garlic, minced
1 c. white wine
½ c. heavy cream
4 Tbsp. Parmesan cheese, grated
1 c. fresh spinach, cut in strips
salt & pepper
8 oz. angel hair pasta, cooked
Marinade (recipe follows)

Prepare Marinade. Marinate chicken breasts for 24 hours. Preheat oven to 350°. Remove chicken from marinade and pat dry with paper towels. Quickly sauté chicken in olive oil in a hot skillet until lightly browned on both sides. Remove from pan and finish cooking in oven until fully cooked (45 minutes). Meanwhile, add to skillet shallots, garlic, white wine, cream, Parmesan cheese, spinach and salt and pepper to taste. Simmer 3-5 minutes until well blended and spinach is limp. Serve sauce hot over chicken with angel hair pasta.

Marinade:

1 c. olive oil
2 Tbsp. garlic, chopped
1 tsp. oregano
2 tsp. rosemary

Blend ingredients and use them to thoroughly coat chicken.

Serves 4

Carrot Bread

2 c. sifted flour
2 tsp. baking soda
2 tsp. cinnamon
¾ tsp. salt
1 ½ c. sugar
1 ½ c. corn oil
3 eggs
2 tsp. vanilla
2 c. carrots, grated

Sift together the flour, soda, cinnamon and salt. Add sugar, corn oil, eggs and vanilla to the dry mixture and beat on medium speed with electric mixer until well blended. Fold in the carrots. Pour mixture into 2 well greased and floured 9 x 5" loaf pans. Bake at 300° for 1 hour or until bread tests done.

Hawaiian Banana Nut Bread

2¼ c. flour
1 tsp. baking soda
2 tsp. baking powder
½ tsp. salt
1 (8¼ oz. can) crushed pineapple, undrained
1 c. mashed banana
⅓ c. orange juice
½ c. butter
1 c. sugar
2 eggs, beaten
1 ½ c. chopped pecans or walnuts

Hawaiian Banana Nut Bread (Cont.)

Preheat oven to 350°. Butter a one pound loaf pan. Sift dry ingredients together and set aside. Combine pineapple, banana and orange juice and set aside. In a large bowl, cream butter and sugar. Add eggs and beat well. Add a small amount of the flour mixture alternately with the fruit mixture, mixing only enough to moisten the flour. Stir in nuts and pour batter into pan. Bake for 1 hour 15 minutes. Note: this bread is much better after a day or two.

Chocolate Cheesecake

Crust:
26 chocolate wafers, crushed
6 Tbsp. butter, melted
½ tsp. cinnamon

Filling:
1½ lbs. cream cheese, softened
1 c. sugar
3 eggs
8 oz. semi-sweet chocolate, melted and cooled
2 tsp. cocoa
1 tsp. vanilla extract
2 c. sour cream

Chocolate Cheesecake (Cont.)

For the crust: Mix ingredients thoroughly and press into a well-buttered 10" spring form pan. Chill. Preheat oven to 350°. In a large bowl, beat cream cheese until fluffy and smooth. Add sugar and beat in eggs one at a time. Stir in chocolate, cocoa and vanilla, beating well after each addition. Add sour cream and continue beating until very smooth and well blended. Pour into crust. Bake for 1 hour and 10 minutes. Cake may appear to be too liquid, but it will become firm when chilled. Cool to room temperature, then chill overnight.

Serves 12

Mocha Chip Cheesecake

8 Tbsp. unsalted butter, melted
2 c. chocolate wafer crumbs
2 Tbsp. sugar
1½ lbs. cream cheese, room temperature
1 c. sugar
4 eggs, room temperature
⅓ c. heavy cream
1 Tbsp. instant coffee powder
1 tsp. vanilla
6 oz. mini semisweet chocolate chips

Preheat oven to 350°. Butter a 10" spring from pan. Combine the butter, cookie crumbs and the 2 tablespoons of sugar. Press onto the bottom and partially up the sides of a springform pan. Chill for 5 minutes. Bake for 10 minutes. Set aside to cool. Reduce the oven temperature to 200°. In an electric mixer, beat the cream cheese until light and fluffy. Beat in the sugar. Add the eggs, one at a time, beating well after each addition. Stir in the cream, instant

Mocha Chip Cheesecake (Cont.)

coffee and vanilla. Beat for 2 minutes. Pour half of the filling into the prepared pan. Fold the chocolate chips into the remaining filling and carefully pour over the filling in the pan. Bake for 2 hours or until a tester inserted in the center comes out clean. Cool completely at room temperature. Refrigerate overnight.

Serves 10 -12

Index

A

Ahi Poke..280
Almond Panna Cotta 259
Anatra al Balsamico 100
Antipasto Salad..140, 141
Appetizers
    Basil Gorgonzola Torte...323
    Brie Wrapped in Puff Pastry..178, 179
    Chili Sweet & Sour Sauce...177
    Crab & Shrimp Cocktail Lahvosh 178
    Curried Stuffed Eggs 346
    Fresh Basil Bruschetta 185
    Garlic Bread...114
    Garlic Chili Beef with Parmesan Baguette Croute........................180
    House Torte Stuffed Mushrooms...322
    Hawaiian Banana Nut Bread..354, 355
    Italian Sausage Stuffed Mushrooms 192
    Provolone Sauté..15
    Roasted Portobello Mushrooms..219, 220
    Salsa...139, 142, 157, 283, 284, 301
    Seafood Stuffed Mushrooms..176
    Spicy Thai Chicken Bites 181
Artichoke Bruschetta...318
Asian Bistro Bouillabaisse..107, 108
Avocado Aioli 278, 279

B

B. J.'s BBQ'd Beans..146
Baby Greens with Strawberries and Sugared Almonds............................127
Balsamic Peppercorn Sauce 100, 101
Basic Bread Pudding with Praline Topping...77, 78
Basic Vinaigrette 252
Basil Gorgonzola Torte 323
Basque Beans 210
Béchamel Sauce 244, 245, 316
Beef Pepper Steak 239
Beef, Lamb, and Venison
    Beef Pepper Steak...239
    Braised Lamb Shanks 215
    Cafe Soleil Lamb Shanks Braised in Red Wine 72

Chicken Fried Steak 231, 232
Garlic Chili Beef 180
General Grant's Pepper Steak 198
Grilled Lamb Chops 209
Mongolian Beef 219, 222, 223
Moroccan Lamb 170, 171, 172
Oxtail Stew in Brown Gravy 208
Rack of Lamb 13, 275
Rosemary Cabernet New York Steaks 329
Rouladen 95
Texas-Style Barbecued Brisket 122, 123
Venison Ravioli 50, 51
Berries Romanoff 264
Black and Blue Caesar Salad 304
Black Bean Chili 285
Black Bean Soup 294
Blueberry Crisp 297, 298
Bourbon Apple Butter 68
Braised Lamb Shanks 215
Bread
Rosemary Brioche Dinner Rolls 268
Wild Horse Ale Cinnamon Bread 151, 152
Bricks BBQ Pepper Prawns 14
Brie Wrapped in Puff Pastry 178, 179
Broiled Mahi Mahi 301
Broth Base 305, 306
Butternut Squash & Leek Soup 16
Butternut Squash Soup 66

C

Caesar Dressing 166, 167
Caesar Salad 104, 128, 214, 304, 327
Caesar Salad Dressing 214
Cafe Soleil Basic Polenta 73
Cafe Soleil Lamb Shanks Braised in Red Wine 72
Cafe Soleil Roasted Bell Pepper Sauce 75
Cakes, Pies and Tortes
Andy's Incredible Apple Pie 235, 236
Blueberry Crisp 297, 298
Cappuccino Cheesecake 58
Carrot Bread 354
Chocolate Cheesecake 355, 356
Cranberry Orange Muffins 332
Flourless Chocolate Cake 38, 39
Ground Almond Torte 344
Italian Rum Cake 30

Mocha Chip Cheesecake..356, 357
    Shortbread...182
Calico Salad..340
Calzone...84
Candied Basil 34, 35
Cappuccino Cheesecake 58
Cappuccino Panna Cotta..76
Caramelized Ginger Scones 266
Carrot Bread 354
Casa Dia 292
Chardonnay Butter Sauce 98
Cheesy Potatoes..342
Chicken & Shrimp Won Tons with Chili Sweet & Sour Sauce 176, 177
Chicken and Grape Pasta Salad 130, 131
Chicken and Rice..209, 210
Chicken Breast Florentine 353
Chicken California Sandwich..81
Chicken Chili Relleno 283, 284
Chicken Cordon Bleu 351
Chicken Eggplant Parmesan Casserole 88, 89
Chicken Fried Steak 231, 232
Chicken Mozzarella...350
Chicken Pesto 17
Chicken, Duck, Turkey, Quail and Pheasant
    Anatra al Balsamico...100
    Chicken & Shrimp Won Tons with Chili Sweet & Sour Sauce.....176, 177
    Chicken and Grape Pasta Salad 130, 131
    Chicken and Rice..209, 210
    Chicken Breast Florentine 353
    Chicken California Sandwich 81
    Chicken Chili Relleno...283, 284
    Chicken Cordon Bleu 351
    Chicken Mozzarella...350
    Coco Chicken 56
    Coral Reef Chicken..62
    Cranberry-Stuffed Cornish Hens 352
    Fajita Wrap 228, 229
    Fettuccine with Quail and Shiitake...48, 49
    Garlic Chicken..113, 114, 115, 141
    Garlic Chicken Dijon Pizza 114, 115
    Gold Pan Pizza...115
    Grilled Tuscan Chicken 43
    Lemon Basil Chicken 187
    Lemon Herbed Breast of Chicken 69
    Mediterranean Chicken Sandwich 277
    Pan Roasted Muscovy Duck..310

Pollo Ripieno.. 223, 224
Roasted Red Bell Pepper Chicken................................... 199
Sierra Chicken Stew 233
Smoked Turkey Tetrazzini 349
Spicy Basil Chicken 111
Spicy Thai Chicken Bites... 181
Spit Roasted Garlic Chicken 248, 249
Szechwan Duck Breast Salad 109
Chili Oil 32, 34
Chili Sweet & Sour Sauce.. 177
Chinese Cole Slaw 339
Chocolate Cheesecake.. 355, 356
Chocolate Mousse... 195
Chocolate, Bourbon, Pecan Tart 253
Chopped Cobb Salad... 42
Christiania Caesar Salad 327
Chutney Butter.. 275, 276
Cinnamon Burgundy Sauce 246, 247
Cinnamon Ice Cream 253, 254
Cioccolati Mousse... 57, 58
Citrus Cilantro Mayo 136, 137
Clam Chowder 24, 26
Classic Caesar Salad 128
Coco Chicken.. 56
Coco Prawns 23
Coconut Shrimp 229, 230
Coral Reef Chicken 62
Corn Husk Salmon 282, 283
Crab & Shrimp Cocktail Lahvosh.................................... 178
Crab Quiche 345
Crab Topped Swordfish 225
Cranberry Horseradish Mayo... 135
Cranberry Orange Muffins... 332
Cranberry-Stuffed Cornish Hens..................................... 352
Creme Brulée 163
Cremosa Polenta Rosso... 57
Crispy Saffron Risotto Cakes... 250
Currant Scones 202
Curried Stuffed Eggs... 346

D

Deluxe Potato Salad.. 348
Desserts
     Almond Panna Cotta 259
     Basic Bread Pudding with Praline Topping 77, 78
     Berries Romanoff 264

Cappuccino Panna Cotta...76
Caramelized Ginger Scones...266
Chocolate, Bourbon, Pecan Tart...253
Chocolate Mousse..195
Cinnamon Ice Cream...253, 254
Cioccolati Mousse 57, 58
Creme Brulée..163
Currant Scones...202
Key Lime Pie 37, 38
Lemon Curd..202, 203
Nut Meringue Cookies...259
Orange Pistachio Biscotti...267
Pear, Ginger, Hazelnut Tart 18, 19
Pumpkin Brulé...333
Root Beer Float Pie...216, 217
Strawberries in Amaretto Sabayon 320
Sweet Potato Tarts 147
Tiramisu..188
White Chocolate Bread Pudding with Whiskey Sauce 45
Yogurt Berry Pie...92
Dijon Herb Paste 275, 276
Dijon Mustard Vinaigrette..67
Dill Sauce 330
Double Pork Chop 309

E

Eggplant and Hot Garlic Sauce 240
Eric Sandwich..293

F

Fajita Wrap..228, 229
Fennel Sausage and Wild Mushroom Lasagna..................................316
Fettuccine with Quail and Shiitake..48, 49
Fire-Grilled Pizza 44
Fish
  Ahi Poke 280
  Broiled Mahi Mahi 301
  Corn Husk Salmon..282, 283
  Fish Mousse...263
  Grilled Salmon...74, 98, 296, 328
  Panevino Cioppino 54
  Peppered Ahi Sashimi...307, 308
  Roasted Striped Bass 319
  Salmon En Croute..263
  Salmon Fusilli...169, 170
  Salmon Gravlax 330

Salmon Spread 337
Salmon Tacos with fresh Mango Salsa 156
Salmone Ai Carcioffi 98
Seared Salmon Salad.. 168, 169
Spanish Ceviche 22
Sunnyside Ahi Fish Taco 282
Tortilla Grilled Fresh Fish... 278
Fish Mousse 263
Flourless Chocolate Cake.. 38, 39
Fresh Basil Bruschetta 185
Fritelle with Crab and Shrimp.. 258

G

Garlic Bread.. 114
Garlic Chicken 113, 114, 115, 141
Garlic Chicken Dijon Pizza... 114, 115
Garlic Chili Beef... 180
Garlic Roasted Smashed Potatoes 286
General Grant's Pepper Steak 198
German Potato Salad... 324
Gold Pan Pizza... 115
Gorgonzola and Pear Salad 252
Grandma Dot's Easy Stir Fry Vegetables 88
Grilled Asparagus and Chili Oil.. 32
Grilled Jumbo Shrimp... 300
Grilled Lamb Chops.. 209
Grilled Lola.. 292
Grilled Medallions of Pork with Bourbon Apple Butter 68
Grilled Pork Tenderloin 146
Grilled Salmon 74, 98, 296, 328
Grilled Sweetbread Salad.. 256
Grilled Tuscan Chicken 43
Ground Almond Torte... 344

H

Harvard Beets... 341
Hawaiian Banana Nut Bread... 354, 355
Herb Mayonnaise 277, 278
Herbed Aioli... 307
Hilltop House Vinaigrette 80
Hilltop Vegetable Soup.. 80
Homemade Garlic Croutons... 128, 129
Hot & Sour Soup.. 238
House Torte Stuffed Mushrooms 322

I

Italian Rum Cake...30
Italian Sausage Stuffed Mushrooms 192

J

Jamaican Jerk Marinade 123, 124
Jamaican Jerk-Style Pork Medallions......................................154, 155, 156

K

Key Lime Pie...37, 38

L

Layered Mexican Delight 347
Lemon Basil Chicken 187
Lemon Curd...202, 203
Lemon grass-Jalapeno Ponzu Sauce...221, 222
Lemon Herbed Breast of Chicken 69
Lentil Soup 48
Linguini Pescatora..99
Lobster Whiskey..264
Louisiana Oyster Fritter Salad...166

M

Mango Salsa 156, 157
Marinated Mushroom Salad 134
Mediterranean Chicken Sandwich...277
Mediterranean Red Clam Chowder 26
Mediterranean Seafood Paella...305
Minted Couscous...246, 247
Mocha Chip Cheesecake 356, 357
Mongolian Beef..219, 222, 223
Moroccan Lamb 170, 171, 172
Moroccan Spice Mixture 171, 172
Mountain Pinto Beans...234, 235
Mushroom Sauce..183, 244, 250, 251
Mushroom Vinaigrette..36

N

Neptune Sauce...162
Nevada Gold Cucumber Salad 153
Nut Meringue Cookies 259

O

Olive Tapanade..277
Omelets and Eggs
    Eric Sandwich..293

Ossobuco..27, 52
Oxtail Stew in Brown Gravy...208
Oysters Rockefeller...261, 262

P

Pan Roasted Muscovy Duck 310
Panevino Cioppino..54
Papaya Cilantro Salsa...194
Parmesan Baguette Croutes..180
Pasta
   Bambi's Macaroni and Cheese...90
   Chicken Pesto 17
   Fennel Sausage and Wild Mushroom Lasagna 316
   Fettuccine with Quail and Shiitake..48, 49
   Linguini Pescatora...99
   Lentil Soup..48
   Pasta Al Boro 192
   Pasta E. Fagioli...184
   Potato Raviolis 257
   Ravioli Fritta 186
   Saffron CousCous...306
   Seafood Lasagne...204, 205, 206
   Spinach & Mushroom Lasagne...244
   Summer Tortellini Salad 91
   Toad in the Hole...204
   Two Colored Linguini 319, 320
   Venison Ravioli...50, 51
Pasta Al Boro 192
Pasta E. Fagioli 184
Pea Salad..340, 341
Pear, Ginger, Hazelnut Tart 18, 19
Peppered Ahi Sashimi...307, 308
Pickled Onions 166, 167
Pickled Red Onion 33
Polenta 57, 73, 248, 249
Pollo Ripieno 223, 224
Pork
   Double Pork Chop...309
   Grilled Medallions of Pork with Bourbon Apple Butter 68
   Grilled Pork Tenderloin 146
   Jamaican Jerk-Style Pork Medallions 154, 155, 156
   Pork Roast in Beer Sauce 96
   Rasta Ribs...120
   Texas-Style Pulled Pork 121, 122
   Texas-Style Ribs 118, 119, 120
   Woodfired Pork Tenderloin 246

365

Texas-Style Ribs..118, 119, 120
Woodfired Pork Tenderloin...246
Pork Roast in Beer Sauce 96
Port Wine and Morel Mushroom Sauce 61
Portobello Mushroom Burger..43, 44
Potato Cabbage Soup..94
Potato Raviolis...257
Prawn Tropicale 60
Provolone Sauté...15
Pumpkin Brulé...333

Q

Quiches
Crab Quiche..345
Quick Garam Marsala...124

R

Rack of Lamb 13, 275
Raspberry Sauce 76, 77
Rasta Ribs...120
Ravioli Fritta..186
Ricotta Gelato with Grilled Stone Fruit...................................34, 35
Risotto Radicchio & Scallops..51
Roast Peppers 33
Roasted Garlic Green Peppercorn Butter 329
Roasted Portobello Mushrooms...219, 220
Roasted Red Bell Pepper Chicken...199
Roasted Red Bell Pepper Cream 287
Roasted Red Potato Salad...129, 130
Roasted Striped Bass 319
Root Beer Float Pie 216, 217
Rosemary Brioche Dinner Rolls..268
Rosemary Cabernet New York Steaks 329
Rouladen...95

S

Saffron CousCous..306, 310
Salad
Antipasto Salad...140, 141
Baby Greens with Strawberries and Sugared Almonds 127
Black and Blue Caesar Salad..304
Caesar Salad 104, 128, 214, 304, 327
Calico Salad...340
Chicken and Grape Pasta Salad 130, 131
Chinese Cole Slaw...339
Chopped Cobb Salad 42

Christiania Caesar Salad.. 327
Classic Caesar Salad... 128
Deluxe Potato Salad 348
German Potato Salad... 324
Gorgonzola and Pear Salad 252
Grilled Sweetbread Salad 256
Louisiana Oyster Fritter Salad.. 166
Marinated Mushroom Salad 134
Nevada Gold Cucumber Salad 153
Pea Salad 340, 341
Roasted Red Potato Salad... 129, 130
Seared Salmon Salad... 168, 169
Spicy Crab Salad 140
Spinach Salad 31, 36
Summer Tortellini Salad 91
Szechwan Duck Breast Salad 109
Texas Taco Salad 234
Thai Cole Slaw 269
Tortellini Salad with Dijon Mustard Vinaigrette............................... 67
Salad Dressing
Basic Vinaigrette 252
Caesar Dressing... 166, 167
Caesar Salad Dressing.. 214
Dijon Mustard Vinaigrette 67
Hilltop House Vinaigrette 80
Homemade Garlic Croutons 128, 129
Mushroom Vinaigrette 36
Salmon En Croute 263
Salmon Fusilli 169, 170
Salmon Gravlax 330
Salmon Spread 337
Salmon Tacos with fresh Mango Salsa 156
Salmone Ai Carcioffi 98
Salsa 139, 142, 157, 283, 284, 301
Sauces
Balsamic Peppercorn Sauce 100, 101
Béchamel Sauce 244, 245, 316
Bourbon Apple Butter 68
Cafe Soleil Basic Polenta 73
Cafe Soleil Roasted Bell Pepper Sauce 75
Chardonnay Butter Sauce... 98
Chili Oil.. 32, 34
Chili Sweet & Sour Sauce 177
Chutney Butter 275, 276
Cinnamon Burgundy Sauce.. 246, 247
Citrus Cilantro Mayo... 136, 137

Cranberry Horseradish Mayo 135
Dijon Herb Paste...275, 276
Dill Sauce 330
Herb Mayonnaise..277, 278
Herbed Aioli 307
Jamaican Jerk Marinade 123, 124
Lemon grass-Jalapeno Ponzu Sauce 221, 222
Mango Salsa 156, 157
Mushroom Sauce 183, 244, 250, 251
Neptune Sauce 162
Olive Tapanade...277
Papaya Cilantro Salsa 194
Parmesan Baguette Croutes 180
Polenta 57, 73, 248, 249
Port Wine and Morel Mushroom Sauce...61
Quick Garam Marsala 124
Raspberry Sauce 76, 77
Roasted Red Bell Pepper Cream...287
Sesame-Cilantro Aioli 225, 226
Sweet & Sour Dipping Sauce 229, 230
Sweet & Sour Sauce 342
Tarragon Cream Sauce 62, 63
Tequila Lime Marinade 194
Thai Red Curry Sauce...310, 311
Tomato/Mushroom Sauce..244, 245
Whiskey Sauce 45, 46
White Clam Sauce 28
Yellow Tomato Tomatillo Salsa 216
Sautéed Prawns...317
Seafood
Asian Bistro Bouillabaisse...107, 108
Bricks BBQ Pepper Prawns 14
Chicken & Shrimp Won Tons with Chili Sweet & Sour Sauce.................176, 177
Coco Prawns 23
Coconut Shrimp..229, 230
Crab & Shrimp Cocktail Lahvosh 178
Crab Topped Swordfish...225
Fritelle with Crab and Shrimp 258
Grilled Jumbo Shrimp...300
Lobster Whiskey...264
Mediterranean Seafood Paella 305
Oysters Rockefeller 261, 262
Panevino Cioppino 54
Prawn Tropicale..60
Risotto Radicchio & Scallops 51
Sautéed Prawns...317

Seafood Gumbo..274
Seafood Lasagne 204, 205, 206
Seafood Stuffed Croissants 90, 91
Seafood Stuffed Mushrooms 176
Shrimp BLT 193
Shrimp Scampi...105
Tempura Prawns... 221, 222
Tiger Prawns and Swordfish 110
Veal and Lobster Roulade 61
Vicky Shrimp 162
Seafood Gumbo 274
Seafood Lasagne 204, 205, 206
Seafood Stuffed Croissants 90, 91
Seafood Stuffed Mushrooms 176
Seared Salmon Salad.. 168, 169
Sesame-Cilantro Aioli... 225, 226
Shortbread...182
Shrimp BLT 193
Shrimp Scampi...105
Sierra Chicken Stew..233
Smoked Turkey Tetrazzini..349
Soup
Asian Bistro Bouillabaisse...108
Black Bean Soup 294
Broth Base 305, 306
Butternut Squash & Leek Soup 16
Butternut Squash Soup 66
Clam Chowder 24, 26
Hilltop Vegetable Soup 80
Hot & Sour Soup 238
Lentil Soup.. 48
Mediterranean Red Clam Chowder 26
Potato Cabbage Soup 94
Spiced Tomato Soup 331
Tomato Bisque 338
White Bean Minestrone... 55
Wisconsin Style Beer Cheese Soup................... 150, 151
Spanish Ceviche... 22
Spiced Tomato Soup 331
Spicy Basil Chicken 111
Spicy Crab Salad...140
Spicy Thai Chicken Bites..181
Spinach & Mushroom Lasagne..244
Spinach Balls 345, 346
Spinach Salad... 31, 36
Spit Roasted Garlic Chicken 248, 249

Summer Tortellini Salad...91
Summer Vegetable Medley 296
Sunnyside Ahi Fish Taco...282
Sweet & Sour Dipping Sauce 229, 230
Sweet & Sour Sauce 342
Sweet Potato Tarts..147
Szechwan Duck Breast Salad 109

T

Tarragon Cream Sauce 62, 63
Tempura Prawns..221, 222
Tequila Lime Marinade 194
Texas Taco Salad..234
Texas-Style Barbecued Brisket 122, 123
Texas-Style Pulled Pork 121, 122
Texas-Style Ribs...118, 119, 120
Thai Cole Slaw 269
Thai Red Curry Sauce 310, 311
Tiger Prawns and Swordfish 110
Tiramisu 188
Toad in the Hole 204
Tomato Bisque 338
Tomato Bruschetta 326
Tomato/Mushroom Sauce 244, 245
Tortellini Salad with Dijon Mustard Vinaigrette..67
Tortilla Breading Crust..278, 279
Tortilla Grilled Fresh Fish 278
Two Colored Linguini 319, 320

V

Vanilla Glazed Vegetables 246, 248
Veal
    Ossobuco 27, 52
    Veal and Lobster Roulade 61
    Veal Joshua...173, 174
Veal and Lobster Roulade 61
Veal Joshua...173, 174
Vegetables
    Artichoke Bruschetta 318
    B. J.'s BBQ'd Beans...146
    Basque Beans..210
    Black Bean Chili...285
    Cheesy Potatoes..342
    Chicken Eggplant Parmesan Casserole..88, 89
    Cremosa Polenta Rosso 57
    Crispy Saffron Risotto Cakes...250

Cremosa Polenta Rosso 57
Crispy Saffron Risotto Cakes...250
Eggplant and Hot Garlic Sauce 240
Garlic Roasted Smashed Potatoes 286
Grandma Dot's Easy Stir Fry Vegetables 88
Grilled Asparagus and Chili Oil... 32
Harvard Beets.. 341
Mountain Pinto Beans 234, 235
Pickled Onions 166, 167
Pickled Red Onion 33
Polenta..249
Roast Peppers 33
Spinach & Mushroom Lasagne 244
Spinach Balls 345, 346
Summer Vegetable Medley... 296
Vanilla Glazed Vegetables 246, 248
Venison Ravioli 50, 51
Vicky Shrimp 162

W

Whiskey Sauce... 45, 46
White Bean Minestrone 55
White Chocolate Bread Pudding with Whiskey Sauce 45
White Clam Sauce.. 28
Wild Horse Ale Cinnamon Bread 151, 152
Wild Rose Morning Casserole 203
Wisconsin Style Beer Cheese Soup 150, 151
Woodfired Pork Tenderloin 246

Y

Yaki Soba.. 42
Yellow Tomato Tomatillo Salsa 216
Yogurt Berry Pie 92

ORDER FORM

IN GOOD TASTE RENO / TAHOE
P.O. BOX 455
GENOA, NEVADA 89411
(775) 782-0035
FAX (775) 782-0296
e-mail: sonnieimes@msn.com
lori@lacey.reno.nv.us
Website: ingoodtastecookbook.com

Please send _____ copies of
IN GOOD TASTE, RENO / TAHOE
@ $14.95 Each

Add $4.50 postage and handling for the first book ordered
and $1.50 for each additional book.
Enclosed is my check for $_____.

Name_____
Address_____
City_____State_____Zip_____

☐ This is a gift. Send directly to:

Name_____
Address_____
City_____State_____Zip_____

☐ Autographed by the authors.

Autographed to:_____

ABOUT THE AUTHORS

Sonnie Imes of Genoa, Nevada is the author of 11 books, including "The Tastes of Tahoe" and "The Tastes of Cruising". She has been writing about food, people and places since 1974, exploring the best cuisine's around the globe. A gourmet cook in her own right, she has taught cooking at Sierra Nevada College. Sonnie also produced and directed a PBS television show, "Taste of Tahoe", featuring chefs preparing their specialties for the camera. From cruise ships to neighborhood delis, Sonnie is tireless in her pursuit of "tastes". When she finds something good, Sonnie finds pleasure in sharing her discovery with the world.

Lori Lacey's fascination for cooking and cookbooks stems from being alongside and standing at the elbows of her grandmother and mother in their Jewish kitchen. Growing up in North Miami Beach, Lori learned from her family that the heart of a home begins with a good recipe. This legacy she shares with appreciative husband, Joe, and teenage sons Mike and Jake, who are only too willing to sample as Lori tries out the dishes selected to be in "In Good Taste Reno/Tahoe".

"In Good Taste" a brain child of Lori, who recognized the need for a new area cookbook to be a guide for locals and a souvenir for tourists, became a reality with the marriage of experience between Sonnie Imes' know how and Lori's imagination.

Lori and Joe have lived in Reno for over 18 years, exploring restaurants and gradually adding to her collection of more than 300 cookbooks while expanding her own gourmet cooking skills.

373